THE INTIMATE MARRIAGE

The Intimate Marriage

HOWARD J. CLINEBELL, JR.

AND

CHARLOTTE H. CLINEBELL

1817

HARPER & ROW, PUBLISHERS
New York, Hagerstown, San Francisco, London

THE INTIMATE MARRIAGE. *Copyright © 1970 by Howard J. Clinebell, Jr., and Charlotte H. Clinebell. All rights reserved. Printed in the United States of America. No part of this book may be used or reproduced in any manner whatsoever without written permission except in the case of brief quotations embodied in critical articles and reviews. For information address Harper & Row, Publishers, Inc., 10 East 53rd Street, New York, N.Y. 10022. Published simultaneously in Canada by Fitzhenry & Whiteside Limited, Toronto.*

LIBRARY OF CONGRESS CATALOG CARD NUMBER: 72-109062

Contents

To John, Don, Susan
Whose lives have enriched our marriage
beyond measure

We can orbit the earth, touch the moon . . . .
And yet this society has not devised a way
(though love propels our very existence) for
man and woman to live together for seven
straight days with any assurance of harmony
and personal growth.

George B. Leonard*

* "The Man and Woman Thing," *Look* (December 24, 1968), p. 55.

Foreword

Intimacy in marriage can bring shared ecstasy, mutual satisfaction, well-being, joy, serenity, and peace. This important and provocative book by Howard and Charlotte Clinebell promotes with clarity and firm persuasiveness the thesis that marriage without intimacy is at best a meager, depriving, and self-defeating way of life. In the following chapters they explore the nature and variety of intimacy, barriers to its achievement, the art of nurturing intimacy, and its spiritual components. Liberal use of illustrative case material shows the reader how relationships between men and women in marriage suffer from innocuous desuetude when they do not venture into communication and sharing. Paths and landmarks are presented by which individuals may extricate themselves from isolation and develop potentials for demolishing the walls built by their attitudes and behavior.

Intimacy is closeness and unity. It presupposes warmth, kindliness, and love, those positive attributes for which mankind has sought throughout the ages. These characteristics have fortified man in his search for health, for growth, for life, for immortality, for a Divine Being. They are understood and realized by a man and a woman in the fleeting but forever lasting moments when a wanted child is created in the ecstasy of loving union.

The task undertaken in this volume is not an easy one. In many subtle ways it is less difficult to discuss aloneness than intimacy. It takes courage to examine man's potential in his closest and most meaningful relations. The authors involve the reader in this search, they also involve him in understanding that each partner in a marriage is unique and can be sufficiently secure to realize that difference can be constructive, stimulating, and even fun. Kahlil Gibran reminds us with beauty of each person's inalienable need to be himself or herself distinct from all others even while sharing in loving intimacy:

> But let there be spaces in your togetherness,
> And let the winds of the heavens dance between you.
> Love one another, but make not a bond of love;
> Let it rather be a moving sea between the shores
>   of your souls.

In spite of man's impassioned search, aloneness, failure, and despair are still common companions to men and women. Perhaps it is because these negative feelings are so evident in the troubled persons who seek help in their personal and family problems that counselors from a variety of professional backgrounds equate growth and hope with the ability to communicate, to accept difference, to share, to be together, to be intimate. A book exploring this equation in depth, illustrating the unique dilemmas and feeling responses of married couples and the methods through which experienced and sophisticated teacher-counselors were able to foster constructive modification, is a real contribution. For me it is a very real privilege to know the authors and to have shared this much of their work.

—EMILY HARTSHORNE MUDD

Appreciation

Within these pages, we have endeavored to apply insights derived from our experiences as a married couple and as marriage and family counselors, to the strengthening and deepening of relatively healthy marriages. Our gratitude to those who have shared their marital pain and struggle, defeats and victories with us in counseling relationships is especially strong. In recent years, participants in our marital growth groups have taught us much about the use of group counseling methods to help functioning marriage partners to communicate and relate more fully. We are indebted to these persons. The anonymity of both counselees and group participants has been carefully guarded by changing identifying data in case material and by using composite cases which are true to life but are drawn from several individuals or couples. Our hope is that some of the things that have become clearer to us as a result of sharing in these experiences will help those who read these pages to enjoy more success in the continuing process of keeping their marriages going and growing.

We approached this project from the professional perspectives of pastoral counseling and social work, respectively—perspectives which we have discovered reinforce and complement each other at many points. Howard had an opportunity to engage in systematic study of marital interaction during a sabbatical year at the Marriage Council of Philadelphia. It was from this experience that the first draft of chapters 1 through 6 emerged. Appreciation is expressed to Emily Hartshorne Mudd and the other staff members of that agency, for their valuable help in the study, and to the National Institute of Mental Health and the American Association of Theological Schools, for fellowship assistance. The drafts which came from that sabbatical provided a starting point for the subsequent revisions and additions by the two of us.

Whatever realism concerning the limitations of marriage we bring to the task and whatever enthusiasm we feel regarding its creative potentialities reflect our own existential involvement in the same marriage for twenty-five years. Our own struggles to overcome the barriers and to achieve greater depth in our relationship are woven into the fabric of what we have written. The joys and frustrations of these years which we have had the good fortune to share have colored the views expressed throughout this manual. The ideas have meaning for us, in our relationship; we hope that they will have meaning for you in yours.

HOWARD AND CHARLOTTE CLINEBELL

Claremont, California
October 1969

How to Get the Most from This Book

Every marriage relationship has many untapped potentialities. This is as true of the relatively functional, successful marriage as of the malfunctioning, deeply pained relationship. Here is a book for those who wish to release the rich potentials of average or better-than-average marriages. It is a book on the *prevention* of serious marital problems by two means—early recognition and correction of problems which could grow, and a continuing approach to strengthening, broadening, and deepening the total relationship. It can serve as a guide to *periodic marital checkups.*

The book is intended to be a resource for use by the following: (*a*) An individual or couple who are interested in achieving on their own, more intimacy in marriage. (*b*) Individuals and couples in marriage counseling. (*c*) Those receiving premarital counseling or instruction, as couples or in groups. (*d*) Participants in courses on marriage and the family. (*e*) Participants in marital growth groups and marriage counseling groups. (*f*) Professional persons functioning in marriage counseling and family-life education.

For couples who are relating well in some areas, but desire more of what Paul Tournier calls a "total marriage," this book may be a useful tool. Its goal is not to present a single, monolithic model of a "good marriage" or an "intimate marriage"; rather, it is to encourage each couple to work at developing that style of relationship, with that degree of intimacy which meets the unique personality needs of themselves and their children.

This is a book primarily for couples who desire to awaken or deepen their marriage relationships. As such, its main purpose is practical—to serve as a resource for helping couples to learn skills of relating in depth. A secondary purpose of the book is to shed light on the nature of intimacy and the process by which it is enhanced. Many couples discover that an *understanding* of the inner nature of creative closeness and the processes by which couples can move toward it is one important step toward satisfying the universal hunger for such closeness. Other steps must follow —action steps—but understanding is like a light on the journey to greater intimacy.

Here are some suggestions to help couples derive maximum benefit from the book:

1. *Read and discuss it as a couple.* The meaning you discover in these pages will be increased by sharing your reactions, thoughts, and objections with your fiancée or spouse. Set aside some regular time alone together to discuss and reflect on ideas that speak to you. If you enjoy reading aloud to each other, perhaps you will want to use it in this way. If your spouse is not interested in the book, you may find it useful in strengthening your side of the marriage.

2. *Apply to your marriage the ideas that are relevant.* This will begin to happen spontaneously, if you take step one. Applying what you read is what makes a book like this a marital growth-stimulator. Don't be surprised if the ideas do not seem to work at first. Intimacy in marriage (or anywhere else) takes some doing. Everything has its cost and the cost of a closer relationship, with better skills, is persistent effort.

3. *Keep trying the* "Taking Action" sessions *at the close of the various chapters. Learning occurs by doing.* Skills of interpersonal relations are something like muscles—they gain strength through use. Couples who used these "lab" sessions between meetings of marital growth groups reported that the main barrier was feelings of self-consciousness and embarrassment because of the artificial nature of the sessions. You may feel somewhat the same at first.

But most couples who persisted until they got into the swing of the communication sessions found that they were useful. Adapt the suggested procedures of a session to your own style of relating. Even if your first effort seems mechanical or worthless, we would encourage you to try several additional sessions. It takes that long to discover what value they may have in reaching a more intimate relationship. A number of the exercises are much more effective in couples' groups than when used by couples alone.

4. *Join or start a marital growth group.* The ideas in the book will come alive more rapidly if you wrestle with them in a group of three to six couples, all striving for more depth in their marriages. One approach is to invite several couples to your home, telling them in advance what you have in mind (so they won't feel they came under false pretenses). Choose couples who have reasonably happy marriages. (A couple with a crippled or disintegrating marriage needs a marital *therapy* group with a trained leader, not a marital *growth* group; their presence in a leaderless group may hurt them and will curtail the group's usefulness to the other couples.) After the couples arrive, the two of you can present some of the ideas that make sense to you from Chapter 1. As others begin to discuss these, your group is off and running. At the close of the evening, ask them if they would like to continue, perhaps with everyone reading a chapter a week before the group meeting. Leadership of the discussion can rotate among the couples. If the group meetings are unproductive or disturbing, it is important to bring in a trained leader.

If your minister or rabbi is trained in counseling and group dynamics, invite him to participate as a guide or resource person. Or, he may suggest someone trained in group marriage counseling. A skilled leader is a major asset to a group; he can draw out the group's potentialities and accelerate the communication processes. Perhaps there is a marital growth or enrichment group already meeting in your church or in a community agency. If not, discuss the matter with your pastor, priest or rabbi to see if he would be interested in initiating a church-sponsored group.

5. *Go deeper on your own.* Some of the ideas in these pages may whet your appetite for deeper understanding. Recommended readings are included in a section at the end of the book. Reading will enhance your head-level understanding. To deepen your insight on the heart level, regular discussion between you may help; or you may decide to join a sensitivity training group, a professionally led growth group, or perhaps a marriage counseling or therapy group.

6. *Obtain professional help if you are unable to achieve what you want on your own.* If your communication system has never been effective, or if it has "gone to pot" through unconstructive conflict, you will need a *trained* third party to assist you in building or rebuilding. Through a series of sessions—individually, as a couple, or in a small group of couples—a skilled marriage counselor often can help couples work through their walls and learn to use hidden resources for mutual need-satisfaction. To seek such help takes honesty and courage. It isn't easy for most of us to admit we need outside help. But by getting professional help, and sticking with it as long as it takes to be effective, a couple can open the door to a more satisfying marriage. In a sense, this is a do-it-yourself book. But a part of doing it oneself effectively is to use needed resources from outside the relationship. Unscrambling severely distorted communication in a marriage on your own is something like giving yourself a haircut—possible in some cases, but exceedingly difficult. If a marriage is frozen, the skills of a competent marriage counselor are essential.*

The first draft of this book was given a trial run in two groups. To illustrate ways of using this book, a brief description of the groups will be given. The first group was a short-term marital growth group composed of five couples in their thirties. They have functional marriages and had indicated an interest in developing more creative intimacy. The group met two hours a week for

* One way to discover the names of qualified marriage counselors is to write the American Association of Marriage Counselors, 3620 Maple Avenue, Dallas, Texas 75219.

four weeks.* Couples read certain chapters in the book prior to each meeting; they participated as couples in the "Taking Action" sessions between group meetings.

Interaction within the group was vigorous: couples began to discuss their own patterns of relating early in the first session. Striking differences among the couples became apparent to the participants—for example, in their ways of handling hostility. The sessions triggered increased marital-partner communication between meetings. After session one, two couples reported that they stayed up until 2:00 A.M. talking about their marriage. Another couple reported at the second session, "We appreciated each other more than usual this week after reading about barriers to intimacy." Group discussions of mutual need-satisfaction and communication produced constructive efforts at these areas. One of the wives commented that it was "exciting to hear how others relate" and to realize that they are different but successful. The group was pointed and candid in its suggestions for improving the book.

The second group was a church-sponsored class on "Deepening Your Marriage Relationship." Three 2-hour meetings were held within an eight-day period. Approximately thirty-five persons were enrolled. During the sessions, key ideas from the chapters of the manuscript were presented. "Practice session" assignments including the checklists of needs, etc., were given. Considerable time was spent during the group sessions on questions, discussion, and feedback from the "homework" the couples had done in *their* own lab sessions.

In spite of the short-term nature of the class, it seemed to stimulate constructive communication among some of the couples. These comments are from the evaluation session at the end of the course:

It opened a variety of areas of marriage where we can work constructively, realizing that a more need-satisfying marriage is possible.

* It is our present view that marital growth groups of at least eight sessions tend to be more productive.

The course started us thinking again about the areas in which we want to grow and suggested techniques that can be *used*.

Gave us some insight into our problems and made us realize that some problems that seemed only personal are really universal.

The series helped to begin new discussions of *us*—who we are and where we expect our relationship to go from here. Even though we didn't agree on some things, at least we are talking more.

My husband and I, for the first time, have discussed many of these areas and hopefully will continue our discussion.

The series confirmed the directions in which we are already moving; we gained courage to experiment more boldly in communication. . . .

It has motivated us to try to develop more areas of intimacy, and to show the deep affection we feel. . . .

. . . made us conscious of our need to grow, to move from the more-or-less satisfying but static level . . . a helpful start to deeper levels of communication.

There was general agreement that the series was too short; the value might have been increased if a part of each session had been spent in smaller interaction groups of not over ten people.

These two groups are described as contrasting examples of two short-term group uses of this volume. Both seemed to be helpful to the majority of couples who participated. Had the groups been set up to meet longer, they undoubtedly would have gone deeper and had a greater impact.

1 *Reaching for Greater Intimacy*

Can you believe that you and I are a state of mind?
Lois Wyse, *Love Poems for the Very Married*[1]

Intimacy is a many-faceted diamond. There are as many satisfying ways of relating as there are constructive relationships. One couple may find satisfaction and intimacy in a comfortable, companionable marriage. Another couple may find it in a tumultuous balance between intense passion and vigorous battle. Most couples find themselves somewhere along the continuum between these two extremes. Intimacy is not so much a matter of what or how much is shared as it is *the degree of mutual need-satisfaction within the relationship*. When interaction is destructive, or the partners live parallel, "live-and-let-live" existences, or when either spouse feels the desire for something more in the relationship, a couple may seek change.

A marriage counselor hears couples asking many questions. Some they ask in words; others they express with feelings too painful to trust to words; some they ask in the silent language of the ways they relate to each other. Their questions are filled with searching and hurting and longing; with anger and hoping and hunger. The questions are crucially important to them. Finding functional answers—answers they can understand and use—can make the difference between a stagnant and a satisfying marriage, between a withering and a growing relationship. In a deeply disturbed marriage, finding answers that work is often a life and death matter—the life or death of the relationship. Couples in relatively stable but nongrowing marriages often ask the same questions, with less desperateness but with the quiet urgency of unmet needs.

If one listens carefully to young couples in the early years of marriage adjustment, some of the questions he hears recurring are these:

How can we learn to get through to each other? We try to talk about our differences, but we end up mad.

How do you get close to another person in more areas than just sex? Sometimes, even when we make love it feels as though we're in different worlds.

How can we work out our differences in habits, and tastes, and values, when each person's way feels right to him?

Why do we fight so much when we really love each other? And without settling anything?

How can I understand her needs when she won't talk? Her feelings get hurt and she clams up. What am I supposed to be —a mind-reader or something?

Why won't he listen to me? Why aren't my feelings important to him?

How do we get over being single? It's as though we are living alone together much of the time.

Is there something in marriage that goes beyond romance? Something more durable? How do we go about finding it?

How can you keep a person wanting to come home? You sleep in the same bed, breathe the same air, and use the same toothpaste tube month after month. How do you keep a marriage from going stale?

How do we learn to live with each other's differences? Now that we're married there seem to be so many things we don't like about each other.

How can we learn to care more about what really matters to each other—especially feelings?

What makes a relationship work so that two people not only can get along but even look forward to a long time together? Frankly, if the next thirty years are going to be like the last two, I'd rather not.

If a counselor listens to couples who have been married for fifteen to twenty years, he will hear some of the same questions, but also others:

How do we get reconnected with each other now that the kids are gone? They were the cement that held us together or maybe kept us from seeing that we were far apart.

We seem to dislike each other and to fight more since the children have grown up.

It's not that we're terribly unhappy—just fed up with nagging and hurting and not relating.

How can we get something *more* in our relationship? Some depth? We go through the motions of marriage—have for a long time—in a kind of empty, shallow way. Sometimes I feel cheated because I know there's more to both of us than we ever give to the other. We're not willing to settle for what we haven't got, any more.

It's when I feel cheated that I think about cheating—and I don't want to wreck what I've got, even though it lacks a lot.

How do two human beings help each other face the future—aging and all that? We've both lost our parents in the last four years. It makes us realize that we haven't got forever to make a marriage.

Something tells me the other woman isn't really the basic problem, although that part hurts like the devil. Somehow we've never stopped keeping each other at arm's length. We're kind of marital strangers. How can we get through our wall?

Sex just isn't what it used to be in the early years of our marriage. We still call it "making love" and usually get around to it once a week or so, if one of us isn't too tired or too mad. When I think of the wild fun we used to have in bed, it makes me cry inside. Is there any way to get the fire back in our marriage? .

What's the trouble with our love life? We're not romantic adolescents any more, of course, but I wish we could still get that delicious feeling of almost merging, when we have intercourse.

Sex never has been any fun for us. Is there some way to learn at this late date?

He's got a lot of worries on his mind—his job is a heavy burden at times. But why can't he talk to me about it and let me share some of the load? I try to reach him but it's no good. He says I wouldn't understand. How can I, if he won't talk or let me near him?

Things have built up between us over the years—hurts, resentments, dead dreams. Now we can hardly see over the barrier. Is there any way to get rid of this? To let the past be past?

These are some of the important questions asked by couples who come for marriage counseling. They have to do with the search for relatedness in marriage. At the beginning of a counseling experience, many couples are too hurt and angry to be able to ask questions which focus on their problems of relating. If counseling is successful, they eventually ask such questions. The ability to ask relationship questions is a sign of hope. Asking the right questions is an essential step toward finding workable answers.

Many couples not in marriage counseling are asking the same searching questions about ways to deepen their relationships. Even those who have relatively effective marriages often are searching for increased richness and depth. Those who have achieved considerable intimacy at one stage of their lives together sometimes find that they must work at developing a new style of closeness as the next stage of marriage approaches. Many couples with relatively healthy marriages are working to make them more so—more satisfying and fulfilling for themselves and their children. They are working as couples, often with the help of a trained marriage counselor who is equipped to be a "growth facilitator" in relationship. In some cases, they are in marital growth groups—

composed of from four to six couples with a trained leader. However they are going about it—alone or with professional assistance, as a couple or in a group—they are motivated by a desire to deepen their marriages.

Here are three couples whose struggles to relate may help make the problems of the search for intimacy more vivid:

Bill White and Amy Jones, ages twenty and nineteen respectively, are engaged. They expect to be married in about four months. Bill is a junior, Amy a sophomore at the state teachers' college. They have known each other for about a year and a half, and have dated regularly during the past year. Their engagement was announced at Christmas and the wedding is scheduled for June. They both expect to work during the summer and to continue college in the fall, with some financial help from his parents.

Bill and Amy are very much in love. Physically they "turn each other on" and their dates include extended periods of physical intimacy, stopping just short of intercourse. Emotionally they often feel on the same wavelength. They find themselves resonating to the same music, movies, and people. They love to discuss social problems and their solutions. In short, they already have developed a number of areas of relatedness which will be invaluable in their marriage. They are using the period of their courtship and engagement to lay the foundation for bridges of communication which can serve them throughout their lives together.

But in spite of the progress they have made in establishing a relationship, Bill and Amy have encountered barriers to closeness. Bill is often late for dates and although Amy resents this, she is uneasy about telling him how annoyed it makes her. Instead, she smolders and withdraws in a way that Bill describes as "aloof." Sue tends to be pushy at times—for example, making plans involving both of them without checking first to make sure Bill is in agreement. Bill is hypersensitive to aggressiveness in women, and reacts by being late or "forgetting" about the activity that she has planned unilaterally. His tardiness or memory gap triggers Amy's aloofness, which makes Bill feel rejected and angry. He expresses this by increased tardiness or forgetting. Both know when the tension between them is escalating and the distance increasing. Eventually the loneliness is too much for one of them and a shift toward reconciliation begins. They "make up," but with little understanding of what has actually been going on between them, or of the roots of this interpersonal drama.

Bill and Amy have hang-ups in a number of areas in which they cannot communicate effectively. One concerns their feelings about being financially dependent on his parents. Bill consciously feels comfortable about this, but he responds defensively when Amy expresses her feelings about the importance of a husband supporting his family as soon as possible. It is as though his adequacy as a male is being attacked by her image of the husband's role; consequently he does not even hear the second part of her statement, the "as soon as possible." Another touchy area is religion. Amy comes from a conventionally religious family. For her, involvement in a church organization is a meaningful part of family life. Bill's background, in contrast, causes him to feel that the essence of religion is ethics and the intelligent person can do better without the institutional expressions of religion, with all their pettiness and irrelevancies. Efforts to "talk through" to some common ground of mutual understanding have ended in a collision with the roadblock of strong, partially buried feelings on both sides.

Bill and Amy have much going for them so far as their prospects for building a strong, mutually fulfilling marriage are concerned. Even without help, they will probably have a better-than-average relationship. But there are blocks in their communication pattern which could grow into walls through the years. Because of their basic desire for the best possible marriage relationship, and their partial awareness of the barriers to it, they decide to join a discovery group for engaged couples sponsored by the clinically trained college chaplain. Their ounce-of-prevention philosophy could have taken them to a counselor for premarital relationship counseling. Either approach would be a good investment in their future happiness.

Carl and Joan Green have been married for about three years. He is twenty-six; she is almost twenty-four. Both are employed—Carl as an engineer, Joan as a medical secretary. Both handle their work with competence. They argue occasionally about how long they should wait to begin their family. Joan worked to help put her husband through his last year of a five-year engineering course. Now that he has been out for two years, she feels that it's time to have a baby. Carl wants another two years without the responsibilities of a child, to improve their financial situation. When they argue about this, Joan accuses him of being more concerned about money than about her happiness. He responds by accusing her of being "irresponsible" in her attitudes toward finances and unaware of how a man feels about such things.

Carl and Joan have resentments, annoyances, and hurt feelings in other areas, too. He feels that she nags him unnecessarily about hanging up his clothes and taking out the trash. Joan sees him as "not holding up his end" of the chores around the apartment, particularly in the light of her full-time job.

The Greens have problems in the area of sex. At times, when Carl makes advances, Joan turns over and says she is too tired. He feels rejected and needles her about her faults. Joan wishes that he would be more tender and interested in her when he hasn't got his mind on sex. He wishes that she would show more pleasure in the physical side of their marriage and take the initiative in sex play occasionally.

In spite of their areas of conflict, the Greens' young marriage is satisfying many of their needs as persons. Yet, both Carl and Joan want a great deal more from their relationship than they are currently getting. Underneath their relatively successful coping with most of the new demands of married life, there is a longing for more closeness. As Joan puts it, "Our times of touching are so seldom and so fleeting." Of course, they are very busy. But even when they have time to try to get inside each other's worlds, they seem to run into an invisible wall. The barrier is higher at some times than at others. On rare occasions, it is low enough to let them share in ways that satisfy their heart-hungers. But more often, when one reaches out to the other, he bruises his outstretched feelings against the wall. The response to this pain is a retreat into frustrated isolation, or an angry attack, either of which increases the sense of distance.

The marriage of Joan and Carl is hurting but it is not on the rocks. They are suffering from problems of relating which are common among couples in the early years of marriage. Their desire for a deeper relationship is strong. If they make the grade to creative intimacy during the early, formative years of their marriage, they will have the basic pattern for a lifetime of growth and mutual satisfaction.

Young adults in general are deeply involved in the quest for greater intimacy in their relationships. The quest is the life task of this stage of growth. Joan and Carl have two significant assets in their quest. They have a shared desire to develop a deeper relationship, and a willingness to work at realizing this desire. Furthermore, they have known moments of genuine connectedness, however brief; thus they have a clear understanding of their goal. If they can learn how to lower the "wall" which limits closeness and communication in their relationship, their marriage will deepen through the years. But if they do not learn how to lower the wall, it will gain height and impenetrability and increase the distance between them. Unless they can learn ways to multiply their experiences of successful communication, each failure will add another rock to the wall.

Bart and Sarah Brown have just celebrated their twenty-second wedding anniversary. Both are forty-three. Two of their three children are now away from home. Their son is in the army in a distant state. One daughter is finishing her first year at a college one hundred miles from home, and a second daughter is a junior in high school. Already, Sarah and Bart are experiencing feelings of bereavement because of the near-empty nest. They have invested much of their emotional energy for twenty-two years in their children. This has been particularly true for Sarah. Their child-centered marriage is losing its center.

Bart and Sarah have been aware of growing distance in their relationship. As Sarah put it in a couples' sharing group, "Before the children came, we had something going; but then we both got so wrapped up in other things we didn't work at our marriage, at least not very often." The "other things" to which she referred were Bart's preoccupation with building his law practice and her heavy investment of herself in the children. Periodically, through their late twenties and thirties, Sarah had expressed a desire for more time together and more communication about nonsurface things. They discussed this and agreed it was a good idea, but little change resulted. Bart's satisfaction from his professional successes made him less sensitive to the growing distance between them. But he too has known that something vital has been missing and, in a vague sort of way, has wished that it weren't.

The wall in the Browns' marriage has grown higher and deep communication has become more difficult through the years as they have neglected their relationship. Because their lines of communication are in bad repair, they lack the basic tool of conflict resolution. Thus, hurts and petty annoyances accumulate, and the pressure of unmet personality needs produces smoldering anger. After a while, the anger, and the painful loneliness and hunger which produced it, are transformed to apathy. Their sex life reflects this apathy. It consists of less and less frequent intercourse, with little passion and no romance. The deep loneliness in their marriage has been masked from their friends, and to some degree, from themselves, by their "successful" involvement in child-rearing, vocational, church, community, and social activities. The only obvious clue to the possible presence of a chasm between them is the emotional disturbance of their younger daughter who is currently failing in school, in spite of above-average intelligence. Otherwise, the Browns give the casual observer the picture of a "successful marriage."

One Sunday, Bart and Sarah heard their minister describe marriages in which "two people are lonely together because they have not continued to work at their relationship." The minister declared, "It's more than simply *doing* things together, although that's important. It's *being* together both physically and emotionally, sharing in each other's worlds of feelings, hopes, anxieties, and dreams, that keeps in good repair the bridge that joins two persons. It's this that makes love grow and flower." Both Sarah and Bart felt inner twinges as they listened and met themselves in the minister's words. Later, over their after-dinner coffee, Sarah got the courage to describe her feelings during the sermon to Bart. He was tempted to dodge behind a denial, but instead he decided to admit that he had had some of the same feelings and that he knew the shoe fitted their marriage. In this way, the door was opened to discussion of their mutual need for more of each other and what they might do to recapture and perhaps even increase the closeness of their early years together.

The awareness of the need for marital enrichment and deepening can dawn on a couple at any age or stage of marriage. Experiences in marriage counseling and marital growth groups indicate that the struggle for increased relatedness may become intense at any time in a marriage. But there seem to be three periods when the search for intimacy is most likely to be active and urgent. The first occurs during the engagement period when the couple is getting acquainted on a deeper level and is experimenting with patterns of closeness and distance. The second is the period of major learning following the honeymoon and usually lasting for from two to five years. This is the time of the meshing of two divergent personalities and sets of needs which were brought to the marriage, and of acquiring the new roles of marital partners. Experimenting with patterns of closeness and distance continues, and, it is hoped, mutually satisfying patterns of relating are evolved through the give-and-take of living together. The third period often occurs during the middle years—the forties and fifties—when the exodus of the children confronts the couple with their own relationship, in the context of their feelings about aging.

These crucial periods could be described as the *three crises of intimacy*. Each of the couples—Bill and Amy, Carl and Joan, Bart and Sarah—represents one of these periods. The nature and intensity of each crisis is influenced by the way in which the earlier search for intimacy was handled. If the degree of meaningful closeness achieved during the engagement period was inadequate, from the standpoint of either partner's needs, the second crisis will be more painful and the necessity for growth more crucial. Similarly, if a couple achieves a relatively high degree of relatedness during the premarital period and early years of marriage, it is likely that they will continue to deepen their marriage through the years and will take the adjustment of the middle years as the opportunity to discover new facets of intimacy. For a relationship is never stagnant; a live relationship is a changing one. If a husband

and wife are not growing together they probably are growing apart. New experiences of intimacy are a continual challenge. Few couples, if any, ever grow beyond the need for alertness to the hazards of a neglected relationship, and awareness of the invitation to adventure in a thriving one.

In Chinese, the word for "crisis" has two characters—one meaning danger and the other opportunity. Crises of intimacy in marriage have both aspects, whenever they occur. The danger in the posthoneymoon period, for instance, is that failure to achieve an adequate degree of healthy intimacy may leave the couple unprepared for coping with the demands of parenting. As Erik Erikson observes, the achievement of intimacy in young adulthood provides essential equipment for handling the life task of the next period, generativity.[2] The opportunity of the young adult intimacy crisis, on the other hand, is that of laying a foundation of mutuality upon which a life of satisfying sharing can be built.

The danger of the intimacy crisis of the middle years is that failure consigns the couple to facing the years of loss in a condition of creeping loneliness and alienation, and fear. The opportunity is that of *another chance* to develop a more meaningful marriage, another chance to achieve deeper trust—trust in a marriage which will allow them to use their longevity creatively and cope constructively with the anxiety of aging and death.

Couples like Bill and Amy, Carl and Joan, Bart and Sarah can achieve greater depth in their marriages providing: (*a*) both decide they want more depth in their marriage, (*b*) both are committed to working persistently toward that goal, and (*c*) both are willing to draw on whatever outside resources—books, growth groups, counselors, etc.—are needed to lower their walls. The vast majority of married couples can, on their own, achieve more satisfying relatedness, providing they are willing to pay the price of self-investment and mutual effort over an extended period.

Couples who have achieved some degree of psychological intimacy can increase it by working at marriage in some of the ways described in this book. The growth-in-intimacy process can be accelerated by joining with a small group of like-minded couples under a leader trained in group marital enrichment, or by obtaining guidance from a trained minister or marriage counselor. Couples who have always had severe trouble getting through to each other or whose communication lines have been neglected for many years find it essential to obtain expert assistance. They will still need to work persistently on their own, but self-help methods alone rarely suffice if the wall is high and thick.

Though most couples have the capacity for a deeper relationship than they have yet achieved, the realization of this capacity is rarely easy. Quite the contrary is true. Time and courage are required and a willingness to express one's own feelings and to understand the other's. Such mutual openness demands of each partner a lowering of defenses, an honesty in recognizing his own responsibility for the relationship. There is a "latent marriage" hidden within each actual marriage relationship; but to bring the latent potentialities of the marriage into actuality takes sweat and struggle by the couple.

THE WILL TO RELATE

There is in the heart of every human being, a powerful longing for a meaningful relationship with at least one other person. For some, the longing is a conscious awareness; for others it remains unconscious, felt only as loneliness or an absence of meaning in life. This hunger is a part of being human with deep roots in man's long infancy and childhood. Personality is formed and deformed in relationships; a person needs others in order to be a person.[3]

The inescapable need for relationships produces a striving in man which could be described as the *will to relate*. It is more fundamental than the striving which Sigmund Freud called the "will to pleasure," or that Alfred Adler described as the "will to power," or what Viktor Frankl terms the "will to meaning." These strivings or desires can be met only in relationships. Pleasure, power, and meaning come into full realization for human beings only in interpersonal relationships. The will to relate is man's most basic striving, upon the fulfillment of which other satisfactions depend. Psychiatrist Karl Menninger declares: "The establishment or re-establishment of relationship with fellow human beings is the basic architecture of normal life. . . . To live, we say, is to love, and vice versa."[4]

In various forms and many degrees, *relationship-hunger* is all about us in our society, as well as within us. In its milder forms it produces loneliness and unhappiness; in more severe forms, it causes the personality distortions of emotional malnutrition; in extreme and protracted forms, it produces relational-starvation and the eventual death of creativity and coping, as seen in mental illness.

The dynamics or driving forces behind the will to relate seem to include both a push and a pull. The push is provided by the need to move away from anxiety and loneliness, the pull by the need to move toward sources of interpersonal satisfactions of personality needs.

One thrust in the dynamics of the will to relate is the desire to satisfy such universal human hungers as the hunger for affection, recognition, caring, esteem, dependency, and sexual satisfaction.[5] The hungers of the heart can be satisfied only in relationships. As sociologist Otto Pollak has put the matter, "Humans are open systems which must exchange input and output with others in order to live."[6] Close relationships provide the opportunity for mutual feeding of the hungers of the heart. The husband, off alone on an afternoon's fishing expedition, thinks of how he will describe to his wife the huge fish that got away. Even the solitary dimension of the human psyche is essentially interpersonal. Joys and sorrows are incomplete until they are shared.

Another expression of the will to relate is the striving inherent in every person to realize his potential. The drive toward self-actualization is deep within every living organism, including man. Because the realization of man's potentialities cannot occur apart from relationships, the inner drive toward self-fulfillment motivates a person to relate. The striving toward self-actualization is the chief ally of every teacher and learner, every counselor and counselee. It is the indispensable resource in any effort to improve a marriage relationship. The growth drive is present in every person, although in some it seems deeply buried. If it can be activated, it will help to provide the motive power for the process of learning new, more satisfying ways of relating. The inner drive toward self-fulfillment and growth is directly linked with the striving to find satisfactions for the basic hungers of the personality. Only as these hungers are met can growth occur. Self-actualization depends on satisfaction of one's basic interpersonal needs, and thus on the quality of one's relationships with significant others.

Feelings of anxiety often stimulate the will to relate. In his studies of gregariousness, Stanley Schachter described to his subjects a frightening experiment and then asked them whether they would prefer to be "together" with others during the experiment, "alone," or "don't care." Nearly two thirds of those with high anxiety chose to be with others, whereas two thirds of the low-anxiety group indicated that they did not care whether they were alone or together. Both groups, with a few exceptions, rejected the choice of being "alone." Significantly, his subjects generally said they preferred to be with others during a frightening experiment whether they were prohibited from talking, allowed to talk only about irrelevancies, or free to discuss whatever they chose. Apparently, the mere physical presence of others was seen as anxiety-reducing. Schachter concludes: "It is clear that affiliative desires increase with anxiety."[7] The drive behind the will to relate in all of us is partly the desire to reduce the pain of anxiety by being near to other human beings.

The depth and intensity of the will to relate can be appreciated most fully by looking at the various dimensions of loneliness. We often think of loneliness as preventable or as the result of unfortunate circumstances which must be endured temporarily until supportive relationships can be re-established. Much loneliness is in these two categories. But there is a deeper dimension of loneliness which makes it a pervasive factor in the background, if not the foreground, of everyone's life. In his book *The Hills Beyond,* Thomas Wolfe declared: "The whole conviction of my life now rests upon the belief that loneliness, far from being a rare and curious phenomenon, peculiar to myself and to a few other solitary men, is the central and inevitable fact of human existence."[8]

Reports of war prisoners, castaways, and hermits all point to the intense suffering of prolonged isolation from human contacts. Such isolation produces rising anxiety and often profound disturbances. The pain increases to a certain tilt point and then, in many cases, decreases sharply. But the pain is frequently replaced by apathy, withdrawal, and detachment, which in extreme cases resembles schizophrenia. Reports describe a tendency to think, dream, and occasionally even hallucinate *about people!*[9] Viktor Frankl's imaginary conversation with his wife, which helped to keep him going during his death-camp experience, is an example.

The awful, aching loneliness of those in such extreme circumstances is cut from the same cloth as the garden-variety loneliness that all of us experience. Recall, for a moment, the ache and emptiness of some lonely period in your life. By recapturing the feelings of such an hour, the pain and fear of loneliness which help to motivate the drive to relate become vivid.

Quite apart from preventable and temporary loneliness, there is man's *existential loneliness*—the loneliness that is inherent in the very nature of human existence. Understanding this is basic to understanding man's reaching out to his fellows and his attempts to form relationships. Man's dilemma is this: at the very moment he tries to escape from loneliness by relating, he is haunted by the dim awareness that he is essentially and inescapably alone. There is an important truth in John Donne's familiar "No man is an island"—our lives are intertwined in a vast network of relationships. But it is also true that, in another sense, *every man is an*

island. Every person is an island of consciousness. He must relate
to other islands of consciousness. Yet, in the final analysis, he is
utterly alone within his world. No one can ever really know how
he sees the sunset, feels a toothache, enjoys or does not enjoy sex,
loves or does not love his wife, how he experiences the color blue,
or how he really feels about death. Even the most intimate and
empathic friend or spouse can only surmise by inference from his
own feelings, how the other really experiences life.

In a moving book entitled *Loneliness,* Clark E. Moustakas
states:

The vastness of life itself produces the emotional climate of existential loneliness, the mystery of a new dawn, the endless stretches of
sea and sky, the immense impact of air, and time and space, the unfathomable workings of the universe. The constant, everlasting weather
of man's life is not love but loneliness. Love is the rare and precious
flower but loneliness pervades each new day and each new night.[10]

Man's existential loneliness is a fact. But how an individual
responds to it determines whether its impact will be destructive
or creative. Frantic activism; endless superficial socializing; leechlike pseudo-mutuality (discussed in chapters 2 and 3); losing
identity in group conformity;[11] use of drugs; compulsive work—
all these are responses to existential loneliness.

These unconstructive responses to existential loneliness result
from feelings of panic. Originally these feelings were the product of
lack of adequate experiences of emotional intimacy with loving,
protective adults in early childhood. The responses derived from
these early experiences of loneliness continue the pattern of lonely
living in adult life by cutting the person off from depth relationships. Whether the lonely person responds by losing his identity
in the anonymous herd, clinging frighteningly to others, or deadens
the inner ache with drugs, overeating or compulsive work, the
price he pays is the increasing loneliness of superficial relationships. The loneliness cycle tends to become self-perpetuating,
separating the person more and more from *the major resource*

for coping with existential loneliness—a depth relationship with at least one other human being!

In contrast, the person who has known enough genuine intimacy in his early, need-satisfying relationships to feel some "basic trust" in his relationships can recognize, confront, and accept the essential loneliness of human existence. When this occurs, existential loneliness provides a foundation for healthy intimacy, Moustakas calls this "exercising one's loneliness." He writes:

> Every lonely man experiences deep joy and gladness, rapture and awe in the presence of a human voice . . . the miracle of a silent eye, the quiet touch of a human hand, the ecstasy of standing face to face, of walking shoulder to shoulder with one's fellow man.[12]

Awareness of aloneness makes more precious the moments of intimacy which with increasing frequency punctuate a growing relationship—moments when one feels as though he does not see the other "through a glass darkly, but face to face." Moustakas puts it this way:

> Loneliness enables one to return to life with others with renewed hope and vitality, with a fuller dedication, with a deeper desire to come to a healthy resolution of problems and issues involving others, with possibility and hope for a rich, true life with others.[13]

Awareness of one's ultimate aloneness stimulates the healthy desire for constructive bridge-building between personal islands of consciousness. A powerful thrust in the will to relate is the realization that the most effective way of confronting and using one's essential loneliness creatively is by relating to another human being in depth.

MARRIAGE AND THE WILL TO RELATE

A good marriage offers the most favorable opportunities in our culture for fulfilling the will to relate. Gibson Winter declares, "Marriage is intended to be an intimate relationship. This is the one opportunity for sharing one's whole life with another person."[14] Because marriage is potentially the most totally intimate of human relationships, it is both the most difficult relationship, on the one hand, and the most rewarding, on the other. It is the place where most adults have the opportunity to lessen their loneliness, satisfy their heart-hungers, and participate in the wonderfully creative process of self-other fulfillment.

The importance of achieving intimacy in marriage is enhanced by the scarcity of depth relationships outside the family. The slope of the psycho-social continent on which we live is away from close relationships; hence the gravitational pull is toward passing without really meeting—like ships in the night. The minister who told his psychotherapist, "My life is characterized by a plethora of contacts and a poverty of relationships," was describing most of us. Many factors in our society militate against depth relationships—the frenzied pace of our lives; the frantic pressures to get ahead which encourage *using* rather than *relating to* people; the constant mobility of many families which contributes to a rootlessness and noninvolvement in community life; the anonymity of megalopolis where people do not know the names of even those in adjoining apartments. Furthermore, a majority of males in industrialized societies is involved in some form of bureaucracy—a corporation, a union, the government, the military, a church's political machinery, a large university, etc. and bureaucracies tend to be inherently depersonalizing, creating manipulative I-It relationships.[15] Basically, it requires *time* and *face-to-face, nonmanipulative interaction* for deepening relationships to grow. For most of us both of these are in short supply outside the family. From his long experience in working with emotionally disturbed children, Bruno Bettelheim declares, "The more we live in a mass society, the more important are intimate relationships."[16]

The importance of achieving an intimate marriage is further increased by the *power of the partner* in monogamous relationships. Marital partners become the key resource persons for supplying the basic foods of the spirit. Each spouse has considerable power to nourish or to starve the other's personality. The covenant of marriage is a commitment to the mutual responsibility for fulfilling the deep personality needs of the other—"to love and to cherish" by so doing. It is not that one is responsible for "making my mate happy." No one can *make* another person happy. But when two people commit themselves to a kind of relationship which necessarily excludes many other sources of personality-feeding, they have an obligation to do all within their power to provide the interpersonal food the other needs. In taking our marriage vows, we agree to become key resource persons to each other. We can fulfill this mutual-nurturing function *only by developing a relationship deep enough to provide channels for satisfying personality hungers.* As Gibson Winter says, "Intimacy is the crucial need in marriage today. It is, consequently, the focus of marital difficulty."[17]

The nurturing of one's partner is much more than an obligation derived from the marriage covenant. It is also an open door of opportunity to participate in the creative process by which the God-given potentialities of two human beings are progressively fulfilled; it is a way of satisfying one of the fundamental needs of every person—the need to give as well as to receive love.

Alone, a man marks time and becomes very set in his ways. In the demanding confrontation which marriage constitutes, he must ever go beyond himself, develop, grow into maturity. When marriage is reduced to mere symbiosis of two persons essentially hidden from one another, peaceful though such life may sometimes be, it has completely missed its goal. Then it is not solely the marriage which has failed but both husband and wife. They have failed in their calling as a man and a woman. To fail to understand one's spouse is to fail to understand oneself. It is also a failure to grow and to fulfill one's possibilities.[18]

Here one encounters the fundamental principle of reciprocity in relationships—it is in the process of *inter*action, of giving and receiving, that one's basic needs are satisfied.

Modern marriage, with its robust emphasis on companionship, communication, and equality, offers unprecedented possibilities for the growth of depth relationships. But the democratic model of marriage also offers more opportunities for conflict and progressive alienation. It puts more demands on the partners than did the older patriarchal model. Roles are changing rapidly and in ways that are threatening to husbands and to wives. The increased communication, mutual sharing, and openness which are at the heart of the new model mean that both partners are asked to give more of themselves to the relationship. There is little place to hide. Inadequacies in our abilities to relate cannot be hidden in relationships which put a premium on transparency. Even the normal need for "distancing" at certain times may be misinterpreted by the spouse as rejection.

Such are the dilemma and the challenge of modern marriage. The same factors—openness, equality, communication, companionship—which create new potentialities for conflict also present us with the opportunity to develop relationships of unprecedented depth and mutual fulfillment. Eric Berne describes what we regard as the goal of modern marriage:

> For certain fortunate people there is something which transcends all classifications of behavior, and that is *awareness;* something that rises above the programming of the past, and that is *spontaneity;* and something that is more rewarding than games, and that is *intimacy.* But all three of these may be frightening and even perilous to the unprepared.[19]

TAKING ACTION

Discuss with each other your reactions to the ideas in Chapter 1. Which ones appeal to you and which do you object to? Set aside thirty minutes to an hour for this, preferably at a time when your chances of not being interrupted are best.

You may find it helpful to jot down the main questions and issues that each of you picked up from the first chapter, including points at which you disagree with the author or with each other. Concentrate on listening to each other and on making sure you understand what your mate is saying. If you are not certain, "check out" the meaning by saying, "Let's see if I am getting what you are saying. . . ." or "Do you see it this way . . . ?"

Discuss the things each of you *likes* about your marriage as it is now. Then talk about the kind of relationship you want to have in a year, in five years, in ten years. It will help if you can begin to understand the goals each of you has in mind. Some understanding of what you *want* will help you move toward it.

You may find it useful to discuss the problems in the relationships of the three couples described in this chapter, comparing them with your own and with other couples you know.

NOTES

1. Wyse, *Love Poems for the Very Married* (Cleveland: World Publishing Co., 1967), p. 29.
2. For a discussion of intimacy and generativity see Erik H. Erikson, *Childhood and Society* (New York: W. W. Norton, 1963), pp. 263–268.
3. In their illuminating study of "Pseudo-Mutuality in the Family Relations of Schizophrenics," Lyman C. Wynne, *et al.*, state: "Movement into relation with other human beings is a fundamental principle or 'need' of human existence. To relate this in psychoanalytic terminology, man is inherently object-related." In N. W. Bell and E. F. Vogel (eds.), *A Modern Introduction to the Family* (New York: The Free Press, 1960), p. 574.
4. Menninger, Karl, *The Vital Balance* (New York: The Viking Press, 1963), p. 295. E. Bentley states this same truth when he writes, "The essence of humanity is to be found in the quicksilver of relationships rather than in the dead weight of isolated being." Quoted by Helene Papanek in "Group Psychotherapy with Married Couples," *Current Psychiatric Therapies,* ed. Jules Masserman (New York: Grune and Stratton, 1965), p. 157. From the perspective of depth psychology, Erich Fromm stresses the same truth in pointing out that the need for love and relatedness are among man's fundamental needs. (*The Sane Society* [New York: Holt, Rinehart and Winston, 1955], p. 124.) A century ago, William R. Alger authored a volume containing penetrating insights concerning the universal human need for relationships. It was entitled *The Genius of Solitude,* with the subtitle, *The Solitudes of Nature and Man or the Loneliness of Human Life.* Alger

observed: "Every man obscurely feels, though scarcely any man distinctly understands, the intimacy and vastness of his connections with his race. It is true that the real world of the soul is an invisible place, removed from the rush and chatter of crowds. . . . Yet the most influential element even of this secluded world and this hidden life, is the element which consists of the ideas and feelings we habitually cherish in relation to our fellow-beings" (Boston: Roberts Brothers, 1867), p. vii.

5. In his experimental studies of the sources of gregariousness, psychologist Stanley Schachter states: "People, in and of themselves, represent goals for one another; that is, people do have needs which can be satisfied only in interpersonal relations. Approval, support, friendship, prestige . . ." (*The Psychology of Affiliation* [Stanford, Calif.: Stanford University Press, 1959], p. 2).

6. Pollak, lecture at the University of Pennsylvania, Spring, 1967.

7. Schachter, *op. cit.,* p. 19. It is noteworthy that Schachter found that the later the subject's birth position, the less likely she would choose "together" (p. 61). Affiliative tendencies were significantly correlated with anxiety mainly in the cases of firstborn and only children.

8. Quoted by Clark E. Moustakas, *Loneliness* (Englewood Cliffs, N.J.: Prentice-Hall, 1961), p. 33. Sensitive persons have always been aware that life, even at best, is a lonely journey. There is a contemporary ring about William Alger's words penned a century ago: "Alas, how widely yawns the moat that girds the human soul! Each one knows its own bitterness, its own joy, its own terrors and hopes; and no foreigner can ever really touch, but only more or less nearly approach, and exchange signals, like distant ships in a storm" (Alger, *op. cit.,* p. 34).

9. Schachter, *op. cit.,* pp. 7–8.

10. Moustakas, *Loneliness,* pp. 33–34.

11. As Erich Fromm showed in *Escape from Freedom* (New York: Rinehart and Co., 1941), loneliness is so painful that men will do almost anything to avoid it, including losing their freedom by fleeing into a totalitarian religious or political system.

12. Moustakas, *op. cit.,* p. 55.

13. *Ibid.,* p. 102.

14. Winter, *Love and Conflict* (Garden City, N.Y.: Doubleday and Co., 1958), p. 71.

15. Lecture by Otto Pollak, University of Pennsylvania, Spring, 1968.

16. Bettelheim, lecture in Los Angeles, 1962.

17. Winter, *op. cit.,* pp. 69–70.

18. Paul Tournier, *To Understand Each Other* (Richmond, Va.: John Knox Press, 1962), pp. 30ff.

19. Berne, *Games People Play* (New York: Grove Press, 1964), p. 184.

2 *The Many Facets of Intimacy*

Someone asked me
To name the time
Our friendship stopped
And love began.

Oh, my darling,
That's the secret.
Our friendship
Never stopped.

Lois Wyse, Love Poems for the Very Married[1]

What is intimacy? Is it something a couple really wants? How do they know when they have achieved it? Is it possible for everyone? What are its varying forms and degrees? Does it stifle individuality or make people too dependent on each other? The dictionary and the thesaurus, in defining intimacy, list such widely divergent words and phrases as "friendship, closeness, communion, familiarity, pertaining to the inmost being, sexual relations, illicit sexual commerce, fornication." The word "intimacy," like "love," is a symbol that carries a freight of meanings as diverse as a peddler's wares. It is clear that some guiding image of intimacy is needed—an emotionally alive picture[2] that will provide guidelines for couples in their search. The picture presented here is tentative. It must be so since exploration of this important human experience is only beginning. One thing stands out sharply: intimacy in marriage can be rich and diamondlike in its many facets. Some of these facets are difficult to describe adequately with the frail vessels of meaning we call words. Certainly, in any depth human encounter, there is a prominent element of mystery. Some of the mystery in the experience of intimacy has been put into words by Gibran in his essay "On Friendship":

> Your friend is your needs answered.
> He is your field which you sow with love and reap with thanksgiving.
> And he is your board and your fireside.
> For you come to him with your hunger, and you seek him for peace.
> When your friend speaks his mind you fear not the "nay" in your own mind, nor do you withhold the "ay."
> And when he is silent your heart ceases not to listen to his heart;
> For without words, in friendship, all thoughts, all desires, all expectations are born and shared, with joy that is unacclaimed.
> And let there be no purpose in friendship save the deepening of the spirit.
> For love that seeks aught but the disclosure of its own mystery is not love but a net cast forth: and only the unprofitable is caught.
> And let your best be for your friend.
> If he must know the ebb of your tide, let him knew its flood also.
> For what is your friend that you should seek him with hours to kill?
> Seek him always with hours to live.
> For it is his to fill your need, but not your emptiness.
> And in the sweetness of friendship let there be laughter, and sharing of pleasures.
> For in the dew of little things the heart finds its morning and is refreshed.[3]

In that most intimate of friendships called marriage, the opportunities and demands for a relationship of depth are pervasive. Intimacy is an art with as many expressions as there are artists to express it. It is often expressed in the sharing of thoughts and ideas and feelings. It is expressed in shared joys and sorrows, in respect for the deepest needs of the other person, and in the struggle to understand him. Intimacy does not suggest a saccharine sentimentalism; it can be expressed in constructive conflict which is the growing edge of a relationship. Intimacy is not a constant, but is expressed in varying degrees in the ebb and flow of day-in, day-out living. And intimacy is never a once-and-for-all achievement but must be nurtured throughout marriage; with this care, it grows and changes with the stages and seasons of marriage.

An intimate marital relationship requires certain qualities of the husband and wife as individuals as well as of the interaction between them.

Intimacy grows as couples dare to risk greater openness. As each partner becomes more honest with himself and more aware of his own faults, and his own need to blame the other for their conflict, the wall between them begins to come down, block by block. Each of us feels the need to hide at times, behind a mask of self-sufficiency or self-justification, particularly when conflict threatens or self-esteem is weak. Only as each individual relaxes his mask and becomes more transparent (openness) can intimacy develop in the relationship.

Carl R. Rogers uses the term *congruence* to describe one aspect of openness.[4] Congruence means being a real person, not being phony or putting on an act. It means knowing and owning one's feelings; it means to "ring true" as a human being. There is a kind of inner honesty and consistency in a congruent person which makes it possible to know and to relate to him.

In order to have peace, many couples put aside certain subjects—those that are emotionally charged—those that are important for their coming to a true mutual understanding. Thus bit by bit the transparent window which the relationship of man and wife should be, becomes blurred. They are starting to become strangers to one another.[5]

Intimacy thus requires mutual openness and the willingness to risk genuine encounter or meeting in areas which are important to either partner.

Intimacy grows as couples learn to be emotionally present to each other. The concept of *presence* is taken from the thinking of the existentialists in psychotherapy.

The immediacy and un-clothedness of our meeting can only be suggested by the word "presence." We are a presence for each other

—a personal presence available to the other. The feeling tone is one of utter lack of alienation and strangeness to each other—of at-home-ness.[6]

Two people can live in the same house for decades without ever being present for each other, without ever experiencing a joining or linking of thoughts and feelings, longings and fears, dreams and delights. The wife who protested, "I feel like you're a thousand miles away" was speaking to her husband who was "absent" in the same room. This was an obvious experience of lack of presence at that moment in their relationship. Cultivation of the quality of presence is essential for the experience of intimacy.

Intimacy grows as couples develop a high degree of caring for each other. Affectionate concern for the partner's safety, well-being, and growth as a person is an essential ingredient in an intimate relationship. It is this mutual caring which makes for responsiveness and complementarity (mutual need-satisfaction). The development of intimacy depends on one's caring enough to make a continuing self-investment in the relationship and in meeting the needs of the other. But it is also true that caring develops as a result of the giving as well as the receiving in the relationship. Mutual giving or complementarity includes being a warm, responsive, earthy, and responsible human being to the other.

Intimacy grows in a climate of trust based on commitment to fidelity and continuity. Couples who enter marriage with the assumption that they can easily dissolve the relationship have already jeopardized its success, at least as an intimate relationship. The commitment of each partner to the other and to the relationship over time, "for better or for worse," is essential to the development of intimacy. Marital partners who find it easier or less demanding of self-investment to meet their sexual or emotional needs outside the marriage will not achieve intimacy. It is the "we're in this thing together" attitude which allows a couple to use periods of crisis, conflict, or even estrangement, as challenges to work harder at deepening and expanding the relationship.

INTIMACY AND AUTONOMY

There is within each of us
A private place
For thinking private thoughts
And dreaming private dreams.

But in the shared experience of marriage,
Some people cannot stand the private partner.

How fortunate for me
That you have let me grow,
Think my private thoughts,
Dream my private dreams.

And bring a private me
To the shared experience of marriage.[7]

One of the marks of genuine intimacy is the respect for the need of each partner for periods of aloneness—for the natural rhythm of intimacy and solitude in a relationship. It is a costly fallacy to assume, as some romantic illusions about marriage do, that an "intimate marriage" is one in which husbands and wives do everything together. Our conformist, group-minded "other-directed" culture, as David Riesmann makes clear, cultivates the idea that aloneness is somehow dangerous or a sign of maladjustment.[8] The popular version of "togetherness" is often a kind of pseudo-intimacy, an attempt to escape from loneliness by blending into the "lonely crowd." If marital partners are too dependent on each other for a sense of self-worth and even identity, there is a kind of compulsive togetherness which is not genuine intimacy. The values of savoring a book alone, for example, are lost. There is a kind of clinging quality which reveals the fear of desertion underlying the sticky quality of such a relationship.

In his study of the "self-actualizing" person, Abraham Maslow found that some persons do not *need* relationships in the same way that many others do.[9] Because they have a firm sense of their own identity and a dependable feeling of worth within themselves, they are able to relish both intimacy and autonomy. There are two major sets of needs in all of us—the needs for dependence, love, and nurturance, on the one hand, and the needs for autonomy, self-fulfillment, achievement, and independence, on the other.[10] The desired balance between these two sets of needs is different for each individual and for the same individual at different times in his life. These differences are reflected in the distance-closeness needs and, at times, in the conflicts of two marital partners. Those who in childhood were forced to sacrifice their autonomy in order to receive love carry a sense of conflict between dependence and independence into adult life.

Creative or growth-producing intimacy depends on each person's sense of his own personhood. Having an identity of one's own is necessary before one can develop a shared identity with another. Having one's own center of meaning and existence—being a person in one's own right—makes intimate meeting and union with another possible. An intimate relation is an I-Thou relationship. For such a relationship to develop, there must be an I and a Thou. In Ross Snyder's words, "At the same time that we have a sense of immediacy of contact with his life, we recognize the otherness of the other person. Each of us is a center and is meant to be a center."[11] The union of intimacy is always only partial. With it goes a sense of *communion*—which requires the presence of two individuals joined deeply, but still individuals. Creative intimacy has respect for needed privacy—one's own and one's partner's—as an indispensable ingredient.

THE DIMENSIONS OF INTIMACY

Many couples are surprised and stimulated by discovering that intimacy is like an instrument of many strings. There are more areas in which creative closeness can grow than most couples even suspect. The music which couples make together comes from playing on a variety of combinations of strings. Each couple should aim at discovering the particular harmony and melody of intimacy which *they* find most satisfying. Their musical pattern will vary at different periods in their marriage. At various times, the music will be interrupted by silence or disharmony.

Most couples who make a serious effort can achieve intimacy in several of the dimensions of their relationship. Here are some of the major opportunities for marital intimacy:

Sexual intimacy is for many couples the axis around which other forms of intimacy cluster. The marital relationship provides the optimum setting in which to develop the blend of sensual-emotional satisfactions which is sex at its best. Sexual intimacy is more than the bringing together of sexual organs, more than the reciprocal sensual arousal of both partners, more even than mutual fulfillment in orgasm. It is the experience of sharing and self-abandon in the merging of two persons, expressed by the biblical phrase "to become one flesh."

Emotional intimacy is the depth awareness and sharing of significant meanings and feelings—the touching of the inmost selves of two human beings. Emotional intimacy is the foundation of all other forms of intimacy. Couples whose inner worlds of meaning overlap become tuned to each other's emotional wavelengths so that they can often sense what the other is feeling long before a word is uttered. Some couples even have dreams which seem to be connected.

Intellectual intimacy is the closeness resulting from sharing the world of ideas. Oliver Wendell Holmes once stated: "A man's mind stretched by a new idea can never go back to its original dimensions." Sharing mind-stretching experiences—reading a great book, studying an issue of joint concern, discussing a stimulating lecture—can bring a special quality of intimacy. There must be a genuine touching of minds based on mutual respect for each other's intellectual capacities. Couples who have a wide discrepancy in educational backgrounds sometimes find intellectual intimacy more difficult to achieve.

Aesthetic intimacy is the depth sharing of experiences of beauty. One couple finds a special closeness in relaxing very near to each other as the stereo plays the soul-moving strains of a magnificent symphony. Another experiences together the raptures of natural beauty—the sun sparkling on whitecaps; a grove of giant sequoia; the fury of a mountain storm; the tranquillity of a mountainside at sunset. Others find it in great art. Drinking from the common cup of beauty, wherever it is found, is an experience of communion for many couples.

Creative intimacy is the intimacy of shared creativity. Conceiving and parenting children is an act involving many forms of creativity—biological, emotional, social, spiritual. The middle years, when "generativity" (Erikson[12]) is the central task of the ego, constitute a period of shared creativity in that the two are joining their skills and persons in generating new life between each other and in the family and community. Creative intimacy often is linked to aesthetic intimacy in that what is created together is something of beauty—a garden, a house, a musical expression, a painting. Creative marital intimacy, at its heart, is the experience of helping each other grow—to be co-creators (not reformers) of each other, engaged in the mutuality of feeding the heart hungers of each other so that each can realize his potentialities as a person. Ross Snyder declares: "A marriage is not just a personal relationship of affection between two people; it is a joint venture into a life of growth."[13]

Recreational intimacy may be for newlyweds synonymous with sexual intimacy. Gradually, the pattern of play broadens to become more inclusive, and to involve other activities. Recreational intimacy is essential to the mental health of the partners, refilling the wells of energy and allowing one's "Child" side, in Eric Berne's[14] terms, to rejuvenate the personality through stress-relieving play.

Work intimacy is the closeness which comes from sharing in a broad range of common tasks involved in maintaining a house, raising a family, earning a living, and participating in community projects. Married partners face many common problems in which they join their strengths and support each other in bearing responsibilities and loads. In work-oriented marriages, this form of intimacy is one of the major channels for developing closeness. Work intimacy needs to be balanced with other forms, particularly recreational intimacy. The shared satisfactions of achieving relatively minor objectives such as redecorating a recreation room and the long-term goals of seeing one's children launched in their marriages and vocations—these are derivatives of working as a team. But the joining of hands in mutual tasks in itself can have a deepening effect on a marriage; the mutuality which stems from the feeling of a job well done is an added bonus of work intimacy.

Crisis intimacy is the strength which stems from standing together against the buffeting of fate; standing together in the major and minor tragedies which are persistent threads in the cloth from which family life is woven. Included are the times of internal testing, when a crisis occurs in the marriage itself as the shifting tides of circumstance and the pressures of aging throw the relationship off balance for a while. This particular form of crisis intimacy, derived from facing and struggling with differences, might be called "conflict intimacy." Coping successfully with the threats of internal and external crisis, through the years, helps to cement marriage ties. One couple said after the ordeal of his near-fatal auto accident and six-month hospitalization: "It was sheer hell while it was happening but it has given us a new love for life and each other."

Commitment intimacy is the core feeling of ongoing mutuality which develops in a marriage in which there is shared dedication to some value or cause that is bigger than the family, something that both partners regard as worthy of self-investment. Being captured by a common cause that turns on enthusiasm and conviction provides a powerful bond in a marriage.

Spiritual intimacy is the nearness that develops through sharing in the area of ultimate concerns, the meanings of life (to both partners), their relationship to the universe and to God. For many it is the sense of a transcendent relatedness which provides a firm foundation or supportive ground for transient human relatedness.

Participation in the life of a church or synagogue, and in the century-spanning heritage of a couple's religious tradition, often stimulates and nurtures the development of spiritual intimacy.

The common characteristic of these various expressions of intimacy is that each has the potentiality for drawing the marital partners together. Collectively, they allow opportunities for the lives of two human beings to touch significantly in an increasing number of areas. Many couples have achieved satisfying intimacy in at least a few areas. The opportunity which is before all couples is to increase the number of areas in which depth sharing occurs. This can happen as a result of planned and persistent effort, choosing the goals that attract both and planning strategy for moving toward them, remembering that there needs to be a balance among the various dimensions of intimacy in order to enrich the relationship and prevent any one facet of the relationship from being overloaded.

Of course, joint participation in any of these areas is no guarantee of intimacy. Some couples participate in one or more of these areas—sexual, aesthetic, recreational, work, for example—without the growth of any sense of organic one-ness. (They are something like nursery children at certain stages who play alongside others but not really "with" them.) In such *parallel marriages,* the pall of loneliness is not really dispelled.

"Intimacy" refers to two different things in marriage: (*a*) a close moment or period of intense sharing; (*b*) an ongoing quality of the relationship which is present even in times of some distance and conflict. The latter is the undergirding "we-ness" of a good marriage. Increasing moments and periods of intense closeness help to establish the abiding sense of dependable oneness. It is important to understand how the quality of intimacy develops.

Complementary interaction produces a *gradual narrowing of the emotional distance* until there is, in Eric Berne's terms, "a genuine interlocking of personalities,"[15] or intimacy. What develops is a kind of psychological union. In both Hebrew and Greek, the verb "to know" is the same word as to have sexual intercourse.

Clearly, to really *know* one's marital partner requires a kind of union. Such a union is the heart of intimacy. In it, the aloneness of a man and a woman's existential condition are transcended and, to some degree, overcome.

Erikson describes the union of personalities which is intimacy when he defines love as "The mutuality of mates and partners in a *shared identity,* for the mutual verification through an experience of *finding oneself, as one loses oneself in another.*"[16] The key ideas here are "shared identity" and "finding oneself [through losing] oneself in another."

The idea of shared identity opens the door to an understanding of the essence of the experience of marital intimacy. As two people continue to relate in the ways we have been describing, the breadth and depth of their relationship increase. Thus develops a new and unique psychological entity—the marital relationship. Psychiatrist Nathan Ackerman calls this entity the "marital pair identity."[17] T. S. Eliot points to this reality of shared identity when he makes one of his characters exclaim to his partner, "The new person—us!"[18] It is this "us" or "we" feeling that identifies the existence of a relationship of ongoing intimacy. Anne Philipe writes with sensitivity to this: "There was this you and this I and this we, which was not exactly you plus me, and which was coming to birth and would surpass us and contain us."[19] In other words, the *marital identity* is more than the sum of what each partner brings to the relationship. It is the sum of these, plus what they become together in their interaction. In the language of *Gestalt* psychology, the marital identity develops when there is an overlapping and a partial merging of psychological fields or worlds of meanings, of the two partners.

In some marriages the "we" feeling never develops. These are the still-born relationships in which the participants continue to live alone together, as though they were still single psychologically. In those marriages in which the "we" feeling does emerge, it does so slowly, with struggle and with frequent retreats into psychological singleness. Anne Philipe recalls:

In the beginning we had only the tiniest part of a life together. . . . We had our moments of elan and restraint. We each still kept to our reserves, watching each other. . . . "One" served as a transition from "I" to "us." We used it for a long time. And then one day the "we" appeared, said as though by accident and then thrown away; no doubt we were still unready. Later the "one" became the exception. *We had started to construct our life,* and the day this was admitted and recognized, we understood that we had been keeping back this desire for a long time. Then all of a sudden we were rich with a hundred moments and happenings we had lived through together, kept in our memories because they had united us. Sometimes the presence of a stranger made us bolder. I would talk about a walk in the rain, or you would say that a cloudy sky can be marvelous. . . . We were laying in our stores. It was a long job of work and it engaged our lives so completely that sometimes it frightened us. At those times we would suddenly turn away without uttering a word and stop seeing each other.[20]

The development of some degree of shared identity occurs in any close relationship. Emerson's familiar statement, "I am a part of every man whose path has crossed mine," states a basic psychological truth—viz., that our relationships become a part of us. The unique opportunity in a good marriage is that of developing a degree of shared identity through a *continuity* and *fidelity* of relating seldom available in any other context. Two people who have lived together for forty years, having experienced the sunlight and shadow of married life and rearing a family, have shared many dimensions of their lives. If there has been what Ross Snyder calls "creative fidelity"—"long term commitment to the growth of the other and to the 'both' "[21]—such a marital pair has a profound and marvelous degree of closeness. The pity is that so many couples are unable to use their years of being together to deepen their relationship.

DEGREES OF INTIMACY

In their study of sexual and marital behavior among affluent couples married for ten years or more, Cuber and Harroff discovered five recurring configurations of male-female relationships in marriages.²² The first was the *conflict-habituated*. These were couples for whom fighting seemed almost a way of life. Their dominant mode of relating was through the exchange of hostility. A kind of intimacy can develop in such a relationship. It may be, as some psychiatrists have suggested, that the need to do battle with one another is the cohesion that holds these couples together.

The second pattern consisted of the *devitalized*. Often these couples reported being deeply in love in the early years of marriage —including spending a great deal of time together and enjoying sex. Now these relationships have become voids. The zest is gone. Sex is much less satisfying qualitatively and quantitatively. Little time is spent together and there are few shared interests. Some seemed resigned to their apathetic, "habit-cage" existence. Others were less accepting; both assumed that "marriage is like this." In such relationships there is occasional sharing, if only of a memory. One man said, "Tomorrow we are celebrating the anniversary of our anniversary."²³ The intimacy in these marriages seems to be mainly an unburied corpse. They illustrate an important truth— that intimacy can never be taken for granted. It can be lost.

The third pattern, the *passive-congenial,* is much like the devitalized, except that the passivity has been there from the beginning. There is little conflict. Things are polite, convenient, and conventional. There is some sharing of common interests. Sex is often regarded, by both partners, as of little importance. Unlike the devitalized, there is no sense of "barren gullies in their lives left by the erosion of earlier satisfactions."²⁴

The fourth mode of marriage, the *vital,* stands in sharp contrast to the previous three types, although these couples say and do many of the same things. The difference is the presence in the vital marriages of a high degree of intimacy:

But when the close, intimate, confidential, empathic look is taken, the essence of the vital relationship becomes clear: the mates are intensely bound together psychologically in important life matters.

Their sharing and their togetherness is genuine. It provides the life essence for both man and woman.[25]

One of the husbands of such a couple reported: "The things we do together aren't fun intrinsically—the ecstasy comes from *being together in the doing*. Take her out of the picture and I wouldn't give a damn for the boat, the lake, or any of the fun that goes on there." People in this kind of vital relationship know that their style of life is not comprehensible to most of their associates. One such couple declared, "The *big* part of our lives is completely mutual. . . ." Their central satisfactions are found in "the life they live with and through each other."

The *total* relationship, the fifth pattern, is like the vital, but there are many more points of vital meshing. In some cases there is vital sharing in all the important areas. One husband described his wife of thirty years as his "friend, mistress and partner."[26] This kind of multifaceted intimacy, as Cuber and Harroff indicate, is rare, in marriage or out, but it does exist.

These five types of marital relationships do not necessarily represent degrees of marital stability. Most of those in all five categories said that they were reasonably content, if not happy. What they represent is five styles of relating and different degrees of intimacy. There are undoubtedly many other styles and degrees of intimacy. It should be noted that there are many factors in addition to intimacy and happiness which play a role in holding a marriage together.[27]

What is the optimal degree of intimacy in a marriage? There is no arbitrary way of determining this. Rather, each couple must work out its own most-satisfying pattern of intimacy. *Intimacy is different for different people*. In all marriages there are cycles of moving toward and moving away from one's spouse. In some marriages contact can be maintained for a brief time only. In others the tolerance for intimacy is so low that the partners seldom, if ever, really touch. Still others, like the *vital* and *total* relationships, can luxuriate in intimacy for longer periods of time. Most of us achieve depth relatedness only a small part of the time and in certain limited areas of our marriages. In spite of the designation "total" relationship in the study cited above, it is our experience that there are at one time or another walls in every marriage, sometimes high, sometimes low. Most of us long for more intimacy than we have found. We hunger for the walls to be lowered. The message of this book is that significant lowering of the walls usually is possible, if a couple is willing to work at developing the potential for joy, pleasure, and creativity in their marriage.

TAKING ACTION

Discuss your reactions to the ideas in Chapter 2. At what points are they relevant to your marriage? Make an inventory of the facets of your marriage in which you feel that you have achieved some degree of sharing and sense of closeness. You may find it helpful to use the "Marital Intimacy Checkup" to identify the areas in which each of you would like to improve your relationship. The form headed "Marital Intimacy Action Plan" may be useful in planning your approach to this improvement. Or you may prefer a less-structured approach to understanding and improving your relationship. Do it in your own way. The important thing is to begin discovering how to apply the ideas that make sense to you, in your relationship.

MARITAL INTIMACY CHECKUP

(Instructions: After discussing each area, check the blanks that apply to your relationship.)

Facets of Intimacy	Both Desire Improvement	Wife Desires Improvement	Husband Desires Improvement	Both Satisfied
1. Sexual Intimacy	——	——	——	——
2. Emotional Intimacy (Being tuned to each other's wavelength)	——	——	——	——

3. Intellectual Intimacy
(Closeness in the world
of ideas)   ——   ——   ——   ——

4. Aesthetic Intimacy
(Sharing experiences of
beauty)   ——   ——   ——   ——

5. Creative Intimacy
(Sharing in acts of creating
together)   ——   ——   ——   ——

6. Recreational Intimacy
(Relating in experiences
of fun and play)   ——   ——   ——   ——

7. Work Intimacy
(The closeness of sharing
common tasks)   ——   ——   ——   ——

8. Crisis Intimacy
(Closeness in coping with
problems and pain)   ——   ——   ——   ——

9. Conflict Intimacy
(Facing and struggling
with differences)   ——   ——   ——   ——

10. Commitment Intimacy
(Mutuality derived from
common self-investment)   ——   ——   ——   ——

11. Spiritual Intimacy
(The we-ness in sharing
ultimate concerns)   ——   ——   ——   ——

12. Communication Intimacy
(The source of all types
of true intimacy)   ——   ——   ——   ——

                    Total   ——   ——   ——   ——

MARITAL INTIMACY ACTION PLAN

(Instructions: In those areas in which both of you desire improvement, discuss specific next steps which you feel can be taken to increase the degree of mutuality and meaningful closeness in each area. If you agree on specific action in one or more areas, decide on how you will go about implementing your plan. If you agree on what you want to do in several areas, decide on which should have priority. Jot down the main ideas for action under the appropriate categories below. If you cannot agree on any concrete plan in any area in which you both desire change, you may need to consult a marriage counselor.)

Sexual Intimacy:

Emotional Intimacy:

Intellectual Intimacy:

Aesthetic Intimacy:

Creative Intimacy:

Recreational Intimacy:

Work Intimacy:

Crisis Intimacy:

Conflict Intimacy:

Commitment Intimacy:

Spiritual Intimacy:

Communication Intimacy:

NOTES

1. Lois Wyse, *Love Poems for the Very Married* (Cleveland: World Publishing Co., 1967), p. 41.
2. We are indebted to Ross Snyder for this conception of guiding images.
3. Kahlil Gibran, *The Prophet* (New York: Alfred A. Knopf, 1940), p. 64.
4. Carl R. Rogers, *On Becoming a Person* (Boston: Houghton Mifflin, 1961), pp. 47–49.
5. Paul Tournier, *To Understand Each Other* (Richmond, Va.: John Knox Press, 1967), p. 14.
6. Ross Snyder, unpublished paper entitled "Married Life," p. 7.
7. Wyse, *op. cit.,* p. 51.
8. David Riesmann, *The Lonely Crowd* (Garden City, N.Y.: Doubleday Anchor Books, 1954), p. 183.
9. Abraham Maslow, *Motivation and Personality* (New York: Harper & Row, 1954).

10. For a classic study of these two sets of needs see John Levy and Ruth Monroe, *The Happy Family* (New York: Alfred A. Knopf, 1938).
11. Snyder, "Married Life," p. 6.
12. Erik Erikson, *Childhood and Society* (New York: W. W. Norton, 1963).
13. Ross Snyder, "Married Life," p. 17.
14. Eric Berne, *Games People Play* (New York: Grove Press, 1964).
15. Eric Berne, *Transactional Analysis in Psychotherapy* (New York: Grove Press, 1961), p. 86.
16. Erik Erikson, *Insight and Responsibility* (New York: W. W. Norton, 1964), p. 128 (italics added).
17. Nathan Ackerman, *The Psychodynamics of Family Life* (New York: Basic Books, 1958), p. 22.
18. T. S. Eliot, *The Cocktail Party* (New York: Harcourt, Brace and Co., 1950), Act two, p. 137.
19. Anne Philipe, *No Longer Than a Sigh* (New York: Atheneum, 1964), p. 34.
20. *Ibid.,* p. 86.
21. Snyder, "Married Life," p. 13.
22. John Cuber and Peggy Harroff, *The Significant Americans* (New York: Appleton-Century, 1965).
23. *Ibid.,* p. 50.
24. *Ibid.,* p. 54.
25. *Ibid.,* p. 55.
26. *Ibid.,* p. 58.
27. For a discussion of the multiple factors influencing marital cohesion see "Marital Cohesiveness and Dissolution: An Integrative Review" by George Leninger, *Journal of Marriage and the Family,* Vol. 27, No. 1 (February, 1965), pp. 19–28.

3 Barriers to Intimacy

It is strange that in our society the things that go into a relationship—the sharing of tastes, fantasies, dreams, hopes and fears—seem to make people more shy and vulnerable than going to bed with each other does. They are more wary of the tenderness that goes with psychological and spiritual nakedness than of the physical nakedness in sexual intimacy.

Rollo May[1]

It is clear that there are forces in all marriage relationships which pull the partners toward intimacy. The sum of these forces we have called "the will to relate." It is equally clear that there are forces which block intimacy and cause husbands and wives to move away from each other. It has been said that men and women appear to pour endless ingenuity into creating new ways to be miserable together. The fact that so many couples achieve almost no genuine intimacy suggests that the counterforces to the will to relate must be very strong indeed. The walls, or barriers, in a marriage are frequently high and thick. The prominent characteristic of such a marriage is not intimacy but distance, not warm mutuality but estrangement. A therapist who does group counseling with couples states: "One basic conflict characterizes all marriage neuroses: need for closeness and fear of it."[2] In disturbed marriages, the conflict (ambivalence) between moving toward and moving away from one's partner is intense. In relatively healthy marriages, the two-way pull is less evident. But regardless of the intensity of the ambivalence, it accounts for the alternate coming together and moving apart that is the rhythm of all relationships.

If the goal is to increase the degree of intimacy in marriage, it is important to gain some understanding of the barriers to intimacy —those ways of interacting which keep people apart. Such understanding may be an essential step toward lowering the barriers.

Basic to any individual's ability to relate intimately with another person is a firm *sense of personal identity*—a dependable core feeling of who one is as a separate individual, of what one really values in contrast to the oughts and shoulds of others— one's intrinsic value as a person not dependent on the whims of approval and disapproval of others. Achieving a firm sense of identity is the focal task of each person during adolescence. Many young people do not succeed at this task and are thus unable to proceed toward genuine intimacy in marriage. None of us ever succeeds fully. But the degree of success in the identity search is at the heart of the first (and each subsequent) crisis of intimacy in marriage. Many young, married partners are still contending with the need to discover their identities more fully and have, therefore, a shaky foundation on which to construct an intimate relationship. Ideally both partners should be far enough along in achieving a sense of identity that they can support each other in the continuing struggle. One reason for the failure of so many teenage marriages is precisely that the young people are still each searching for themselves; they have not had the time nor the experience which is required in our culture for the establishment of a strong self-identity.

Erik Erikson, who has thrown more light on the identity struggle than any other student of humanity, states:

Identity proves itself strongest where it can take chances with itself. For this reason, love in its truest sense presupposes both identity and fidelity . . . . only graduation from adolescence permits the development of intimacy, the selflessness of joined devotion, which anchors love in mutual commitment.[3]

The distant person has difficulty relating to others because he has difficulty relating to himself. He is out of touch with his own feelings and so cannot recognize or respond appropriately to the feelings of others. The impact of this lack of self-other awareness on a marital relationship is to block communication of feelings and meanings, and therefore to interfere with mutual need-satisfaction. It is difficult to know when to feed a person if neither he nor you knows that he is hungry.

The point is that one cannot truly give of himself in any relationship until he has found himself, and therefore has something to give. A person who is not sure of himself will find intimacy too threatening simply because it requires him to lose himself to some degree in the relationship. As a person becomes more sure of himself, he increasingly seeks intimacy in relationships.

An illuminating insight in understanding the dynamics of nonintimacy is the realization that the same forces which prevent a person from relating closely with others also block him from being intimately related to himself. If a person is cut off from vital relations with others, he is also cut off from vital areas within his own life. The barrenness of his person-to-person contacts is an extension of the arid desert of his inner landscape. In her brilliant exploration of the dynamics of detachment, Antonia Wenkart points out that, fundamentally, detachment is a way of attempting to cope with relationships by moving away from other people *and from oneself.* "The movement away from life experiences and from relationships . . . the distance from the individual's own feelings causes estrangement, alienation from himself."[4] The highly detached person becomes "a stranger to himself."

Although the absence of a firm sense of identity is most critical in the intimacy crisis of early marriage, it is also basic to the achievement of intimacy at each subsequent stage. Failure at one stage compounds the difficulties at the next. The growing ability to achieve the we-ness or marital identity described in Chapter 2 depends upon each partner's firm sense of personal identity.

It should be re-emphasized that identity is not an absolute or a once-and-for-all achievement. There is a wide variation in the degree to which it is achieved by each individual during adolescence and young adulthood. There is also a difference in the way each individual feels his own identity from time to time. When things go well the inclination is to feel a strong and good sense of self; when things go badly or in the midst of crisis, the sense of self is often severely threatened. Nonetheless, it is true that a certain ongoing core of inner identity, strength, autonomy and self-love, is necessary in order for an individual to be capable of relating creatively and intimately with another person.

What can be done when a person has not achieved a strong enough self-acceptance? If his lack is severe, he should get some kind of psychotherapy which will help him to discover some answers to the two big identity questions—"Who am I? What am I worth?" Marriage partners who wish to strengthen and affirm their own and each other's feelings of identity can do so in many ways. Given a certain basic feeling of self-worth, couples have the ideal opportunity to grow in their individual and their shared identities. Through group experiences together, through affirming each other's masculinity and femininity, two people who are learning to trust each other can practice the leap of faith which allows them to discover that it *is* possible to be safely close to another person. (Some specific ways of doing this will be discussed in chapters 4 and 5.)

A number of barriers to intimacy grow out of an inadequate sense of identity. One of these barriers is *emotional immaturity*. In a sense, the degree of emotional maturity of a couple equals their capacity for intimacy. The operation of emotional immaturity in marriage takes many forms: giving primary commitment to parents rather than to the marital relationship; remaining stuck in premarital "I-ism"[5]—thinking and making decisions in terms of psychological singleness; thinking in terms of getting rather than of giving-and-receiving; demanding that the other person "make me happy"; wanting to be taken care of in a kind of childlike dependency without putting much into the relationship; showing little control of impulses and self-centered whims in the relationship. The over-all tone of marriages in which emotional immaturity is a prominent element is one of mutual demandingness, an individualistic "living one's own life," and the lack of a sense of responsibility for the shared task of creating a relationship in which all persons can grow.

The *fear of being hurt* in close relationships is rooted both in unfinished identity and in emotional immaturity. The fear in such cases has the quality of fear of smothering, being swallowed, losing one's autonomy, or even oneself, in relationships. Those who in early life had to sacrifice their strivings toward independence in order to be loved and accepted by parents, tend to experience any closeness as a threat to their feelings of strength and adequacy. They are tortured by loneliness and a crying need for closeness, and at the same time by the fear of being hurt or crippled if they let another person near them. To illustrate: Alice's parents used praise to manipulate her during her childhood; consequently, as a thirty-two-year-old adult, she experiences her husband's sincere appreciation as frighteningly controlling, even though she is also hungry for his affirmation of her.

Low self-esteem and *guilt feelings* are twin barriers to intimacy which, in turn, are closely linked with unfinished identity. A sturdy sense of self-worth is an essential element in the feeling of identity; it makes a person "cope-able." The person who pictures himself as of little value feels unlovable, and therefore expects rejection. Rather than risk the pain of being rejected, he may avoid the closeness which would expose him to that risk. He may hide his feelings of worthlessness behind a façade of pride, grandiosity, or phony humility. If he marries it will be to *get,* since he feels that he has nothing to *give.* He will want in his spouse the qualities he feels he most lacks—strength, competence, worth, givingness. Frequently, he will attach himself to another person of damaged self-esteem who is looking for the same things and who also has a façade which hides deeper feelings of self-rejection.[6] Both will want the impossible—to be richly fed while keeping at a safe distance.

Guilt blocks intimacy by breeding low self-esteem and *self-alienation*. Erikson shows how distortions of conscience can make a man his own worst judge. "The resulting inhibitions and repressions could be expressed in terms of alienation, for they can turn man's most intimate wishes and memories into *alien territory*."[7] Neurotic guilt feelings cause a person to fear the exposure which he expects will occur if he allows a close relationship to develop. The husband who said to the counselor, "If my wife really got past my shell, she'd find out what a phony failure I am," is a case in point. His guilt was not about some gross and obvious dereliction such as marital infidelity; rather, it was his feeling that he was not as competent or always-genuine as he thought his wife believed him to be. His need to maintain the picture in his own mind of what he assumed to be his wife's picture of him created the fear of loss which he felt would result from exposure of his human frailty. Through joint counseling, eventually he was able to let go of his cruelly perfectionistic self-image, to discover that his wife was quite aware of his weaknesses, and loved him as much because of them as in spite of them.

Whether the fear of discovery is derived from low self-esteem or guilt feelings (neurotic or rational), or both, a vicious cycle usually comes into operation: the fear forces the person to build higher and higher interpersonal walls; the higher they become, the more his anger and guilt accumulate behind them; and the more oppressive these painful feelings become, the higher and thicker must grow the walls. The sense of relief and release which comes from learning that discovery by others does not necessarily bring rejection, and often brings acceptance, is an experience of indescribable burden-lifting for such a person. Feeling accepted for oneself regardless of one's frailties is, as one member of a marital growth group put it, "a juicy taste of the grace of God in my marriage." When two people with the guilt-fear-hiding vicious cycle marry, the wall-building proceeds from both sides with an intensity bred of fear of discovery.

The fundamental feeling of vulnerability which is grounded in unfinished identity and its by-products—emotional immaturity, fear of being hurt, low self-esteem, guilt—brings a barrage of relationship-damaging defenses into action whenever closeness with another person threatens to develop. These commonly used defenses constitute further barriers to intimacy. They are the defenses by which one or both of the marital partners attempt to control the relationship in order to avoid intimacy and the anxiety it produces. Robert W. White states:

> . . . Personal relationships are easily injured by anxiety and defenses . . . . defenses freeze the repertory of safe social behavior and block the attempting of new responses. Suppose that a person has learned to cover social discomfort by fast, superficial chattering, thus avoiding both the silences that would make him anxious and the serious discussions that would challenge his competence. His discomfort forbids him to stop chattering; thus he never learns how people would respond to him, or how he would respond to them, in other kinds of interaction. Social learning is peculiarly vulnerable to the working of anxiety and defense.[8]

People who are partially immobilized by big, painful feelings are unable to use their inner resources fully and flexibly in their relationships.

Among the defenses which are often used to avoid intimacy is the substitution of *pseudo-intimacy* for the real thing. Jean-Paul Sartre tells the story of Henri who is impotent, and Lulu who is afraid of sex.[9] He paints a powerful word-picture of the revulsion-attraction in a relationship of leechlike attachment, a "zipper relationship" based on rigid, interlocking neuroses. Henri and Lulu are people who can draw close to each other only in limited ways. Theirs is the blind clinging of people held together by their intense fear of loneliness. For many people such relationships are the only alternative to utter loneliness, but they do not represent creative intimacy or produce growth.

There is a variety of forms of counterfeit intimacy which are further removed from creative intimacy even than that described by Sartre. Counterfeit intimacy is closeness without mutuality or concern; it is closeness whose purpose is manipulation or exploitation of the other, without regard for his or her needs. Salesmen often try to get close to potential customers in order to gain the emotional leverage necessary to make a sale. The same manipulative use of closeness may occur in marriage. It should be apparent that the issue of pseudo-intimacy as a barrier to growth-producing intimacy is a continuation of the intimacy-autonomy discussion in Chapter 2. The price of closeness in pseudo-intimacy is the sacrifice of healthy autonomy. Lyman C. Wynne writes: "In pseudo-mutuality, independence of expectations and affirmation of a sense of personal identity, is experienced as demolishing the entire relation."[10] In contrast, genuine intimacy thrives on the differences which distinguish the uniqueness of each individual. In pseudo-intimacy, one's marital partner is perceived as an extension of oneself, not as a separate person with wants and needs of his own. There is a symbiotic quality—a kind of mutual parasitism—in this kind of clinging-vine, compulsive attachment. The Siamese-twin closeness leaves no spaces in the togetherness of marriage. It therefore strangulates growth of the individuals. There is little mutual respect, particularly of the right of each to realize his own unique personhood.

Another form of pseudo-intimacy is physical familiarity without interpersonal relatedness. Adolescents and older persons who are still adolescents emotionally often confuse a kind of mechanical sexual gratification with genuine human sexuality which must include relatedness. Impersonal sex is dehumanized sex; it lacks that which makes human sex more than animal sex—an ongoing multi-leveled interpersonal relationship.

Pseudo-intimacy is sometimes characterized by endless superficial contacts with masses of casual acquaintances. One hundred years ago, William Alger wrote of "the thick solitudes called social." He pointed to discomfort with one's inner being as one cause of this: "They whose thoughts are in a fair and hurry within, are sometimes fain to retire into company to be out of the crowd of themselves."[11] Oversocializing is a way of protecting oneself from depth relationships. Sociability, however, is never a satisfactory substitute for intimacy, for it leaves the person with a consuming loneliness based on the feeling that no other human being is really in touch or understands.

It is possible to view *chronic busy-ness* as another barrier to intimacy. Certainly it is true that love and intimacy require time to grow. Middle-class adults (and children) are frantically overscheduled. That this constant breathless running blocks out the occasions for closeness is undeniable. We live in a society in which it is easy to be too busy—a society in which people trying for their first heart attack are rewarded by social approval of their "drive," "ambition," and "success." However, busy-ness is also *a symptom of our fear of intimacy*. We run so we won't have to relate in depth! Could it be that our society's pressure toward superficial relatedness is an expression of general fear of intimacy —with self and others?

Mishandled hostility is often a barrier to intimacy in marriage. There are hidden volcanoes of stored-up anger in many long-standing marriages. Because the partners are afraid to face the anger and work it through, it comes out in a constant trickle of sniping and "cutting each other down," or in a variety of other expressions such as psychosomatic illness (anger turned on the self to manipulate the other). Buried hostility is often expressed in a vicious cold war in which there is mutual refusal to communicate and to feed the other's needs. Frozen rage is frequently at the root of sexual difficulties such as impotence and frigidity.

When rage is kept "under the lid" for a long time, the pressure builds up like steam in a teakettle with the spout sealed up. The explosion which eventually comes can take many forms—a temper tantrum of uncontrolled aggression, a striking out at the other by having an affair, a period of severe depression, or a "nervous breakdown" in which the person's coping abilities are temporarily immobilized by a flood of frightening impulses. If rage is imprisoned within a person for a long time or if, at the other extreme, a person knows that he has poor control of his hostile impulses, he may avoid intimacy because he is terrified that he might do harm to anyone who gets close to him. Avoidance of dealing with the negative feelings in a marriage is the equivalent of storing dynamite in the cellar of one's house. Long-hidden anger often produces an explosion which seems to justify the fear that caused the anger to be hidden in the first place.

The healthy alternative to overcontrol of negative feelings in a marriage is not the absence of control. Chronic expression of hostility is also a sign that basic needs of the marital partners are not being met in the relationship. Unsatisfied hunger inevitably produces anger. Chronic anger and attack compound the damage to self-esteem resulting from the unsatisfied needs. To this is added the appropriate guilt produced by hurting each other.

In marriages in which fighting seems to be the chief recreation, the function of hostility is to allow a touching without intimacy. The partner who feels engulfed by the proximity of a mate will often experience panic causing him to try to salvage his sense of identity and autonomy by means of a hostile attack. If intimacy threatens to develop, one or both will pick a fight. This move gains both distance and a sharpened sense of identity in the experience of fighting one's partner. It is usually done in such a way as to make the initiator appear to be the innocent victim, thus simultaneously providing an excuse for not having sex or relating in other ways, and making the other person seem to be the one responsible for the schism. Such use of hostility in a kind of wild reaching-out to each other may seem to allow the couple to eat its cake and have it too. Actually, the "cake" of deeply satisfying relationships is neither tasted nor retained, since intimacy is sabotaged consistently. The persons are saying neither Yes nor No to relating— only a kind of unsatisfying "maybe at a distance." Edrita Fried points out that "Every new recourse to hostility, while undertaken of necessity and as an emergency measure, simultaneously reinforces the unhappy conviction that happiness is out of reach."[12]

The process of relating, in such cases, involves a pushing away of love and intimacy as the person tries again and again to get these in self-defeating ways.

It is important to make clear that creative intimacy is not dependent on the absence of hostility, resentments, and other negative feelings from a marriage. If it were, there would be *no* intimacy, since negative feelings are persistent and valuable threads in the cloth from which all close human relations are cut. The crucial issues are: the sources of such negative feelings; their intensity; whether they are appropriate to the present relationship or left-over from past relationships; whether they are balanced by loving feelings, and whether the relationship possesses enough trust and openness to allow the feelings to be faced and worked through. Couples who can deal with their mutual resentments openly, within the wider context of their affection and respect for each other, can "fight clean" without always attacking the other's self-esteem. They can move *through* their conflict to greater intimacy. For such couples, a good healthy fight occasionally clears the air and gives their marriage a new vigor. Besides these benefits, as one husband observed, "Making up is great fun!"*

Still another barrier to intimacy in marriage is the *manipulation* of one spouse by the other in order to make him fit into a prescribed mold. Manipulation often is a two-way game, with each partner trying to outmanipulate the other. There are several forms of interaction in which manipulation is the basic ingredient. One of these is *ghost marriages.*

Some lively ghosts are still spooking around in most marriages, influencing and undermining the present relationship. All of us are, to some extent, prisoners of the past; in no area is this more apparent than in marriage. Maturing emotionally—the process of cutting one's ties to past relationships and learning to live in present relationships—is a slow, painful struggle in which even

* An illuminating exploration of the function of healthy fighting in the achievement of intimacy is found in *The Intimate Enemy* by George R. Bach and Peter Wyden (New York: William Morrow, 1969).

the most fortunate of us is only partially successful. Those who are caught in past relationships which are carried within them tend to create *ghost marriages*. Manipulation is required when one partner needs to fit the other into his unresolved and ever-present past.

Marriage-influencing ghosts come in various forms, shapes, and sizes. The most common are those involved in "parentifying one's spouse."[13] The essence of neurotic family relationships, as Otto Pollak has observed, is seeking in the family you have created by marriage what you wanted in the family created by your parents, and in not being able, therefore, to enjoy your present family.[14] What is sought when a person projects the image of a parent-figure onto his spouse is both the good things one got as a child from parents and the things one wanted but didn't get because of inadequacies in them. Fulfilling such dual and extreme demands is impossible for any spouse. Both husband and wife experience frustration and anger, including the intense anger left over from childhood deprivations. The anger and guilt produced by parentifying a spouse contribute to the inability to enjoy the real satisfactions which potentially are available in the marriage. The tricky thing about the spooks in a marriage is that they often function without the couple being aware of them. One's own ghosts are particularly difficult to see; one's partner's ghosts are somewhat more recognizable (not to him, of course). A husband says, "You're acting just like your mother," or "You want me to treat you like your father did." These are examples of how awareness of the operation of a spouse's ghosts is used to clobber him or her. The context of hostility in which such observations occur usually vitiates the possibility of the wife achieving increased self-understanding by accepting whatever truth is in the husband's statements. In a somewhat more objective context such as marriage counseling, it is often helpful to a couple to discover how their relationship is being damaged by their respective ghosts.

The internalized parental ghosts are of two types—good ghosts and bad ghosts. Carl G. Jung held that each of us has two sides to his inner image of the mother—the good, giving mother and the bad, withholding mother. The images of the madonna and the witch are symbolic ways of putting outside ourselves this inner split in the mother image. The same dichotomy exists in the father image. There is the good, protecting father and the bad, punishing father within each marital partner.

The man who has not met and made peace with his own "witchy" side will tend to project this withholding mother image onto a woman and fight it there. Mother-in-law jokes indicate that she is a favorite target and a way to avoid facing not only one's negative feelings toward one's own mother, but particularly toward that part of one's mother that one carries around within him. In marital conflict, the split mother image often gets projected onto two different women—the bad mother onto the wife and the good mother onto the "other woman" who "understands." Since the mate now bears the projected image of the witch, the husband's angry "Child" side can, with less guilt, burn her at the stake, symbolically, in the fires of vicious attack. Intense feelings of rejection in sick relationships, and in relatively healthy marriages in stormy periods, are the results of perceiving the spouse as almost entirely a bad parent figure, without the sprinkling of good, feeding qualities which redeem the anger in most marriages. In healthy marital fights there seems to be a point at which the bad-parent projection is counterbalanced by the good-parent image, leading to a reconciliation, as the couple pulls itself out of a tailspin of mutual attack and retaliation.

The image of the bad parent, when projected onto the other, tends to produce alienation in the marriage. The good-parent image may serve as a bridge for establishing greater intimacy with the mutually nurturing sides of each spouse. The reason for this is that if one treats his spouse in a warm, appreciative way, he will tend to respond with his good, giving side. Conversely, if one treats his spouse like a witchy-bitchy parent (withholding, punishing, or controlling), that side of the spouse will tend to be elicited.

The understanding of the positive and negative cycles involved here is crucial to increasing the need-satisfaction qualities of a marriage. What is operating is a "self-fulfilling prophecy"—negative or positive.

Pete had a bad day at work so that he was feeling low in self-esteem. When he came in the door of his home in the suburbs, his first remark was a gruff "What's for supper?" Marjorie sensed his irritated tone and assumed that he was mad at her. She responded with a defensive, "Can't you even say 'hello'?" Since her sense of adequacy was frayed from a less-than-satisfying sexual experience in which she had not had an orgasm the night before, her feelings were hurt by Pete's "forgetting" to kiss her. Instead of asking for what she wanted (which she couldn't do without risking rejection or, at best, spoiling what she really wanted—spontaneous affection from Pete), she made a critical remark about his neglect of paying the gas bill. His response was, "What have *you* been doing all day?"

Thus began a four-day fight between Pete and Marjorie. Wounded self-esteem on both sides increased the need to attack. Each attack increased the pain of their feeling-wounds and, consequently, their urge to counterattack. As they treated each other like withholding, punishing parents, they tended to bring out precisely that side of each other which seemed to justify the attack. Eventually, their guilt, loneliness, and underlying need and love for each other tilted their interaction toward the restoration of positive need-satisfaction. When Pete reached out with a gesture of reconciliation and Margorie responded, they began a cycle leading toward intimacy—i.e., a cycle of reciprocal need-satisfaction.

What is described here is a process that operates in even the healthiest marriages at times, causing temporary alienation and loss of intimacy. The self-perpetuating cycle phenomenon is basic to understanding both marriage conflict and satisfaction. Rejection spawns rejection and satisfaction elicits satisfaction; mutual rejection or satisfaction, like snowballs rolling downhill, grow in both size and momentum. The difference between a viable, functioning marriage and a dysfunctional one is not the absence of negative cycles in the former. Rather, it is the ability of the couple in the relatively healthy marriages to interrupt their own anti-intimacy cycles and to keep the pro-intimacy cycles predominant.

Ghosts are particularly active in interfering with full sexual intimacy. For example, when a husband projects a mother image, with all the attached feelings, onto his wife and reacts as if she were his mother, he collides head-on with incest taboo which is deep in all known cultures. Unconscious fears and fantasies from that period in his life (three and one half to six) when he wished to replace his father in his mother's affections* are stirred up. The result is painful anxiety which interferes with full sexual pleasure. Sexual contact produces guilt, often on an unconscious level, which takes the edge off the ecstasy of intercourse or may even cause impotence or a renunciation of interest in sex as forms of self-punishment.

The sibling-rival marriage[15] is another variation of the ghost marriage. In such relationships, the power-struggle is intense. Each tries, by hook and by crook, to stay "one-up" on the other. The competition may take many forms—vying for control of the money, of the sexual relationship, of the children, of each other; competing for attention from parent-figures; being jealous and resentful of the other's successes and hypercritical of his weaknesses and failures; automatically taking the opposite position on most issues, thus ensuring a constant struggle. Paul Tournier describes "the competitor"[16] who feels he must prove himself better than everyone with whom he relates. He likens such a person to those chess champions who can carry on thirty games simultaneously with able opponents. When this kind of person marries, he tries to prove his worth at the expense of and against his mate. He will project onto his spouse the image of the sibling with whom he competed as a child for the love and approval of his parents. In the case of a wife who has an underlying resentment of what she sees to be the unfair advantages and opportunities of males in our society (and in her childhood family), rivalry with her husband

*This is the "Oedipal period." See Chapter 8 for a fuller explanation.

will be intense. Because wives are not supposed to have such feelings (according to our cultural myth), she must express her rivalry in covert undercutting rather than in open opposition.

One manifestation of ghost marriages is what Eric Berne calls *marital games*—stereotyped patterns of mutual manipulation learned in childhood by observing the games one's parent's played.[17] A "game," in his system of social psychiatry, is an interpersonal transaction in which each person has an ulterior motive. In other words, it is mutually manipulative. It is socially programed in the sense that it follows an automatic, predictable sequence. It is when relationships become nonmanipulative, when they lose their hidden motivations, and become individually programed, that is, spontaneous and expressive of the person, that intimacy begins. Games, as Berne makes clear, are substitutes for intimacy. The degree of intimacy which a couple achieves is usually in proportion to their success in extricating themselves from their games. The intimacy-damaging games are between the Parent side or ego state of one partner and the Child side or ego state of the other. These ego states are the results of early-life relationships.

Berne holds that most marriages have one or two games which provide the motifs for all interaction. Dating is a process similar to casting for a play. It is a search for someone who will play the same games. The unconscious contract in a marriage is the non-verbal agreement between the two parties that they will play each other's games "so long as we both shall live." An insightful wife described in counseling the prolonged temper tantrum which her husband was having because she was no longer interested in playing the Parent-Child game which had been their unconscious marriage contract; the game had been that she would continue to baby him like his mother had, putting up with his egocentric, inconsiderate behavior in return for the feeling of power this gave her. When one partner stops playing "their game," for whatever reason, the other invariably reacts with a sense of betrayal and with anger.

Many couples take turns being "Parent" to each other. For a

while, one is the strong, adequate one and the other the helpless "Child." Then the game is reversed. In other marriages, one partner consistently plays "Parent" to the other in most (but usually not all) areas of the relationship. The basic intimacy-denying dynamic in all marital games is *mutual manipulation.* The spouse playing "Child" controls by means of helplessness, sickness, "brattishness," and various forms of passive-aggressive maneuvering—bungling, being messy, and keeping others waiting, for example. The spouse playing "Parent" manipulates in more obvious ways—e.g., by being the giver, controller, and decider. The pattern of manipulation between the sexes is deeply rooted in our culture. For example, in dating practices, the boy often uses his initiative-taking prerogative to keep the girl in suspense; she retaliates by playing one boy against another or by keeping him waiting when he comes for a date. Behind the need to manipulate and control others is the fear of being controlled and the fear of real intimacy with mutual transparency. I cannot be genuinely close to someone to whom I cannot "show my hand." Manipulating, hiding, and emotional distance go together.

It should be observed in passing that there are times when both husband and wife need each other to be the good mother and the good father. When a man is feeling discouraged or hurt by the frustrations of his job, for example, some gentle and understanding nurturance from his wife can be a step toward intimacy. Let's bring Pete home again:

Pete had had a bad day at work so that he was feeling low in self-esteem. When he came in the door of his home in the suburbs, his first remark was a gruff, "What's for supper?" Marjorie heard his irritation and sensed that his ego had been under fire that day. She responded by putting her arms around him in greeting. "Roast beef, and it's almost done. Let's sit down and relax a few minutes before dinner." Over an intimate cup of coffee Marjorie let Pete know that she sensed his misery and gradually he could accept her "mothering" and tell her about it, thus helping to ease the pain.

Of course, Marjorie's response presupposes that she was not

angry this time over a poor sexual experience the night before, and that they had a trusting enough relationship that Pete could share his fears and failures with her. Similarly, there are times when a woman needs to be fathered by her husband. This kind of mutual need-satisfaction is of a different quality from the marital games which involve parentifying the spouse. It also assumes that both spouses do not happen to need parenting at the same time, or that if they do, they can recognize and deal with it.

Closely related to ghost marriages and marital games is the *conflict of role expectancies*. This is the clash between the inner images or pictures which each partner brings to the marriage, of what constitutes "right" roles for men-women, husbands-wives, fathers-mothers, fathers-sons, fathers-daughters, mothers-sons, mothers-daughters etc. Every person brings literally dozens of these images, absorbed unconsciously in his family-of-origin. These inner pictures tend to determine how he feels and behaves and how he expects his mate to feel and behave in the varied roles each takes in marriage.

To some degree, expectations determine what a person feels he needs in the marriage. One study showed that women from blue-collar families, with less than high school education, expect little psychological intimacy in marriage and therefore are not demanding in this area.[18] This contrasts sharply with the middle-class woman's expectation that marriage "naturally involves sharing, closeness and communication."

The greater the discrepancy between the inner images which two persons bring to marriage, the more likely that they will have severe conflicts. If basic expectations are radically different, severe need-deprivation is bound to occur, producing anger, frustration, conflict, and a decline or absence of intimacy. Two young people from roughly the same religious and middle-class backgrounds often bring divergent pictures of what a wife should expect of a husband and vice versa, who does what and when, who takes out the garbage, sees that the auto gets lubricated, cleans the basement, who takes the initiative in sex, what patterns of sex-play are "normal," who makes decisions in dozens of areas, who takes what role in the religious practices of the family, how responsibility is divided in rearing the children, etc. When two people come from different social or ethnic backgrounds, the inner models of appropriate behavior and feelings are even more divergent. The task for every couple after the honeymoon is that "somehow the two must integrate into a satisfying partnership and conjoint career plan, two designs for family living, two sets of expectations for the relationship, and two dreams for the future."[19]

The contemporary model of the democratic "companionship marriage" and the fuzziness of changing male-female roles complicate the role-expectation problems. A social worker who has done group counseling with engaged couples states: ". . . former guidelines for role behavior of husbands, wives, and children are no longer valid in our society."[20] The emergence of women as "equals," and the resultant struggle to redefine male-female roles and relationships in a thousand areas, produces role diffusion in both sexes and enhanced fear in men of being controlled by women. These problems are particularly acute in young adults who are still searching for a sure sense of their identity as persons and as male or female. The decline of the patriarchal family model has produced confusion and fear of matriarchy which is allayed only to the extent that a couple finds a more adequate model, within which each can receive that degree of need-satisfaction required for feelings of security and adequacy.

Differences of role images and expectations produce varied responses. One of the marks of a relatively healthy marriage is the ability to cope constructively with differences. A nonconstructive response, which many young marrieds experience, is the attempt at mutual reform to make the other fit the pattern of one's own inner expectations. The Pygmalion-type marriage is an extreme example of this. Pressure to reform is brought in a variety of ways: "Dear, you ought to . . ." or, its more subtle and sneaky form, "Darling, why don't you . . ." Manipulation may use the lever of making the other feel guilty and thus rendering him malleable.

Sex is a favorite bait—given as a reward for "good" behavior or withheld for "bad" (good meaning that which fits the manipulator's inner demands). Whether or not Pygmalion pressures produce reform (and they usually don't), their consequences are a Parent-Child relationship and the resentments which go with manipulation.

Two crucial barriers to intimacy will receive major consideration in subsequent chapters. These are *lack of communication skills* and *mutual need-deprivation*. Since both are results as well as causes of the other barriers, learning to deal with them will automatically help in lowering all the barriers.

In the present chapter we have been putting under the microscope some of the ways in which we interfere with our own satisfactions in marriage, defeating our own deep longings for meaningful closeness with at least one other human being. The picture which comes into focus is indeed a sobering one. The variety of barriers and the price we pay for their operation is impressive. The high cost of distance is a twofold price: it takes a major investment of energy to maintain the distance and keep the barriers intact; and the separation cuts one off from the renewal of self that can occur only in relationship. The fact that so many of us are willing to pay this high price shows how important it feels to avoid intimacy. But the need for intimacy will not disappear because we fear it. The will to relate is woven into the very fabric of our souls.

TURNING BARRIERS INTO BRIDGES

Some couples may experience discouragement, as a result of focusing on the barriers in their marriage. It helps to remember that most barriers can be lowered by becoming aware of what they are, communicating about them, and joining in an effort to improve the "connection" in the relationship. It is important to focus simultaneously on increasing the satisfactions and reducing the frustrations. Almost all couples like more about each other and their marriage than they are aware of in periods of conflict. Becoming aware of the successes already achieved in marriage helps keep up a couple's courage and motivation for the struggle necessary to overcome the barriers by deepening the relationship. The chapters ahead will deal with how to transform marital barriers into marital bridges by increasing mutual need-satisfaction and sharpening communication.

TAKING ACTION

Share your thoughts about the barriers discussed in this chapter. Discover the points at which your perceptions of the barriers in your marriage coincide and differ. Compare your inventory of the areas in your relationship in which you have achieved some degree of closeness, with the areas in which you feel distant or blocked.

As you discuss the barriers, it's a good idea also to talk about the bridges and positive resources in your marriage. Strengthening these may be more helpful than a direct attack on the barriers. As you talk about what you find frustrating, also discuss what you find good and pleasurable in your marriage. Avoid getting bogged down in a kind of post-mortem exercise. There *is* vitality in your relationship (or you probably wouldn't be motivated to read this book)! It *is* possible to increase this marital aliveness by the process in which you are now engaged.

Sometimes it proves worthwhile to try to identify some of the "ghosts" within oneself which interfere with close relationships. Some couples can help each other recognize when they are playing a destructive Parent-Child game. But such games may be difficult to see in one's own relationship. They are usually loaded with big feelings which may make the attempt to identify and change them the occasion for unproductive anger and mutual attack. For these reasons, a marital growth group with a trained leader is the best setting for zeroing in on your self-defeating ghosts and games.

Here is an action-plan[21] designed to help a couple lower the barriers in their marriage: (a) By means of discussion, pick a barrier which you both want to lower, which hasn't always been present in your marriage, and which you both believe can be lowered. Start with a barrier that is already relatively low rather than one which is very high. Don't try to move Mt. Everest at the outset; instead choose a foothill on which you will probably succeed. (b) Decide what you want *positively* in place of the barrier. Concentrate on this rather than on the barrier. (c) Commit yourselves to positive action, aimed at building a bridge in place of the barrier. (d) Use the strengths in your marriage rather than concentrating on repairing the weaknesses. Build on the existing strengths in each of you and in your present relationship, strengths which you probably aren't using fully now. You have more "going for you" than you're aware of most of the time. Becoming aware of these latent strengths will give you hope to grow on. Try to call forth each other's strengths. (e) As you begin to succeed in bridge-building, enjoy your success. This payoff makes it worth the struggle. Enjoy the new precious moments that are occurring. (f) Keep choosing manageable-sized goals—things you can do in the next 24 hours that will improve yourself or your side of the relationship. Act on these realistic goals. (g) Avoid trying to reform your partner. Concentrate your rebuilding on the side of the relationship for which you have responsibility and the ability to control—your side.

NOTES

1. Rollo May, *Love and Will,* in *Psychology Today,* Vol. 3, #3, August 1969.
2. Helene Papanek, "Group Psychotherapy with Married Couples," *Current Psychiatric Therapies,* ed. Jules Masserman (New York: Grune and Stratton, 1965), p. 158.
3. *Insight and Responsibility* (New York: W. W. Norton, 1964), p. 128. In Erikson's approach, intimacy is "to lose and find oneself in another" (*Identity and the Life Cycle,* p. 166). *Psychological Issues,* Vol. I, No. 1, 1959, Monograph 1, International Universities Press, Inc.

"It is only as young people emerge from their identity struggles that their egos can master the sixth state, that of intimacy. . . . Body and ego must now be masters of the organ modes and of the nuclear conflicts, in order to be able to face the fear of ego loss in situations which call for self-abandon: in orgasms and sexual unions, in close friendship and physical combat, in experiences of inspiration by teachers and of intuition from the recesses of the self. The avoidance of such experiences because of fear of ego loss may lead to a deep sense of isolation and consequently self-absorption" (*Childhood and Society,* p. 229).

4. Wenkart, "Detachment—Living in an Ivory Tower," summary of lecture presented under auspices of Auxiliary Council to the Association for the Advancement of Psychoanalysis, p. 1, 1949.
5. The term "I-ism" is from a counselee. It reflects his understanding of the dynamics of egocentricity.
6. For a further discussion of this matter see Virginia M. Satir, *Conjoint Family Therapy* (Palo Alto, Calif.: Science and Behavior Books, 1964), Chapter II, "Low Self-Esteem and Mate Selection."
7. Erikson, *Insight and Responsibility,* p. 103 (italics added).
8. White, *Lives in Progress, A Study of the Natural Growth of Personality* (New York: Holt, Rinehart and Winston, 1952), pp. 340–341.
9. Jean-Paul Sartre, "Intimacy," *The Wall and Other Stories,* trans. Lloyd Alexander (New York: A New Direction Book, 1948), pp. 148–149.
10. Wynne, "Pseudo-Mutuality in the Family Relations of Schizophrenics," in Bell and Vogel, *A Modern Introduction to the Family* (New York: The Free Press, 1960), p. 575. The concept of "pseudo-mutuality" is very close to what is meant by pseudo-intimacy. Wynne writes: "In describing pseudo-mutuality, we are emphasizing a predominant absorption in fitting together, at the expense of the differentiation of the identities of the persons in the relation. In contrast, each person brings to relations of genuine mutuality a sense of his own meaningful, positively-valued identity, and, out of experience or participation together, mutual recognition of identity develops, including a growing recognition of each other's potentialities and capacities" ("Pseudo-Mutuality," p. 575).
11. William Alger, *The Genius of Solitude* (Boston: Roberts Brothers, 1867).
12. Edrita Fried, *The Ego in Love and Sexuality* (New York: Grune and Stratton, 1960), pp. 40–43.
13. Aaron L. Rutledge, *Pre-Marital Counseling* (Cambridge, Mass.: Schenkman Publishing Co., 1966), p. 42.
14. Pollak, lecture, University of Pennsylvania, February 10, 1967.
15. Rutledge, *op. cit.,* p. 43.
16. Tournier, *Escape from Loneliness* (Philadelphia: Westminster Press, 1962), p. 30.
17. Eric Berne, *Games People Play.* In Berne's terms the parentified marriage and the sibling-rival marriage are Parent-Child and Child-

Child games. In a sense, Berne's games are detailed descriptions of how the ghosts interact in a marriage. However, it should be noted that Berne regards each of the ego states (Parent, Adult, Child) to have a valuable function in the person's contemporary relationships. Thus they are seen as resources to be kept in balance rather than ghosts to be laid to rest. This seems to be a useful way of approaching this matter.

18. Mirra Komarovsky, *Blue-Collar Marriage* (New York: Random House, 1962), p. 349.

19. Dorothy F. Beck, "Marital Conflict: Its Course and Treatment as Seen by Caseworkers," *Social Casework* (April, 1966), XLVII, No. 4, p. 212.

20. Dorothy R. Freeman, "Counseling Engaged Couples in Small Groups," *Social Work* (October, 1965), Vol. XLVI, No. 8, p. 36.

21. We are indebted to Billy Sharp and H. Rhea Gray for several suggestions incorporated into this plan.

4 *The Growth of Intimacy*

> How beautiful, how grand and liberating this experience is, when couples learn so to help each other. It is impossible to over-emphasize the immense need men have to be really listened to, to be taken seriously, to be understood. . . . No one can develop freely in this world and find full life without feeling understood by at least one person.
>
> Paul Tournier, *To Understand Each Other*[1]

Inherent in every problem is a possibility. The very barriers which seem at times insurmountable also provide the potential for the growing edge of intimacy. A relationship in which there is growing intimacy rarely just happens. Rather, it is the continuing achievement that results from the self-investment of two persons who are determined to work at deepening the relationship—at turning the problems into possibilities. The art of intimacy, or relating in depth, like other artistic skills, must be cultivated through disciplined practice. Skill comes more easily for some than for others. Most of us have to work at intimacy throughout our marriages if it is to flower. Although the results of such efforts may be discouraging at times, these efforts are also the sources of new joy. The joint efforts necessary to deepen a marriage can be, in themselves, pleasurable forms of sharing.

A couple should ask themselves periodically, *"What are we creating together in our marriage and family?"* If they want marriage to give them more satisfactions, the place to start is for each to put more into the relationship. Two basic principles of mental health are involved here: (1) we reap what we sow, and (2) everything has its cost. These principles are abundantly true in marriage. Mutual investment pays rich dividends. Or, to use the other figure, sowing the seeds of intimacy by continuing to work toward greater mutual need-satisfaction gradually produces the harvest of a richer, more joyful relationship. Some of the sweetest satisfactions available to human beings come through this process. In working together for more intimacy, a couple is moving toward strengthening and lengthening the precious moments in their marriage.

Intimacy grows as personality needs are met in a marriage. In healthy marriages, "positive complementarity"[2] is strongly evident. This term refers to the couple's mutual enhancement of identity through meeting each other's needs. It can be done only in a relationship of love. By love, we mean sensitivity and responsiveness to each other's needs and wants.[3] Nurturing each other by mutually satisfying heart-hungers is the essence of a loving and growing marriage.

Intimacy is nurtured as a couple develops complementary ways of living. The central problem in achieving intimacy is described by Levy and Monroe in *The Happy Family* as "combining the distinct and often antagonistic needs of two individuals into a workable, satisfying union."[4] There are, of course, many successful patterns of meeting the needs of the other in marriage. The challenge that confronts each couple is to discover that unique pattern which produces maximum mutual satisfaction and minimum frustration *for them*. In a growing marriage there is substantial agreement (not entirely on a conscious level) on the main features of this pattern—features which have been discovered through trial and error.

Mutual nurturance starts with the exchange principle. Relationships obviously must be two-way exchanges. Erikson, in discussing the Golden Rule, suggests that the reciprocity of both prudence and sympathy should be replaced with the principle of mutuality which he defines as "a relationship in which partners depend on each other for the development of their respective strengths."[5] Ross Snyder calls this the ability to "evoke the other into fuller personhood."[6] Erikson states:

Seen in the light of human development, this means that the doer is activated in whatever strength is appropriate to his age, stage and condition, even as he activates in the other the strength appropriate to his age, stage and condition. Understood this way, the Rule should say that it is best to do to another what will strenghen you even as it will strengthen him—that is, what will develop his best potential even as it develops your own.[7]

Persons who approach their marriages in terms of "What can I get?" instead of "What can I give and receive?" end up getting little or nothing from the relationship. Moving beyond the exchange principle of the marketplace in a growing marriage is reflected in what Ross Snyder calls "creative fidelity." This could be described as the ability to maintain commitment to a marriage during those dry periods when one's needs are not being adequately met. Snyder puts it this way: "Creative fidelity means to bear with their plateaus, regressions, imperfectness in such a way that these are transformed into new possibilities. Creative fidelity is to be for and with them, come hell or high water."[8]

Creative fidelity is vital in a marriage because it frees the partners from complete dependence on the adequacy of the giving quality of a particular period of relating. If a couple gets caught in a negative cycle, as all couples do occasionally, they will be able to interrupt it if one or both has sufficient feelings of self-worth to be able to give love and nurturance even though he is not receiving it at that moment. An inner sense of worth is derived from previous experiences of having been loved, fed, and esteemed.* When both parties have limited inner resources of self-esteem to draw on in such crises, cycles of mutual retaliation often develop and whirl on with increasing momentum.

* Psychologist Abraham Maslow points out that persons who have this inner sense of worth are able to have "being love" for others (unselfish love of a person's very being), as contrasted to "deficiency love" (self-seeking love based on getting one's deficiencies met).

Relatively healthy marriages have the capacity to interrupt the negative cycles of mutual need-deprivation before the walls become insurmountable. The cycles are interrupted when the couple begins small experiences of mutual-feeding. If the pattern of giving and receiving satisfaction is maintained, a self-reinforcing cycle of mutual satisfaction will replace the negative cycles. Learning how to interrupt negative cycles sooner is a vital skill for enhancing intimacy.

There are several ways in which the degree of mutual need-satisfaction in a marriage can be measured. First, the partner's feelings about the marriage provide a rough index of the extent of need-satisfaction. Warm, positive feelings—happiness, acceptance, safety, joy, liking the other—are indicators that the person's basic needs as he feels them are being adequately met. Second, what the relationship does to the persons' feelings about themselves is significant. Does the relationship leave them with feelings of increased strength and value, or of weakness and self-rejection? (All human relationships can be judged by this one criterion.) A third measuring device is the extent to which the marital partners turn in upon themselves (in day-dreaming, self-comforting through overeating, etc.) or look outside the marriage for the satisfactions they should get within it. Infidelity (emotional and/or sexual) is almost always a symptom of a severe hunger in the relationship. So is the common phenomenon of spouses finding much greater pleasure emotionally in the company of other persons of their gender, than in their relationship with their spouses.

THE BASIC HEART-HUNGERS

Since troubled marriages are essentially hungry marriages, and since the road to fulfillment and intimacy is mutual need-satisfaction, it is crucial for married people to learn about their basic needs. Research at the Marriage Council of Philadelphia shows that the problems about which clients complained (with the exception of stresses such as poverty or illness) fall "within the broad category of lack of consideration . . . for the other's feelings, needs, values or goals, or acts in disregard of them."[9]

Dorothy W. Baruch describes the basic emotional foods that everyone needs and craves:

> We need *love* in good measure, and we need to give it. We need to feel that we are *wanted and belong*. We need to feel that we are capable of *adequate achievement* so that we can manage to meet life's demands. We need *recognition* for what we achieve. We need to know that the *pleasure which our senses and our body can bring us* is permissible and good and that our enjoyment does not make us "bad." We need to feel *accepted and understood*. And finally we need to feel *worth while and essentially worthy in being uniquely the self that we are*.[10]

These may be summarized as the need for security, the need to give or to be needed, the need for self-esteem, the need for pleasure, the need for limits, for freedom, and for faith. All of these are ingredients in the deepest need, the need for love. Marital partners can do much to provide for each other the food which will satisfy these hungers of the heart.

Security is the inner feeling of stability and safety that comes to a person in a relationship in which he feels a sense of identity, acceptance, belonging, and being wanted. How can one help one's spouse to experience this kind of security? There are many facets to such an experience. To exercise "creative fidelity" by letting one's spouse know that one is in the marriage "for better or for worse" and to refuse, in moments of angry desperation, to succumb to the temptation to use threats of leaving or separation to manipulate the other—these are ways of helping to satisfy this need. A stable marriage is the best answer available in our society to the hunger for continuity in the midst of the flux of relationships.

Another way of enhancing one's partner's sense of security is to accept him *with* his weaknesses and imperfections. Gibson Winter writes: "Acceptance in marriage is the power to love someone and receive him in the very moment that we realize how far he falls short of our hopes."[11] Acceptance includes not treading on one's partner's areas of vulnerability. There are touchy spots in everyone's psyche. Living with a person in marriage allows one to discover what these are—the points at which the partner is easily threatened and made anxious. This knowledge gives one a responsibility to respect these areas and to resist the temptation to "stick the needle in where it hurts most" in moments of anger.

Accepting a mate's defenses and vulnerabilities is closely related to respecting his differences. Some persons need much greater distance from the other, in order to feel safe, than do their partners. Jean observed that her husband of ten years, Mark, "needs more time alone than I do. He's that way and his wanting to be alone isn't necessarily an attack on me, as I thought it was early in our marriage." Jean had come to recognize that Mark couldn't feel comfortable with as much intimacy as she could. Because she had learned to accept his need for distance, she no longer added blame—of herself or him—to the frustration of her need for greater closeness.

The need for security, then, can be satisfied by the mutual efforts of husband and wife to stand by each other in all circumstances, even times of conflict, of weaknesses, and of differences.

In helping to satisfy the partner's need for security, husband and wife can both help to satisfy their own *need to be needed,* to have something to give in the relationship. Giving love to others is a fundamental human need. Marriage is an ideal place to satisfy this need to be needed and to invest one's life in others. It is a breakthrough moment in one's life when he discovers that giving spiritual food away does not lessen one's supply in a relationship of mutuality. Everyone has within him a deep inner hunger to make his life count with at least one other person. "If you pour yourself out for the hungry and satisfy the desire of the afflicted, then shall your light rise in the darkness, and your gloom be as noonday" (Isaiah 58:10).

When one's mate is hungry for affection or afflicted by disappointment, grief, or pain, a wonderful opportunity to give oneself to another is at one's fingertips. In a good, growing marriage, the response is a spontaneous reaching out to the need. The opportunity for mutual dependency in marriage gives each partner the chance to be needed. The parenting role as described in Chapter 3, when used in a healthy, nonmanipulative way, is an example of this. The wife who can sympathize and soothe when her husband comes home from work shattered and angry, and the husband who can listen without being threatened or critical when his wife has had a bad day with the children, are satisfying their own need to be needed as well as the other's need to be temporarily dependent.

The *self-esteem* of each partner can be enhanced by the other. The awareness that one is valued, recognized, and affirmed by others can be steadily strengthened by one's spouse. The following is good advice to married couples at every age and stage: *Whatever else you neglect, don't neglect your mate's self-esteem.* A robust sense of one's own worth is an essential part of a firm sense of identity; as such, it is a necessary foundation for depth relationships. It is very easy to give or receive an "ego bruise" in a marriage relationship by a rejecting word, lack of thoughtfulness (as in forgetting a birthday or an anniversary), or the attack of "putting the other down." The consequence of such a bruise is predictable—retaliation, a striking at the esteem of the other. The negative cycles described earlier start in this way. Positive cycles of mutual strengthening of each other's esteem contribute to the fun of being married. One husband described how his wife frequently starts a cycle of mutual caring and affirming: "Barbara makes me feel good about myself with a pat high on the ego."

Walt brought a yellow rose, Patricia's favorite flower, and put it in a vase on her dresser where she would find it on her return from the grocery store. She responded in a loving way which affirmed him as a man and a lover. His gift message of affectionate affirmation, communicated through an act of thoughtfulness, triggered an ongoing cycle of mutual giving.

As young couples "in love" know intuitively (but married

couples often forget), appreciation is the language of love because it is the food for nurturing self-esteem. Being appreciated by one's mate helps one survive in a world that often eats away at feelings of significance and worth. It also helps us to be the kind of persons we would like to be. Complimenting one's wife on how shapely she's looking makes it at least *slightly* easier for her to resist that second hot fudge sundae.

One form of self-esteem strengthening is particularly crucial in marriage—affirming one's partner's sense of sexual attractiveness and strength in the case of a male, or sexual attractiveness and soft loveliness in the case of a female. No compliment is sweeter to the heart or cherished longer than one which appreciates the masculinity or femininity of one's partner. Conversely, no hurt is deeper, no attack remembered more painfully, than one directed at one's sexual adequacy. The art of giving silent compliments, as well as verbal ones, is a valuable marital art. An illustration of this is bringing one's wife a gift which says powerfully without words, "I'm glad you're a woman and I'm a man; I luxuriate in the fact that you're *very much* of a woman!"

If one's need for being esteemed by others was well met in childhood, a person brings to marriage a solid inner-core feeling of self-worth. This is reaffirmed and supported against the buffeting of the world in a good marriage. Those who come to marriage with low self-esteem are easily hurt and rejected. Their sense of inner depletion makes it very difficult for them to give. They need particular support from their spouses in order to maintain that minimal sense of adequacy which every person must have to be happy and cope with life. In all marriages, what one does to strengthen his partner's self-esteem will increase his or her ability to give in the relationship. A cartoon showing a man consulting a psychiatrist had this caption: "Doctor, my wife has developed an inferiority complex. I want to know how to keep her that way." If he could get what he asked for, he would not like it, since those with low self-esteem are difficult to live with. This is because the *ability* to esteem others depends on the ability to esteem oneself.

The basic need for individual *freedom* in marriage has been discussed in Chapter 2. Partners who can allow each other the inner freedom to grow toward the realization of God-given potential, who can allow each "to drink from his own individual cup"[12] do much to meet each other's need. In some marriages there is a conflict between the desires of the partners for dependence and protection, on the one hand, and for independence and freedom, on the other. Some acceptable balance between these two sets of needs is essential. To be able to lean at times but then to be free to launch out on one's own—this is the alternating rhythm of a good marriage. A newly married couple in a church-sponsored growth group agreed with the husband's description of their problem in this area: "We struggle with being ourselves but not our *single* selves. Both of us agree that the other should be able to do his own 'thing' and that our marriage will be better because of it. But we sometimes do our thing in ways that collide with the other person's thing. When we feel this happening, we try to stop, take a careful look at things, and decide what has to change."

Every person has a need for the *pleasures* of the mind and the body; these include sexual, intellectual, aesthetic, interpersonal, and spiritual satisfactions, as well as adventure derived from new experiences. Sexual play and ecstasy can infuse the total relationship with "oomph" and lift. Marriage is the most dependable way of gaining ongoing sexual satisfaction in our culture. In addition to sex, a couple should find other forms of play which bring them both personal revitalization. Otto Pollak has pointed to the human need for regular times of regression in appropriate company and circumstances.[13] Encouraging such healthy regression (a vacation from the burden of adult responsibility) is a vital function of marriage. It occurs in the ecstatic pleasure of sex and in the relaxation of the inner "Parent" during periods of "letting down one's hair" in various forms of play.

Each of us needs a sense of living within a dependable structure —the laws of nature, the principles of the psychological and spiritual life, the requirements of responsive and responsible relationships. This need for *limits* is satisfied in a good marriage in several ways. These include the dependable rituals and routines which develop within such a relationship, the essential process of adjusting one's needs to the needs of the other, and the way in which a marital partner can hold up reality to help the other face it and satisfy his needs within it. Particularly in a young marriage, one of the major helps each can give the other is to prevent inappropriate regression—unconstructive excursions back to childish gratification. For example, in the relationship between Doug and Marilyn, when he had a sudden urge to buy a color TV which both knew they couldn't afford, Marilyn gently and without attacking his self-esteem as a providing male, reminded him of the realities of their financial condition. Teenagers and young adults who marry are often still mastering the art of distinguishing appropriate and inappropriate gratification of their impulses. Marital partners can be of help to each other in this process. For a person who grew up in a rigid home and has internalized over-control of impulses, a spouse can help him loosen up and learn to enjoy letting his "Child" side play.

The concept of relationship—the "we" of marriage—as it influences the awareness of a couple, has a limiting function that can be constructive. The individual no longer thinks of his needs in isolation; rather, it is "my needs in relationship to your needs." The recognition dawns that love and limits are not necessarily contradictory elements in marriage. Instead, what David Roberts called "wise love,"[14] always includes dependable limits. In a good marriage, self-discipline is integral to growing love. Mutual responsibility—each person holding up his end of the relationship —is essential to the growth of intimacy. To live with a firm but not oppressive sense of responsibility provides a sense of self-mastery which enhances self-esteem. It also prevents the appropriate guilt feelings which accompany irresponsible relating.

Every person has a fundamental need for a satisfying philosophy of life, a hierarchy of personal values, and a *faith* which gives meaning to life. One of the challenges and joys of a good marriage is the opportunity to work together at discovering the particular forms of belief and practice that will meet the spiritual needs of both partners and their children. The nature of these spiritual needs and ways of satisfying them in marriage will be explored in Chapter 9.

Love is the experience of knowing that another person cares—deeply, warmly, acceptingly and dependably; this is the most indispensable need of any human being to which all the other heart-hungers are tributaries. To have a steady source of warmth and affection helps to offset the chill of depersonalizing experiences in the outside world. Such love—given and received in a marriage —feeds self-esteem. A husband said, "Knowing that she loves me through all our ups and downs makes me feel ten feet tall." Love helps one define his identity more sharply as he experiences himself vividly in both passionate and quiet caring. It reinforces feelings of inner security by making the marriage a harbor where one is safe from many of the storms and threats of everyday life. Love is the force which welds a relationship at its points of meeting. The ancient insight of St. Paul has been confirmed and reconfirmed in the social sciences, counseling relationships, and successful marriages—"the greatest of these is love" (I Corinthians 13:13).

The kind of love which is the glory and wonder of a marriage —growing love—represents an integration of all the facets of intimacy which the couple has cultivated in their relationship. The integration of sexual, emotional, and spiritual intimacy, for example, makes each of these facets of intimacy richer and more soul-satisfying. Tenderness and passion, comfort and confrontation, dependence and autonomy—all are woven into the multicolored fabric of the emerging "we-ness" of marriage.

The maturation of a love relationship takes time—something that many couples find in short supply. Will and Jenny handle the usual middle-class dilemma of overscheduling by planning so that they have time alone together, however brief, nearly every day. This is not easy, but it pays dividends. An occasional weekend at a cabin in the mountains, away from the children, also helps to keep their love fresh and growing. A frequent "night on the town" —a night when each dresses up for the other and they enjoy a "date"—helps to keep romance alive in their marriage. The dailyness of married life often eats away at romance. Couples like Will and Jenny, who are willing to continue their courtship of each other, discover the amazing secret (amazing to youth, at least)—that there is "a romance for the maturing which has a depth and breadth not possible for youth."[15] By continuing to invest themselves in the creativity of building a life and a family together, they keep their marriage from becoming a "tired friendship."

These, then, are the vitamins, minerals, and essential food elements of human personality. They are the needs of both husband and wife. Learning how to say Yes to one's partner's needs is the essence of the art of being intimately married. Each person has a unique blend of these needs—with certain needs that are more insistent and others that are less pressing. A part of the journey toward maturity which is a growing marriage is the mutual discovery of each partner's individual pattern of needs, and how best to meet each other's special hungers.

HEALTHY VS. NEUROTIC NEEDS

If the need-satisfaction path to greater intimacy is to be a useful one to a couple, it is important for them to recognize that some needs cannot and should not be satisfied, even in the best marriage. Relationships which thrive do so because the two parties have learned to find the middle ground between what each wants from the relationship. The ability of each to sacrifice a part of his cherished fantasies and to bear the frustration of this sacrifice in the interests of the larger good—the marriage—is essential to marital happiness.

It is also important to realize that there are some neurotic elements in the desires of everyone and that these desires often cannot be met in any relationship. There are two reasons for this. First, neurotic "needs" or desires are exaggerations of normal desires, often to such an extent that no human being could possibly meet them. They register with the partner as unfair demands, which they are. There is a kind of craving, demanding quality to such desires—akin to the insatiability of addictions. Usually the craving is for constant approval, reassurance, and appreciation. Frequently, such demandingness produces a vicious cycle.

Jane has a deep chronic sense of inadequacy which causes her to demand excessive protection and approval from Bob, her husband. His resentment of her demands causes him to become withholding of emotional support, which intensifies her frantic grasping for approval. The more she grasps and demands, the more he withdraws, producing a spiral of increasing mutual starvation.

Persons like Jane and Bob often make little headway toward intimacy without professional marriage counseling or personal psychotherapy. In less extreme situations, a couple may face together the points at which their requests of each other are excessive and unrealistic. Some couples can learn to face the need to let go of excessive demands—demands which deprive them of the normal give-and-take in their marriage. They can come to accept the truth that in adult life it is unrealistic to expect any relationship to be all-giving and all-nurturing. We have to settle for less. By surrendering excessive demands we become free to enjoy the genuine satisfactions which *are* present in the marriage. To illustrate, a person who relinquishes his insistence that his marriage supply far more intimacy than is possible in that relationship, can then enjoy and value the closeness that is actually there.

The other reason that the neurotic element in our desires cannot be met in marriage is that there is inevitably a *conflict* within the person between contradictory desires. For example, a wife often wants a masculine, dominant man upon whom she can lean, but who will not interfere with her own domineering behavior. As one wife in her twenties, who had learned to recognize her ambivalent feelings, said, "I want Mac to be strong so I can lean on him while I dominate him." The husbandly counterpart is the man who wants to maintain his self-image of masculine independence and strength, while at the same time receiving total mothering from his wife. The essence of neurotic needs is wanting to eat one's cake and have it too. But the realities of relationships are such as to make this impossible. A good illustration of a conflicted or neurotic need is the powerful fear of intimacy in a person whose painful loneliness makes him crave closeness intensely. Consequently, his behavior is a baffling pattern of reaching out toward others in a way that invariably pushes them away. As psychiatrist Lawrence Kubie says, "A major source of unhappiness between husband and wife is to be found in the discrepancies between their conscious and unconscious demands on each other and on the marriage, as these are expressed first in the choosing of a mate and then in the subsequent evolution of their relationship."[16] The "Parent-Child" games described by Berne (Chapter 3), usually involve such conflicted needs in both parties.

To some extent, there are tensions and conflicts between the various needs in everyone. (This is called "normal ambivalence" by counselors.) Every husband has some need to be nurtured or mothered by his wife, but he also has a contrary need to feel strong, independent, and masculine. When this kind of conflict is severe, it disrupts relationships. The danger in all conflicted needs is that ordinarily the individual is aware of only one half of his needs; the other half is unconscious. A husband who has an intense need to feel self-sufficient (and whose need for dependence and nurturance is hidden from himself) may pull away from his wife and then blame her for not being attentive enough. In other words, he has avoided seeing the contradiction within his own desires by projecting the conflict on his wife. In most such cases, the wife has a parallel conflict which matches and reinforces his. Marital partners who can become aware of their ambivalence— the ways in which they are both projecting their inner conflicts on the screen of the marriage and trying to manipulate each other —can begin to take steps toward mutual need-satisfaction.

BECOMING MORE NEED-SATISFYING

The process of assisting a couple in marriage counseling often follows these steps: The first is to help them discover how the needs and desires of each are being denied and deprived by their present patterns of relating. Second is to assist them to find and experiment with alternative patterns of relating which will produce a higher degree of mutual need-satisfaction. Third is helping them to improve their communication skills, which allows them to feed each other more fully, resolve conflict constructively, and discover compromise solutions to the problem of divergent or conflicted needs. These steps can be used in self-help efforts by relatively healthy couples.

The place to begin is diagnosis: What are the feelings of each partner regarding the extent to which his heart-hungers for the "foods of the spirit" listed above are being satisfied in the marriage? Is each person aware of how the other feels about the points at which he feels satisfied and the points at which he feels deprived? Once these are out in the open, the partners may be able to begin experimenting with changes in their way of relating that will result in a more balanced diet for both. Whatever empathic understanding develops through this process is relationship-enhancing in itself. Putting oneself in the other's skin, even to a limited extent, obviously increases the intimacy in the relationship. It is remarkable how many couples have never asked themselves: "I wonder how my spouse really feels about this behavior on my part?" For a wife to begin to empathize with the pressures and insecurities of a man's world with its fear of failure, its pressure to deny dependency and to maintain a godlike image of autonomy, and the threat of changing sex roles, can be a growth experience for her and her husband. The same applies to the husband's awareness of the unique self-esteem problems of women faced with changing sex roles, the continuing dual-standard in many areas, the increasing period of life after the children are raised and the problem of finding significance therein, and the preparation for creative widowhood which faces the vast majority of women in our culture. Whatever understanding of each other's "worlds" a couple can achieve will put them on the road to greater intimacy.

The second step is to begin to experiment with alternative patterns of relating which may prove to be more mutually satisfying. Mat and Laura, married seventeen years and in the middle of rearing a family of four children, confessed to each other that each was dissatisfied with the direction their relationship was taking. They agreed that they were overinvested in the children and underinvested in their marriage. Mat asked half rhetorically, "How much time have we spent alone with each other during the past month, except when we were asleep?" Both knew the answer and both sensed that here was a part of their problem. Some restructuring of their schedules made a place for regular face-to-face time together. During their discussion, Laura told Mat that she sometimes wondered if he still had some of the feelings about her as a female—feelings that went far beyond interest in sex, per se. Mat recognized that she was feeling a lack of affectionate appreciation and that he had probably been careless about expressing tender feelings that mean so much to a spouse. At this point he was able to talk about his feeling that Laura seldom demonstrated her interest in him sexually by initiating sex play. In this process, they were talking with some openness about their unmet hungers and needs, and providing each other with fresh opportunities for saying Yes to these needs. It is clear that an important channel of need-satisfaction is better communication (the focus of the next chapter).

Some couples discover that, if they try, they can increase the points at which they have connections with each other, thus broadening the range of their intimacy experiences. For example, couples who have little or no relationship in the area of creative or artistic sharing may discover a new point of touching when they take a course in painting or creative writing or music appreciation together. There is some poetry and music in nearly everyone's soul; marital partners can help bring it out of each other through mutual encouragement and sharing. Shared experimentation in the areas of intellectual interests, recreational pursuits, and spiritual searching may result in the adding of another facet of intimacy to a couple's relationship.

GROWTH IN INTIMACY

The process of growth in intimacy is understood well enough so that several key points can be emphasized. For one thing, acceptance of the valuable aspects of the *present* relationship gives a necessary launching pad for growth in the future. John Levy and Ruth Monroe state: "The first step toward a happier marriage, however achieved, is freedom to value the relationship as it is."[17] Again, a marriage in which there is even a minor degree of intimacy can provide some nurturance and openness by which greater intimacy can grow over the years. In this sense, a good marriage is a therapeutic relationship. It can be an experience of being close to another person with safety; as each partner learns to risk being more caring and more honest in sharing his feelings with the other, healing of the wounds of the spirit takes place.

Another point worth emphasizing about growing intimacy is that no degree of intimacy can erase the sense of mystery in the relationship. This is the answer to the worry that too much intimacy destroys the mystery that is essential to love. Anne Philipe in *No Longer Than a Sigh* describes her feelings about her husband:

I look at you asleep, and the world you are in, the little smile in the corner of your lips, the flicker of your eyelids, your naked relaxed body, all these are mysteries. I swim at your side in warm transparent water, or I wait for you to appear in the frame of the door under the wisteria. You say good morning and I know what you have dreamed and your first thought at the edge of sleep—and yet you are a mystery. We talk: your voice, your thought, the words you use, are the most familiar in the world. We can even finish the sentences begun by the other. And yet you are, and we are, a mystery.[18]

Like a scientist's experience in probing the intricacies of nature, each discovery in the intimacy of marriage opens up a dozen new dimensions of mystery.

Another key point about growing intimacy is that intimacy is *a road and not a goal.* The achievement of intimacy is always only partial—the closeness and mutuality only fragmentary. One couple said: "Our marriage is not perfect; we often make each other miserable. Nevertheless we like living together. This life together, difficult as we find it, is still more satisfying than any other."[19]

In this chapter we have been focusing on some down-to-earth issues: (1) How can a couple overcome the walls in their marriage, replacing them with bridges? (2) How can they stimulate the growth of creative closeness? (3) How can they increase their skills in intimate relating?

Our approach to these issues has been to emphasize the crucial significance of mutual need-satisfactions. We have begun to describe what might be called, "The Care and Feeding of a Growing Marriage." The key to this whole process is skill in sharing meanings—i.e., skill in communication. This idea was implicit in the words of Tournier with which we began this chapter. Heart-hungers are satisfied as two people communicate effectively and in depth. How this ability can be increased will be our concern in the next chapter.

TAKING ACTION

Spend some time talking about the strengths of your marriage. Tell each other what you like and admire about the other. What are the things you value about your relationship? How can you make the most of these strengths and values in increasing the intimacy between you?

Discuss your relationship. Talk about the ways in which each of you does or does not receive satisfaction of the various needs described in this chapter. In other words, do an inventory of your marriage as a need-satisfying relationship. Differences and similarities should be discussed so that each can understand how the other sees his own and the other's needs. The "Self-Other Fulfillment Checklist" may be useful in taking your inventory. In those areas in which you agree that improvement is needed, plan strategy for experimenting with new ways of relating which may be more need-satisfying.

Remember that unhappiness and conflict occur in a relationship because of a lack of mutual "want" satisfaction. Some needs and wants of marital partners are mutually exclusive; others are not. During conflict periods, each person withholds satisfactions from the other because he himself is feeling so unsatisfied and therefore angry. This produces a cycle of mutual emotional starvation. The less each gives, the less he receives from the other.

When you experience conflict in your marriage, try these steps as a way of interrupting the negative cycle: (*a*) Clarify, in your own minds and with each other, what you aren't getting from the marriage (e.g. affirmation, affection, sexual satisfaction). (*b*) Concentrate, not on the areas in which your needs are mutually exclusive or contradictive, but on the "areas of overlap"[20] of your two need systems. Focus on those needs which represent positive things you both want in your marriage. (*c*) Pick a realistic goal which you both will find enjoyable and fulfilling if you achieve it. (*d*) Decide what you must do to achieve this goal and begin this action. Don't worry now about the areas in which your wants are in conflict. By working together in the area of overlap that area will tend to grow. By doing something positive to move toward a mutually-chosen goal, you'll begin to feel better and this will make it possible for each of you to meet the needs of the other more fully. A satisfaction-cycle may well replace the vicious cycle that operates during conflict.

If you are using the book in a marital growth group, it may be helpful to role-play a situation in which barriers to intimacy are present. Experiment with new ways of handling such situations, which may result in more mutual need-satisfaction. For example, experiment in role-playing with various ways in which a couple might handle a breakdown of communication on a subject such as disciplining children. Reversing husband-wife roles is a useful method for seeing each other's perspective. On some issue on which there is disagreement, the husband plays the wife's role as he understands her viewpoint, and vice versa. Five- to fifteen-minute sessions of role-playing are usually long enough to provide the group with grist for the mill of productive discussion. This technique should be used only in a group with a trained leader.

SELF-OTHER FULFILLMENT CHECKLIST

(Instructions: This instrument is designed to stimulate discussion of mutual need-satisfaction within your marriage. After discussing each need, check the blanks which apply. Then plan specific steps by which at least one need of each party can be met more fully.)

Basic Heart Hungers	*Wife Feels Fulfilled*	*Husband Feels Fulfilled*	*Plan of Action Needed to Increase Ful-fillment*
Security (from feeling ac-ceptance and belongingness)	——	——	——
Service (giving love to others, investing one's life, meeting others' needs)	——	——	——
Esteem (feeling valued, recognized, affirmed by the other)	——	——	——
Enjoyment (sexual, in-tellectual, recreational, aesthetic, spiritual)	——	——	——
Love (knowing the other cares—deeply, warmly, and dependably)	——	——	——

Limits (the need for
responsibility, dependable
routines, respect for re-
ality and the rights of others)　　——　　　——　　　——

Freedom (the need for
autonomy, distance, respect
for differences)　　　　　　 ——　　　——　　　——

Faith (the need for a
philosophy of life, values,
and trust in God)　　　　　　——　　　——　　　——

NOTES

1. Tournier, *To Understand Each Other* (Richmond, Va.: John Knox Press, 1962), p. 29.
2. Nathan Ackerman, *The Psychodynamics of Family Life* (New York: Basic Books, 1958), pp. 85–86. The principle of complementarity—each bringing to the relationship what the other lacks—is closely related to the idea of "marital balance" as described by Dorothy Fahs Beck in her insightful analysis of marital conflict; marital balance is "a dovetailing of the partners' needs and patterns of reciprocity in meeting them such as will maintain over the long run an equilibrium in gratification that is acceptable to both. This balance in satisfaction and rewards is apparently essential for the long-term stability of the family as a system. The concept does not imply that all the needs of each partner must be met, but simply that the core needs specific to a given marital relationship must be satisfied. The level of giving and receiving needs not be equal provided the ratio of gratification to frustration is acceptable to both . . . . the needs met may also be either 'neurotic' or 'healthy.' The relationship . . . is seen as one that fluctuates with the changing needs, growth of family members, changes in family composition, and stress and crisis" "Marital Conflict: Its Course and Treatment—As Seen by Caseworkers," *Social Casework,* April, 1966, p. 212).
3. This definition is from Regina Wescott.
4. John Levy and Ruth Monroe, *The Happy Family* (New York: Alfred A. Knopf, 1938), p. 148.
5. Erikson, *Insight and Responsibility* (New York: W. W. Norton, 1964), p. 231.
6. Paraphrased from Ross Snyder, "Married Life," unpublished paper, p. 13.
7. *Insight and Responsibility,* p. 233.
8. *Op. cit.,* p. 13.

9. Emily H. Mudd, *et al., Success in Family Living* (New York: Association Press, 1965), p. 175.
10. Baruch, *How to Live with Your Teen Ager* (New York: McGraw-Hill, 1953), p. 23.
11. Gibson Winter, *Love and Conflict* (Garden City, N.Y.: Doubleday and Co., 1958), p. 115.
12. James A. Peterson, *Education for Marriages* (New York: Charles Scribner's Sons, 1956), p. 237.
13. Pollak, lecture, University of Pennsylvania, January 18, 1967.
14. See David Roberts, *Psychotherapy and a Christian View of Man* (New York: Charles Scribner's Sons, 1953).
15. Clark Ellzey, *How to Keep Romance in Your Marriage* (New York: Association Press, 1954), p. 4.
16. Lawrence S. Kubie, "Psychoanalysis and Marriage," in *Neurotic Inter-Action in Marriage,* ed. Victor W. Eisenstein (New York: Basic Books, 1956), pp. 14–15.
17. Levy and Monroe, *The Happy Family,* p. 177.
18. Anne Philipe, *No Longer Than a Sigh* (New York: Atheneum, 1964), pp. 30–31.
19. Levy and Monroe, *op. cit.,* p. 178.
20. This phrase and the general approach to conflict resolution are from the work of Billy Sharp and H. Rhea Gray.

5 Communication: Key to Creative Closeness

> If there is any one indispensable insight with which a young married couple should begin their life together, it is that they should try to keep open, at all cost, the lines of communication between them.
>
> Reuel L. Howe, *Herein Is Love*[1]

Communication is the means by which relating takes place. Its quality determines how a relationship is established and whether it is continued or terminated. Good communication is the ability to transmit and receive meanings; it is the instrument for achieving that mutual understanding which is at the heart of marital intimacy. Words are not the only communicators. The wife who responds to her husband's end-of-the-day greeting with cold silence conveys a powerful message, as surely as though she had used an angry verbal outburst. Communication in any close relationship occurs on literally dozens of levels simultaneously. One way to measure the depth of a relationship is by the number of levels on which communication can take place.

The message pathways between and among people have been likened to telephone lines with intertwined wires of various colors. Some carry ideas, some carry feelings, some carry the behind-the-scenes involvements which have brought the relationship to its present status and which color any subsequent communicational interchange.

Suppose the same wife greets her returning husband with the words, "I thought you'd never come home." Her husband hears

87

her words, but also receives simultaneously several other messages. There is the tone of her voice and its inflection: is it a whine or a caress? Her facial expression and the movement of her body tell him something: is she smiling or frowning? Does she turn her back or reach out to him? Whatever the husband believes to have been the meaning of similar remarks in the past also colors the quality of the message. This is the pattern and relationship context. The fact that this is a marriage relationship also influences his interpretation of the message—the same statement from his employer would have a different meaning. There is also the implied expectation in his wife's remark, sometimes called the "demand quality" of communication. What response is she expecting from him? An apology for being late? A return caress such as, "I missed you, too"? An attack: "Can't you let me live my own life?" Or is she asking for a lingering embrace. At the same time, the husband's own experiences since he left his wife that morning help to determine how he will receive his wife's greeting. Thus, it becomes obvious that even the simplest communication is a complicated exchange. The husband's ability to understand his wife's greeting depends on his ability at that moment to sort out and weigh the multilevel messages he receives.

Meantime the wife is also required to translate the many cues she is getting from her husband. Communication is always a two-way street. Both husband and wife are simultaneously sending and receiving messages. Her statement can probably be understood only in the context of what happened between them before he went to work that day. The husband also sends several nonverbal messages as he enters the front door. The time he gets home, the way he walks, the droop or set of his shoulders, his greeting both verbal and nonverbal—all must be interpreted by the wife even as he is interpreting her messages. The meaning of a remark in a continuing relationship cannot be separated from the network of communication in the total relationship as it extends over time. Communication has a circular character with each person behaving and responding in part according to what each has become through interacting with the other over a period of time. A particular interchange, positive or negative, is the product of complicated relating, which in an ongoing relationship follows a predictable pattern.

The ability to communicate in mutually affirming ways is the fundamental skill which is essential to the growth of marital intimacy. Marriage provides an opportunity for multilevel exchanges of meaning. It provides the opportunity for communicating at increasingly deep levels about the things that matter most to husband and wife.

STRENGTHENING COMMUNICATION

In order to strengthen communication in a marriage, a couple needs to learn to use the varied lines through which the messages and meanings are transmitted. There are many ways to say, "I love you!" A fond glance, a tender or playful touch in an appropriate spot, a thoughtful gift, choosing to sit close in a crowded room, listening with genuine interest, a kiss on the back of the neck, a note, perhaps with a private joke, left where it will be found, a word of sympathy or support, a sly wink, preparing a favorite dish, a bowl of flowers carefully arranged, a phone call in the middle of the day, and even, perhaps, remembering to take out the trash are but a few. A part of the joy of marriage is this opportunity to develop an almost endless variety of transmission lines for the meanings that are important to each partner.

Another step in improving communication in marriage is for both partners to learn to listen more fully. A complaint that is frequently heard in marriage counseling is: "My husband (wife) doesn't listen to me," or "What I say goes in one ear and out the other." The meaning of "not listening" varies, depending on the couple. It may be a passive-aggressive husband (or wife) who "turns off his hearing aid," to block the manipulating, demanding behavior of his spouse which he is afraid to resist openly. Or it may be that husband and wife are so busy with concern each for his own unmet needs that neither can hear the other's pain. The husband may be worried about his job because of the events of the day. The wife is feeling lonely and frustrated because she has been cooped up with the children all day and needs some warmth and love from an intimate adult. She interprets her husband's worry and preoccupation as a rejection of herself, while at the same time he interprets her reaching out to him as another demand which he cannot meet. Each is immediately lost in protecting himself from the further hurt which is expected, and cannot stop to wonder what the other is *really* feeling. Such distortions in receiving messages produce a maelstrom of misunderstanding. The husband has sent a message: he is worried about his job. The wife misperceives its meaning: she feels rejected. She responds with a message based on the misperception: an angry accusation. Now he feels rejected and misunderstood. If neither is able to take the initiative in interrupting the cycle by saying, "What's really going on here?" or by communicating warmth and caring, the chain of distortions may be compounded until all hope of understanding has evaporated.

What is needed here is deep listening. Such listening is seeing the world through another person's eyes. It is "walking awhile in the other fellow's moccasins." It is being led on an unfamiliar pathway while someone is pointing out the significant features of the landscape. It is watching a flower-bud blossom slowly through time-lapse photography. It is the confidence that what is now only partly heard and understood will eventually be more fully known.[2]

Gabriel Marcel has said that there is "a way of listening which is a way of refusing—of refusing oneself—and there is a way of listening which is a way of giving—of self giving."[3] To really listen to another means both giving oneself and being willing to receive the other within oneself.

Such listening in depth is essential for both partners if there is to be depth sharing in a marriage. Paul Tournier writes:

Deep sharing is overwhelming, and very rare. A thousand fears keep us in check. First of all there is the fear of breaking down, of crying. There is especially the fear that the other will not sense the tremendous importance with which this memory or feeling is charged. How painful it is when such a difficult sharing falls flat, upon ears either preoccupied or mocking, ears in any case that do not sense the significance of what we're saying.

It may happen between man and wife. The partner who has thus spoken in a very personal way without being understood falls back into a terrible emotional solitude.[4]

When self-esteem is low and needs are high, true listening may be experienced as a frightening invasion of one's inner world. If one listens one may hear criticism of oneself. Or he may hear a demand that he cannot meet, or be required to change a preconceived notion or opinion. Fears of the closeness we all want but resist may get in the way of listening. "If I really listen to him, then he may really listen to me, and then I will be known as I really am." It is difficult to listen if one is afraid of becoming aware of his own feelings which threaten his self-image, or if he fears blame or advice from the other.

If a couple is not severely crippled in its communication skills, the ability of each to listen can improve with both partners working at it together. Central in this process is what is known as "checking out meanings." The point at which communication frequently breaks down is not in the speaking or the listening, per se, but in failing to check frequently to see if one really hears and understands what the other means, feels, and intends. Many messages in marriages, as well as elsewhere, are ambiguous. The simple process of checking out meanings by asking questions such as, "Do I hear you correctly?" or "Is this what you are saying?" can break up some of the log-jams in communication that grow rapidly otherwise. When a person talks, is silent, listens superficially, doesn't listen at all, or listens in depth, he is communicating something. The best way for each person to keep in touch with what the other is feeling is to check out meanings regularly.

There is something more basic in marital communication than simply saying and hearing words accurately. Communication is more than a problem in mechanics. What is fundamental is the willingness to consider each other's point of view; this willingness is rooted in a degree of mutual respect. Two people can say and even understand an endless flow of words back and forth between them. But unless each cares enough about what the other is saying, and about what his own words mean to the other, communication will not occur, except perhaps on a surface level. Caring about what another person says and thinks and feels is, of course, the same as caring about that person as a person.

Once a couple has set about learning really to listen, there are a number of road signs for which they can watch that point the way to satisfying communication. One of these has been touched on above. It is the importance of checking out meanings. Virginia Satir says that "a person who communicates in a functional way can: a. firmly state his case, b. yet at the same time clarify and qualify what he says, c. as well as ask for feedback, d. and be receptive to feedback when he gets it."[5] Couples frequently have difficulty when they assume that the other knows or should know what is wanted. "If my husband really cared, he'd know what I need." This wife expects her husband to be a mind-reader. The magical expectation is that somehow he will know what she desires. Her anger when her needs are not met is in response to her unrealistic expectation. Checking out meanings is especially important when one or the other does not respond verbally to a message sent. It is impossible *not* to communicate something, if one is in a relationship and still breathing. Complete silence, for example, is often a way of communicating anger or of saying, "My needs are not being met!" or "I'm keeping my distance from you!" The trouble with silent communication is that it tends to be ambiguous, like a Rorschach inkblot. People project their own inner feelings and attitudes onto the silent person and respond in terms of these. What is projected may have little resemblance to the person's actual feelings.

The process of checking out meaning can help both partners to improve the ways in which they send messages and their skill in listening. The effort to find out what the other really means and feels, affirms him and says in a nonverbal way, "You are important to me."

Another road to productive communication is for both husband and wife to learn the skill of *saying it straight*. Each person can help the other to understand by asking himself, "Am I saying what I really mean?" This involves learning to be aware of what one is actually feeling and developing the ability to put the feeling clearly into words. Direct rather than devious, specific rather than generalized statements are required. A wife criticizes her husband as he sits at the breakfast table hidden behind his newspaper, "I wish you wouldn't always slurp your coffee." What she really means is, "I feel hurt when you hide in the newspaper instead of talking to me." Saying it straight involves being honest about negative as well as positive feelings, and being able to state them in a non-attacking way: "I feel . . .", rather than "You are. . . ." Some risk is required in the beginning of this kind of communication, until both husband and wife can trust the relationship enough to be able to say what they really mean.

James Farmer tells a story about a woman who acquired wealth and decided to have a book written about her genealogy. The well-known author she engaged for the assignment discovered that one of her grandfathers had been electrocuted in Sing Sing. When he said it would have to be included in the book, she pleaded for a way of saying it that would hide the truth. When the book appeared, it read as follows: "One of her grandfathers occupied the chair of applied electricity in one of America's best known institutions. He was very much attached to his position and literally died in the harness."[6] The meaning in some attempts to communicate between marriage partners is almost as hidden and confusing. It is usually better to "say it like it is," gently if necessary, but clearly. (We are not suggesting that all secrets be confessed. The help of a well-trained counselor may be needed to help one decide if and when secrets which might damage the relationship, should be confessed.)

Becoming aware of one's own, and learning to translate the

other's *coded and conflicted messages* are steps along the path to good communication. Feelings and thoughts of which an individual is unaware or incompletely aware are often communicated in nonverbal ways. Such messages are often hard to decode because they are derived from underlying conflicting feelings in the communicators. Conflicted messages get conflicted or confusing responses, or no response at all. On a verbal level, a wife says loving things and in various ways indicates that she is feeling amorous; but on a behavior level she sends another and contradictory message by being careless about personal cleanliness in a way that drives her husband away. All of us send such contradictory messages occasionally simply because we all have conflicted feelings. It helps to resolve this block if couples can help each other to bring such conflicts out into the open and discuss them. In this case, the wife discovered through marriage counseling that her inner conflicts about herself as a woman with sexual needs and feelings were expressing themselves nonverbally.

Decoding messages (verbal and nonverbal) is a useful skill in marriage. The hidden or implicit messages which destroy rather than cultivate relationship are usually critical, attacking, or condescending. A couple which says, "We just can't communicate!" usually is sending a barrage of messages that attack each other's self-esteem. The attack may occur in the words said or in the disguised message behind the words. "She won't communicate" may mean, "She won't say what I want her to say." Nagging may be a way of saying, "You're not giving me what I want in this relationship." The wife who interrupts constantly may actually be saying, "Pay more attention to me." The couple that can become aware of the meaning of their nonverbal and coded messages can often prevent a serious cycle of mutual attack and need-deprivation from beginning.

Karen had been involved a considerable part of the day in a perplexing decision involving her parents. As she worried and wondered about it, she thought how good it would be to talk the whole matter over with her husband when he returned that evening. But when he got home from work, his self-esteem was a bit frazzled from the day; consequently, when Karen opened the subject, Jack immediately stated curtly, "Why don't you stop worrying about that and just do the obvious thing? It's silly to knock yourself out about it!" The message, between as well as on the lines, which Jack transmitted to his wife was critical and condescending. It lacked awareness of what she was feeling. Consequently, this response terminated conversation abruptly.

Later, when Karen and Jack were able to talk more dispassionately, she was able to tell him that the feelings that she picked up in his words were these: "The solution is obvious and why are you so stupid you can't see that it is? Stop dragging me into your squabbles with your neurotic family!" As they talked, Jack explained that he was feeling "beat" as a result of a trying day at the office and that her timing—confronting him with her problem the minute he stepped through the door—elicited a response from him which did not really represent his major feelings about the problem of her parents.

Relatively healthy couples like Karen and Jack can usually learn to decipher and unscramble their hidden and conflicted messages; through practice they can learn to send clear, unambiguous messages which contribute to mutual empathy.

Of course, not all coded messages are negative. The husband who brings his wife a bottle of perfume "for no reason at all" probably is saying, "I love you! You're an attractive woman! I like being married to you!" As someone has said, when a man brings his wife a present for no reason, there is a reason! Couples whose nonverbal communication is on a positive level most of the time are continually saying to each other, "I care."

COMMUNICATION AND CONFLICT

"A relationship which spells closeness also spells conflict."[7] Some conflict, unhappiness, frustration, and anger are inherent and inescapable in every marriage relationship simply because they are in the fabric of all human relationships. Marriage is like other human relationships, only more so. That is, marriage is the most difficult and the most demanding, but also the most potentially rewarding of all human relationships, because it is potentially the most intimate. Because it is the most intimate, it also holds the greatest potential for conflict.

Conflict in itself is not a block to intimacy. People who feel strongly about each other are bound to fight occasionally. A man who described himself as a "teacher of human relations" was being interviewed on a radio program. The major selling point for his course was, "My wife and I have been married for forty years and we have never had a fight." The interviewer's remark was, "Isn't it sort of dull?" The interviewer knew more about human relations than did the teacher of human relations. Either the marriage has died of indifference and is no more than two people in possession of a marriage license, or all strong feelings have gone underground because of the fear of anger. Couples who can learn to value their conflicts can use them to improve the communication skills which make possible the growth of intimacy. Anything alive experiences struggle and conflict. A couple can learn to learn from their fights; they can learn how to keep them from becoming physically or emotionally destructive, how to interrupt them sooner and how to grow closer because of them. Intimacy grows when conflicts are faced and worked through in the painful but fulfilling process of gradual understanding and compromise of differences. Democratic marriages in which the couple strives to develop a basic spirit of mutual respect and equality tend to bring conflict to the surface and out into the open where it can be wrestled with. Temporary estrangement during periods of need-deprivation resulting from unresolved conflict is par for the course in even the most effective marriages. The experience of many couples confirms a statement by Terentius, a playwright of ancient Rome: "Great love was never lost by small quarrels. Love after the quarrel was greater than before."[8]

Conflict often produces a *distancing cycle* in a marriage. The need-deprivation causes anger and attack, which results in counterattack and the increase of interpersonal distance, which in turn produces greater need-deprivation and greater anger. Relatively healthy couples usually interrupt this cycle after the mutual attack has given them an opportunity to drain off some of their pent-up hostility, and has produced guilt, the fear of abandonment, and the desire for the re-establishment of closeness. The partner with the stronger self-esteem at the moment, or in whom the processes just described operate more strongly, usually initiates a peace offer or makes a reconciliation gesture. If the other still needs to attack, for whatever reason, the offer or gesture may be thrown back into the partner's face, and the conflict will continue with renewed vigor, fed by the new hurt. If not, intimacy will be re-established. In a less healthy marriage, the forces driving the mutual attack are so strong that the cycle gains momentum rapidly until it is like a large stone rolling down a steep hill. Couples whose need for ventilating negative feelings and gaining elbow room in the marriage is relatively mild tend to have short fights. Those whose needs in this direction are strong often have hot or cold wars lasting for days, months, or even years.

When couples have tried unsuccessfully to communicate, over a long period of time, they often begin to use words mainly to confuse and attack, rather than to attempt to transmit meanings. One husband began to use large words, only semiappropriately, whenever he felt rejected or otherwise threatened by his wife. His words were an attempt both to hide his real feelings and to express his hostility toward her by making her feel "snowed" by verbiage. His use of a string of such words was a way of saying, "I can't reach you; I'm giving up." Such unsuccessful communication often causes couples to store up dynamite by denying and repressing hurt and angry feelings. An escape valve such as beating up the pillow while making the bed, or "knocking the guts" out of the punching bag hanging in the garage can often help to drain off violent, angry feelings while the issue is being resolved. Healthy assertiveness sometimes helps to reduce unproductive conflict. Many people who are depressed or hostile most of the time are simply struggling to hold down their natural aggressiveness and to avoid becoming aware of negative feelings. The use of words with vehemence, even anger, can be an alternative to physical violence. Such words are often a way of letting off pressure in the inevitable frustrations of any close relationship. *Occasional* outbursts may make it possible for the marriage partners to be more caring and compassionate at other times. A relationship strong enough to take such outbursts in its stride is a healthy one. Providing a place where one can safely drain off hostility that has accumulated in the outside world is one of the important mental health functions of a good marriage. There is validity in the jest that, "If it weren't for marriage, husbands and wives would have to fight with strangers." (Chronic verbal attacking is *not* a means of maintaining a healthy marriage.)

Effective conflict-resolution communication focuses on *issues* rather than attacking personalities. This is the chief characteristic of productive, as distinguished from futile, arguments. Furthermore, conflict resolution deals with *specific issues* on which decisions and compromise action can be worked out. It stays away from global accusations and from tackling the whole problem all at once (a sure way to fail). The "issue" in unproductive arguments is often only an excuse for attack upon the other partner. The hidden purpose is to increase one's own sense of power by "putting the other down."

Effective conflict resolution in marriage, then, results from several steps in the communication process. Both partners must first be willing to hear each other's complaints and to accept feelings, however vehement, about them. The couple must then make efforts to narrow down the generalized accusations to the particular issues or differences about which something can be done. They must learn to focus on one issue at a time. Each must state how he himself sees the problem and how he thinks the other sees the problem. When this "checking out" has helped to resolve the negative feelings, the couple can begin to make concessions, compromises, and plans for dealing with their differences. A relatively healthy couple in which both partners have a strong sense of identity can really *use* their conflicts for growth by following these steps. If the conflict is too severe or if the couple is unable to communicate constructively, they need to seek the guidance of a marriage counselor or to join a marital growth group.

A couple may find it helpful to ask themselves questions such as these: Is this really an issue worth fighting over or is my self-esteem threatened by something my spouse has said or done? In relation to this issue or problem area, what do I want and what does my partner want that we are not getting? What middle-ground, or compromise, solution might be worked out in this area to help increase the degree of mutual need-satisfaction? What must I *give* in the relationship in order to satisfy the needs of my partner and myself in this area? What small next step can we take right now toward implementing this decision, made jointly through the give-and-take of discussion?

When the issue is apparently insoluble in spite of sincere effort on both sides, it is sometimes well to agree to abandon it for awhile and to focus on other areas where mutual need satisfaction is possible. Sometimes the conflict evaporates, in which case it was probably merely an excuse for releasing pent-up hostilities. It is more likely, however, that the unresolved conflict can be approached again from another angle when the partners have reconnected their communication lines in other areas.

RHYTHMS IN COMMUNICATION

It is unrealistic to expect that any couple can (or should) communicate in significant depth *continually* through the hours and days of their relationship. Anne Philipe gives a vivid picture of the normal fluctuations in the depth and intensity of intimacy, and of the periodic renewal of significant communication which revivifies a good marriage:

The inhuman city rhythm would sometimes separate us for several days. . . . In, out, telephones, sleep. For a while the communication would be broken, the light between us dimmed, but we knew that the next Sunday would see us reunited and we would tell each other then all that the interminable week had brought to us both: thoughts about ourselves, things we had heard, things we had observed each in the other without seeming to, as we had seemed absorbed. I liked it when you noticed my new sweater after you hadn't said a word about it the morning I put it on for the first time.[9]

A communication rhythm which helps husband and wife to affirm each other's self-esteem will increase the depth of intimacy in a marriage.

Learning to communicate verbally and nonverbally their warm, loving "I care" messages can have the same effect. Effective use of the sense of touch—a hand on the arm or forehead or buttocks—is often worth a thousand words. No spouse should ever assume that "he (she) knows I love him (her)." A growing sense of intimacy should not require minute-to-minute reinforcement; but even the healthiest husbands and wives have enough doubts about themselves as persons worth loving to need regular affirmation from each other.

A recent magazine cartoon showed a husband and wife leaving the office of the marriage counselor. The husband was saying to the wife, "Now that we've learned to communicate, shut up!" It is obvious that learning to be aware of, and to communicate, real feelings in words is not the whole answer to the problems of communication. Need-satisfying communication becomes interpersonal *communion* as richer, more multileveled interaction becomes a channel for caring. Couples who have been intimately married for a long time often communicate on deep, subconscious levels. Such communion is something far beyond the mere sending and receiving of messages, as important as these are. It is the result of depth intimacy, the strong *marital identity* which is the strand of gold thread in a marriage covenant.

TAKING ACTION

Take a look together at your ways of getting through to each other. Discuss the things that block efforts to communicate, par-

ticularly during conflict. Think of ways for increasing the opportunities for communication—more face-to-face time together,
for example. Do something to increase the number of areas in
which you can talk the same language. Perhaps learning something
about an interest of your spouse or reading a book that both of
you are interested in might help.

Here are some additional communication exercises which many
couples find useful in sharpening their skills in transmitting meanings: (*a*) *Look in each other's eyes* for at least a full minute and,
without words, try to read what the other is feeling. The eyes are
a direct pathway to the inner being of a person; their messages
therefore are revealing. (*b*) *Let one person say the other's name
repeatedly,* changing the tone and intensity, until that person
senses that it "feels good" or affirms him. Then reverse the exercise
and let the receiver become the sender. This exercise can help
you to become more aware of the nuances of intimate communication. (*c*) *Practice listening and understanding.* Let one person
share something about which he has strong feelings in the here
and now. The other limits his responses to one thing—saying to
the first person what he perceives him as feeling. The responder
may begin with a phrase such as "Let's see if I understand how
it looks to you . . ." and then he paraphrases what he thinks the
other is expressing. (*d*) *Switch roles* and try to state each other's
position and feelings on one issue on which you have obvious
differences of viewpoint. (*e*) *Practice nonverbal communication* by
attempting to get messages through to each other with the use of
touch, facial expressions, body movements, gestures, eye communication. (*f*) *Try arguing at a distance with your backs to each
other;* then turn around and continue as you are face-to-face, holding hands and looking into each other's eyes. Be aware of the
changes in your feelings in the two positions. It may surprise you
how much difference physical and eye contact makes. (For a
discussion of some of these and other similar communication exercises see William C. Schutz, *Joy, Expanding Human Awareness*
[New York: Grove Press, 1967].)

These techniques are especially helpful when used in marital growth groups with a trained leader.

If you simply can't communicate on any but a superficial level ("Pass the butter," "Looks like rain") in spite of determined efforts on your own, or if your are unable to achieve the kind of communication which satisfies your needs as a couple, it is essential to seek professional help with your communication blocks.

NOTES

1. Reuel L. Howe, *Herein Is Love* (Valley Forge, Pa.: The Judson Press, 1961), p. 100. Howe writes: "One can pull himself from the pit of loneliness only by the ropes of communication.

   "Without communication, the possibilities for a relationship become hopeless, the resources of the partners for the relationship are no longer available, the means for healing the hurts that previous communication may have caused are no longer present. . . ." (P. 99.)
2. Robert Brizee, notes on communication.
3. Gabriel Marcel, quoted by Perry LeFevre, "On Being 'With' Another," *The Chicago Theological Seminary Review* (December, 1966), Vol. LVII, No. 3, p. 24.
4. Paul Tournier, *To Understand Each Other* (Richmond, Va.: John Knox Press, 1962), pp. 28, 29.
5. Satir, *Conjoint Family Therapy* (Palo Alto, Calif.: Science & Behavior Books, 1964), p. 70.
6. Quoted by Ralph McGill, *Atlanta Constitution*, April 24, 1968, p. 1.
7. Otto Pollak, lecture, University of Pennsylvania, January 18, 1967.
8. Quoted by Howard Whitman, *Philadelphia Sunday Bulletin*, January 15, 1967.
9. Anne Philipe, *No Longer Than a Sigh* (New York: Atheneum, 1964), pp. 48–49.

6 *Enriching the Seasons of Marriage*

> To everything there is a season, and a time to every purpose under the heaven.
>
> Ecclesiastes 3:1, AV

> It takes guts to stay married. . . . There will be many crises between the wedding day and the golden anniversary, and the people who make it are heroes.
>
> Howard Whitman[1]

A depth relationship is a living process, with its ups and downs, its ebb and flow, its continuing succession of change. Each stage in the marital cycle has its unique demands, frustrations, worries, joys, and satisfactions. At every stage, the demands on each partner are different. The pattern of needs changes from stage to stage, altering the nature and intensity of the will to relate. Thus the style of intimacy changes through the years. Sociologist Otto Pollak declares: "There is no peace in human relationships; no marriage is ever settled."[2] Marriage need never be dull. Just when a couple has mastered the skills of one stage (or given up, or become bored), a new and unprecedented stage arrives requiring the acquisition of new skills. The periods of transition from one stage to another can be occasions of pressure and crisis as the couple struggles to let go of the familiar, comfortable past and master the demands of a new stage. Old methods of gaining need-satisfaction, and of relating, no longer work as they have in the past. Such periods of transition can be opportunities for discovering new ways of relating, new joys and satisfaction which can give new depth and height to intimacy.

> The central truth is that the tide of happiness in *any* marriage ebbs and flows. The marriage is ecstatically happy at times, excruciatingly painful at others, a mixture of good and bad in between. . . . Even the best marriage has its periods of desperation.[3]

A marriage is built from the everyday-ness of living together—from what seem like the trivial as well as the obviously significant experiences, encounters, sufferings, and satisfactions. Movement on the marital journey is not always ahead. There are times in most marriages when couples regress, or take a detour or a side road that turns out to be a dead end. A *growing* relationship, however, has an over-all movement toward greater depth which results from shared experiences of many kinds. There are changes in the intimacy pattern in the various stages of the marriage, but there is also a tendency for the couple to maintain a general continuity of relationship style over the years. This style can be one of gradual deepening, of stagnation, or of continuing retreat from intimacy. A strong marriage relationship is constructed by two people who are willing to work at it, year-in and year-out, "for better, for worse, for richer, for poorer, in sickness and in health, to love and to cherish, till death us do part."

For couples in the early stages of marriage, it is reassuring to know that a marriage, like Rome, isn't built in a day. A perceptive young wife commented, after a marital growth group session, "I was helped by discovering that no one begins with a perfect relationship. I see now that I blamed us both for not having a full marriage experience. . . . I had been unhappy with the time it took to mature our relationship—felt guilty that ours appeared to me not as deep as those of my acquaintances who have been married twice as long. . . . I think I'll be able to enjoy what we have and be more sensitive to us, instead of comparing us with them."

One of the essential functions of a good marriage is for the partners to provide encouragement and support to each other as they go through anxiety-producing periods of crisis—pregnancy, illness, children growing up and leaving home, deaths of parents, husband's retirement. Couples who are able to support each other and to learn new ways of coping during such periods of stress achieve increased depth as a result of weathering the storms together. The bond which unites a couple that has had a mutually giving relationship for twenty, thirty, forty or more years, has something of the same power and intensity as that which unites soldiers who have come through battlefield experiences together. Other couples, who are unable to support each other and whose communication systems crumble under pressure are pulled further apart by each new crisis.

STAGES OF THE MARRIAGE CYCLE

An overview of the marital journey provides the perspective a couple needs if they are to work at deepening the marriage relationship. The following pages will help to identify the various stages in the marriage cycle and will suggest some guidelines for growth and creativity within each.

There are various ways of defining the stages of the life cycle of a marriage. Here is one.[4]

Stage 1: Courtship and engagement

Stage 2: Wedding to beginning of first pregnancy

Stage 3: Parents of preschool children

Stage 4: Parents of school children (ages 6 to 13)

Stage 5: Parents of adolescents (ages 13 to 19)

Stage 6: Parents of children leaving home

Stage 7: Empty nest to retirement

Stage 8: Retirement to death of one spouse

It is obvious that stages 3 through 6 overlap if there is more than one child. Each stage of marriage and family life has its "developmental task"—certain goals which need to be achieved if the couple is to cope with that stage, continue to grow in intimacy, and prepare for later stages.[5]

Stage 1: Courtship and Engagement. The process called court-ship and engagement is the first stage in the establishment of a relationship of growing oneness. Dating is a process by which young people develop more fully whatever skills they learned as children in relating to persons of the opposite sex. Those who marry with little satisfying practice in relationships with persons of the other sex usually have difficult problems during the first few years. What occurs before marriage—in dating, courtship, and engagement—is immensely important as preparation for growing intimacy.

Dating serves a particularly important preparatory function with reference to the modern mode of companionship marriages. Dating patterns of adolescents should provide them with a varied experience of companionship and communication with persons of the opposite sex. Spending a major part of one's leisure time in dating, as many teenagers do, helps them to acquire the habits of relating and enjoying each other's company, which are essential in a companionship marriage.

Serious dating serves the function of "shopping," of sizing up the potential candidates for marriage in terms of an essential criterion: "To what extent can I expect this person to satisfy my basic personality and sexual hungers?" Although the question is seldom consciously asked, it is *the* guiding consideration which makes some persons more and some less attractive as potential marital partners. When two persons have reason to feel that their needs, both healthy and neurotic, will be met to a substantial degree by the other, their mutual attraction will be intense. The concept of the search for a relationship which will produce mutual need-satisfaction is related to Eric Berne's view that selecting a mate is a process of discovering someone who will play the same marital games.[6]

There are a number of factors which militate against the full use of the dating years to acquire relationship skills and as a time for making a wise choice of a marital partner with whom one can develop growing intimacy. Most dating takes place in leisure time when there is little opportunity for discovering how the person relates in the kinds of nonleisure activities which compose at least 90 percent of married life. Furthermore, there is a good deal of hiding, of putting one's best foot forward, and of playing defensive games which mask real feelings and attitudes. Aaron L. Rutledge states:

> Early in development children are taught by example, if not by word of mouth, to conceal their real feelings about many things. All too often this is taken over to the dating stage by youth, basing their experience upon the "line" of a deceptive front . . . .
> . . . Without specific and deliberate intent to do otherwise, courtship and engagement may serve only as a continuation of subterfuge and camouflage of the basic personalities under a smoke screen of passionate love, and as an opportunity for more intense and exclusive rights to individual satisfaction.[7]

The pressure exerted by powerful feelings and drives sometimes pushes people into unfulfilling relationships. Sex drives are intense during the late teens; the pain of loneliness is also a compelling force, as is the fear of being passed by in the mate-selection years. The latter fear is prominent in many girls. Family pressures may make it nearly impossible to terminate an engagement, even though the couple senses a basic inadequacy in their relationship.

Premarital pregnancies increase the problems of making a wise decision while at the same time making such a decision all the more crucial. The only rational procedure, consistent with the welfare of both the couple and their unborn child, is for the couple to resist any pressures to rush into marriage. Instead, they should evaluate carefully whether they have a reasonable possibility of building a sound marriage. This means facing honestly such issues as their emotional maturity, capacity to bear the responsibilities of child-rearing, and their deep feelings about each other. A trained counselor can give invaluable help in this complex decision by the couple. If their relationship has little or no potential for a viable future, it is much better for everyone concerned for them not to marry, and to give serious consideration to what will be the best course to follow for the child.

Premarital sex, whether or not a pregnancy is involved, can be a problem for couples in later stages of their life together. Couples who have engaged in premarital intercourse, sometimes find guilt feelings plaguing them in marriage. If this is the case, they may need to seek counseling to resolve the feelings which cause difficulty or distancing in the marriage.

The engagement period, in the words of a song from *The King and I,* should be a time of "getting to know you, getting to know all about you." It should also be a time of getting better acquainted with oneself. Problems in marriages usually result from emotional blind spots in the partners. The operation of unconscious and conflicting needs sometimes makes mate selection a hit-or-miss matter. Bill White, whom we met in Chapter 1, illustrates the way in which conflicting needs create problems within a relationship. On the one hand, he reacts negatively to aggressiveness in women, suggesting that he needs to feel in control of such relationships. Yet his hidden dependency-needs cause him to be attracted to Amy Jones, who tends to take charge of situations. In other words, his unresolved conflicts about his own aggressiveness and dependency cause him to "need" two qualities in a woman which are actually contradictory—compliance and a managing quality.

Honesty and openness with each other are, of course, indispensable. Those who live a lie consciously or unconsciously during their engagement usually pay a high price in their marriages. Engagement provides an invaluable opportunity for a couple to work at strengthening communication skills by practicing communication on dozens of diverse topics, *particularly those which are hard to talk about.* Areas of conflict, disagreement, and easily hurt feelings are crucially important; learning techniques of resolving conflict and compromising differences is essential to marital happiness. Avoiding or submerging conflict is "chickening out" of the developmental task of the engagement (or any other) period. It hurts to face it, but the price of "peace at any price" is too high.

It is healthy for engaged couples to broaden their relationship by exploring many dimensions of sharing—intellectual, aesthetic, creative, work, commitment, and spiritual intimacy can be added, in addition to the usual pattern of emotional, recreational and romantic relating.

Many engaged couples profit from joint participation in a premarital growth group or sensitivity training experience. Bill and Amy found that their group experience, extending over some eight months, helped them to lower the barriers in their relationship, before they were married. Bill came to see his lateness as a passive-dependent way of manipulating others and Amy discovered some of the roots of her aloofness and problems in communication. Getting these and other matters out into the open and discussing them freely, both in the group and by themselves between sessions, helped Amy and Bill to interrupt some of their relationship-blocking patterns.

Premarital counseling, on an individual, couple, or group basis, is crucially important if one or both parties evidence a high degree of emotional immaturity. Such counseling should be started as long as possible before the wedding and should continue for whatever period is needed to stimulate the maturing process. Counseling of this variety is very different from what is often meant by "premarital counseling"—i.e., one to three instructional interviews preceding the wedding by a few days or weeks. Longer-term premarital counseling and growth group experiences can prove to be excellent investments in a couple's future happiness and marital creativity.

The engagement period can be an invaluable opportunity for beginning:

1. The total process of learning to understand and relate to each other in all circumstances. "I" and "you" become "we."
2. Undoing unwholesome attitudes developed through earlier conditioning and dating experiences, and exploring the male-female likeness and differences in general and as applicable to each couple.
3. Understanding and evaluating each of the parents, the parents' relationship to each other, the relationship of each to his parents, and the future relationship of the new family to the old family.
4. Determining the kind of marriage and family life desired by the

couple, and the beginning of thinking, feeling, and reacting in this context.

5. The continuation of individual growth and acceptance of responsibility, in an atmosphere of love and appreciation, with the "push" of sexuality as one of the driving forces.

6. Working out attitudes and plans for work and family financing.

7. Exploring attitudes toward children, and coming to a beginning plan of how they should be reared.

8. The exploration of personal development and of family life in the larger context of social and spiritual reality.

9. Solution of problems in the feeling and expression of affection, including specific preparation for sex life.

10. Planning the general and specific details of the wedding.

11. The development of long-range family goals, life purposes and values.[8]

Marriage is an intricate system of roles, needs, relationships, responsibilities, and satisfactions. A couple's motivation to work at the developmental tasks and goals of the engagement period is an indication of the vitality of their growth potential.

Stage 2: Wedding to First Pregnancy. During the early years of marriage, with or without children, a couple faces its most difficult developmental task. The major effort is "to form the basis of a new family system distinct from their background families."[9] Each partner needs to provide a new anchor for the other—an anchor of intimate association to replace the parental anchor. If the partners can do this, they become the *primary resource persons* for satisfying each other's personality hungers. Only as a person has an anchor of gradually increasing intimacy and trust in the new relationship can he relinquish his dependency on old parental relationships and reduce his dependency on "the boys" or "the girls." Unfortunately, because of the superficiality of many premarital relationships, the major interpersonal reorientation required by marriage must begin with a person who is essentially a stranger. In most cases, it takes some time to give up the defensive games of courtship and engagement, and to move toward intimacy-enhancing openness.

Based on her experiences in counseling with young married couples, Miriam Jolesch summarizes the developmental tasks of early marriage:

> During the early years of marriage, a young couple is likely to be exposed to a number of sources of potential conflict. Each partner must *effect emotional separation from his own family;* each must *learn to accept the role of husband or wife.* Together the partners must *gain a sense of identity as a family unity,* over and above their identity as separate individuals. Accomplishing these developmental tasks may be so difficult for one or both of the partners that the marriage becomes threatened.[10]

Becoming a need-satisfying and adequate husband or wife— what Jolesch calls learning appropriate spouse roles—is the developmental task of the first years of marriage. Mates can support each other in the struggle with understanding and acceptance of the feelings of inadequacy and inevitable anger which accompany it. Acquiring spouse roles is even more complicated if the couple simultaneously must acquire new and demanding roles as parents. No matter how adequate a couple's engagement experiences were, there are many problems to be met in the early postwedding years. Most of the problems of marriage aren't really problems until after marriage actually begins. They have little reality for the couple until an existential collision with the problems occurs in the actual business of living together.

One of the necessary but painful transitions is from the euphoria of the honeymoon and first months of marriage to the more down-to-earth matters of compromising the many differences which each brought to the relationship, and working out reasonably need-satisfying ways of communicating and relating.

The shock of discovering that one's new bride or bridegroom has faults and deficiencies, perhaps serious ones, sometimes leads to efforts at reform. While there will be some changes in both husband and wife as each strives to meet each other's needs, both partners must learn to accept (though not necessarily like) each other's imperfections. Marriage has been described as the relationship of "two reasonable human beings who have agreed to abide by each other's intolerabilities." Havemann writes:

> The romantic aura attached to marriage in our society lifts us out of ourselves for awhile. We feel bigger and better than life. Then, as the intoxication wears off, we are saddened and hurt to find that we really have not changed at all. We are still merely human, and so is the husband or bride we have just acquired.[11]

A part of the disenchantment is the discovery that by getting married one has given up a significant amount of personal freedom and that to develop a sense of "we," each must give up thinking mainly in terms of "I." Those who do not face the fact or are not willing to make the investment, do not "build a marriage" though they may continue to live alone together.

Some couples erroneously believe that their love has died when they experience the disenchantment and the grinding of the interpersonal gears which are required to enable them to grow together. The fact is, however, that giving up unrealistic expectations frees the couple to enjoy their relationship more.

A common illusory expectation is that one's partner will be a gratifying parent figure who will both continue the satisfactions one enjoyed in one's childhood family and also make up for what one felt one missed in that family. Since this expectation is usually unconscious, it persists long after the realities of the marriage make its unrealism obvious to a relatively objective observer such as a marriage counselor.

The early years of marriage were described in Chapter 1 as "the second crisis of intimacy." Each partner brings to the marriage different patterns of need for closeness and distance. The grinding of the gears between them in this area is their attempt to evolve a workable compromise between the differences in these two patterns. Miriam Jolesch reports that, among the young couples counseled by her, the chief complaint voiced by the wives "had to do with [her] feeling that [her] husband wanted to maintain his separateness from [her] and [her] distress at the emotional distance between them."[12] Typically, the husbands were threatened by the wives' desire for closeness.

According to Erik Erikson, young adulthood is the time when the major life (developmental) task of every individual is to develop his capacity for rich emotional and sexual intimacy. The time usually coincides with the early years of marriage. As pointed out in Chapter 3, a key factor in the successful resolution of the intimacy crisis is the possession of a firm sense of personal identity as a foundation for intimate relationships. Young couples who have not completed the central task of adolescence—achieving a sense of identity—have a difficult time. They both desire and fear intimacy. It is difficult for them to let go of their dependency on parents and the wider peer group. They fear change and therefore hold on to old sources of satisfaction rather than taking the risk of discovering whether marriage can become their chief resource. Because of this, in-law problems often are acute. Since parents naturally have mixed feelings about losing their offspring's dependency, they may foster this unwittingly, not recognizing that it is hurting the marriage.

Whether or not a wife shall work outside the home is often an issue which causes conflict. Some discussion of it should have taken place during the engagement period. The actual business of living with whatever has been decided may raise the question again. How each partner *feels* about the wife's working is the crucial issue. If a wife doesn't want to work but needs to for financial reasons, if she wants to work but her husband feels that woman's place is in the home, or vice versa, serious problems which need to be openly dealt with may occur. As working wives become more and more common, the problem may arise at any stage of the marriage cycle.

Healthy couples can use the crisis of early marriage as an opportunity for growth. They make the discovery that the most meaningful married love could not be experienced during the engagement except in a rudimentary way. Married love is "love with its eyes open." It includes more of the mundane, but it can also be deeper and richer in many ways than the intense, romanticized love of courtship. This dawning experience can make the second stage of intimacy wonderful and lively in spite of the inevitable stress.

There are a number of ways to maximize the growth of a marriage during these first critical months or years:

1. Recognize and discuss the fact that it *is* a time of stress for both. Frank facing of the fact that it is a period of major re-orientation helps in coping constructively with the demands.

2. Accept the necessity of giving up some of the freedom and individualized decision-making of singleness, in the interests of achieving a relationship and the benefits of marriedness.

3. Do everything possible to support each other emotionally in learning the new wife-ing and husband-ing roles and skills. Warm emotional support of each other will help to offset the frustrations which result from lack of competence in these roles and skills. Appreciation is the language of love. Use it generously. Say "Yes" to each other whenever possible.

4. Work at the nurturance of the various facets of intimacy. Discuss mutual needs and what each finds satisfying; learn to enjoy the art of feeding each other's heart hungers.

5. Attempt to separate ghost-feelings left over from earlier relationships, from feelings and reactions appropriate to marriage. Do everything possible to avoid using regressive defenses to deal with the normal anxiety of the identity crisis; "Going home to mother" (physically or psychologically) is an illustration of trying to escape the uncertainties of a new relationship by seeking to return to the comfort of an old one. In the long run, regressive solutions aren't real solutions. They only increase the difficulties of the marital adjustment. It is better to stay and fight it through to a compromise solution in which each gives up some of his cherished wishes but each also gains some satisfactions.

6. Work together in consciously shaping the unique *image of the kind of marriage you want,* with its own identity, basically

different in some ways from the marriages of either set of parents. Keeping the goal in mind will alert both husband and wife when they are moving toward it and away from it.

7. Keep building bridges as a couple with other couples of various ages. Those who are compatible can become part of the extended family; they can influence the shaping of a unique marital image.

8. Balance time alone together as a couple with time shared with others.

9. If you have serious or escalating conflicts, obtain *professional* counseling help, rather than turning to relatives and friends for advice. Broken hearts often require more professional skill than broken arms.

10. Resist efforts to reform each other. Concentrate on mutual need-satisfaction.

Throughout the early months and years of marriage, it is important for couples to exercise the virtue of patience with each other, recognizing that growth takes time and struggle and living together. For both, it is a difficult period of unlearning old patterns and learning new ones. The young adult intimacy crisis is *the* crucial period. Building on whatever beginnings were made before marriage, newlyweds are working to finish the foundation upon which a lifetime of growing intimacy can be built.

Stage 3: Parents of Preschool Children. For the average couple the prechildren stage of marriage lasts just over two years. Thus, Stage 3 also usually begins during the young adult intimacy crisis. Major adjustment to parent roles must be made while the couple is still working on husband and wife roles. As in the previous stage, the husband and wife need to support each other as they struggle to learn fathering and mothering skills and roles and, simultaneously, seek to integrate these roles with the newly learned or partially learned spouse roles. Permitting each other to find "additional anchors of intimate association in children"[13] is essential and inevitably changes the nature of the intimacy-distance pattern in the marriage. In some marriages, a crisis is produced by the impact of the needs of a child for an intimate relationship with the parents. At each of the child's growth stages, the demands on parents change; with these changes come new opportunities for and strains on marital intimacy.

Out of the many occasions for sharing in the early stages of intimacy there gradually develops a *community of experience* which sets that marriage apart from the rest of the world and produces the "we-ness" of the marriage identity. The birth of the first child broadens the community of experience. A deepening sense of oneness flowing from the joint act of creativity and the mutual fulfillment of producing children together is now possible.

In all cases, pregnancy confronts couples with the need to change and grow. In some husbands, the pregnancy of their wives stirs up ghost feelings of fear from their early lives—fear that their wives will die in childbirth, for example. To the extent that oedipal feelings still remain unresolved in either or both partners, these may be activated by pregnancy. Conflicted feelings from this source may make the wife ambivalent about her new status as mother. The awareness that he is now "married to a mother" may cause the husband to respond in nonrational ways which prevent him from being warm and supportive during a time when his wife needs his support very much. Many couples, of course, are drawn closer by being able to share the experiences of pregnancy and of preparing themselves psychologically and otherwise for the arrival of their child.

Having a baby in the family imposes many strains on husband-wife intimacy. Physical fatigue resulting from the demands of caring for a completely dependent little creature sharply reduces the emotional energy which the wife has for investment in the marriage. The time which mothering and fathering takes depletes the time available for them to be alone together. Conflicts between the wife's pictures of what constitutes the appropriate roles of a mother and a father and the husband's pictures of these roles, call for reconciliation of differences. New responsibilities and pressures (financial and emotional) are on the husband, at the very point where he feels some sense of deprivation of satisfactions from his wife. Jealousy, often hidden from the person himself as well as from others, is frequently present in the husband's feelings toward the baby. If he has "parentified" his wife or if he was an only child, and had no experience in sharing his parents' love with siblings, competitiveness with the baby may be strong.

There are several ways to help make Stage 3 an intimacy-enhancing rather than an intimacy-depleting experience. Before, they had become "one flesh" symbolically in the emotional-physical-spiritual merging of loving intercourse. Now they have become "one flesh" *literally,* in the blending of their biological heritages in a child. Unless a couple is emotionally blocked, they will develop new depth in their relationship, and in themselves individually, by sharing the heartaches, fears, rewards, frustrations, and joys of parenting. It is during this stage and the subsequent three stages, that the primary developmental task (for adults), (what Erik Erikson calls "generativity") is to generate new life and to pour one's energies into the stream of history by investing in the new generation. This is a demanding, frightening, and exciting task involving the transmission of both the culture's heritage and the family's own unique heritage. The capacity to participate in this creativity and self-giving depends on the couple's success in achieving a sense of marital identity and mutually satisfying intimacy. As personal identity is the foundation of marital intimacy, marital identity and intimacy are the bases for generativity.

The periods of pregnancy involve a variety of coping crises for a couple. New expenses occur, often at the very time when income will be cut drastically by the wife's having to quit her outside employment. Sexual relations, housing arrangements, and division-of-labor balances, all demand adjustments and offer new opportunities for conflict. In many ways, their relationship is tested. If it has been founded mainly on physical attractiveness and sex, and is deficient in companionship and communication, pregnancy will threaten the marriage. Useful guidelines for Stage 3 include:

1. Share the responsibilities and satisfactions of parenting. Being an involved father is definitely "in"! Helping to care for the baby and young child is good for both father and the child. In spite of a father's interest and involvement, the main load of childcare will usually be carried by the mother simply because most husbands are at work forty hours or more a week. The trapped-mother-of-young-children syndrome is a danger which can be lessened, if the husband fulfills his highly important role of *supporting his wife* emotionally during this period. This involves expressing his love and respect for her, creating opportunities for continued sharing on as many levels as feasible in light of the new demands of parenthood, encouraging her to maintain at least one satisfying interest outside the home and the marriage, and taking over the parenting role regularly to give his wife a "chance to come up for air," as one young mother put it. If the husband is to be able to do this consistently, *he* will need periods of special attention and support from his wife.

2. Continue to work at developing mutually gratifying patterns of husband-wife companionship. The words "Things went well until the children came along" are heard so frequently by marriage counselors as to be almost a refrain. The point at which many marriages jump the track is in *overinvesting in children and under-investing in the marriage*. In the long run, an overinvestment in children proves to be a poor investment even from the standpoint of their welfare. The very intensity of the experience of childbirth and its sequelae tend to pull attention away from the companionship-intimacy activities of the couple. Active redevelopment of these activities, after the child is born, is often necessary. This includes *re-courtship*. Spouses can resist the centripetal pressure of children on their relationship by planning definite times alone together, without the children. These should be daily, however brief. Regular nights out "on the town," with other couples, can do wonders to keep the relationship batteries recharged. This requires having a baby-sitter in whom one has confidence, or perhaps making arrangements with another young couple to take turns sitting

for each other. It may be expensive but it's an essential investment in the future of the entire family.

3. Keep the lines of communication open by continuing to discuss how each of you feels about all aspects of your relationship, yourself in your new roles, and your mutual interests outside the home and family. It is usually *hidden* feelings of guilt, hostility, and resentment that sabotage a marriage. Of course, irrational feelings in the open can do the same thing. If feelings such as these don't grow weaker when discussed openly, and continue to create problems in the relationship, the help of a professional psychotherapist (psychiatrist, psychologist, or specialist in pastoral counseling) or marriage counselor should be obtained without delay.

4. Acquaint yourself with the characteristics of normal child development to allow you to keep otherwise perplexing aspects of child-raising from interfering with your marriage. One husband reported being disturbed by his four-year-old son's obvious preference for his mother. It was reassuring to him for the counselor to point out that it is normal for a child to have strong sensual and exclusivistic feelings about the parent of the other sex during the three- to the five-and-one-half year period. Actually, this "oedipal period" helps prepare a child for eventual marriage, by giving him a basic experience of relating to a person of the other sex.

Stage 4: Parents of School Children (age six to thirteen). Starting to school is a vital step in the process which will culminate in the children of a couple leaving home and establishing new families. The school-age child gradually widens his world of significant relationships with both peers and adults. The process makes him gradually less dependent on his parents, which means that the parents must depend less on the satisfactions derived from the child's dependency on them. In order to let him grow, they must progressively release him. Evelyn Duvall observes: "Fathers and mothers who continue their growth as persons beyond their roles as parents do better in letting their children go."[14]

Couples who "live for their children" have trouble encouraging their healthy, increasing autonomy.

The couple successful in accomplishing this developmental task is usually one who keep their love for each other central in their family life. Children are loved, of course, but the husband-wife relationship remains paramount. Such a couple finds many a chance to slip away, for a Saturday afternoon or a weekend together, for a little holiday, with perhaps the wife going along on a business trip and making it a "second honeymoon." They maintain the kind of companionship as a couple in which they can get through to each other fully—enriching, renewing, recreating, and creating together within the fullness of marriage.[15]

Life in a family with one or more school-age children teems with activities. Pressures on both parents are often heavy. The community makes demands on them too, and the husband's job responsibilities are pressing because he is striving to get established or "get ahead" in his occupation. The pressures are different from those of the preschool child years, but no less intense. Marriage partners are tempted to become so absorbed in the flurry of their multiple responsibilities that their own relationship is more and more neglected.

During the school years, the identity of the family as a unit reaches its strongest form. Although children are beginning to pull away, they are still deeply involved in their families, and enjoy sharing in all manner of joint activities—family camping trips, holiday celebrations, church activities, family projects and problems. Experiences of family cohesiveness and sharing can be satisfying for everyone concerned. They can add a richness to the intimacy of the marriage relationship, surrounding it with a supportive context of family intimacy. Close relationships between school-age children and parents of the same sex are particularly important for the formation of the children's sense of sexual identity and roles. These relationships can be satisfying to parents, too; as such, they can enhance family life generally and the marital bond in particular.

Guidelines for working to enhance Stage 4 are essentially the same as those in Stage 3, with the following additions:

1. Plan both family experiences such as outings, trips, vacations, and father-children, mother-children experiences. See that boys participate in male activities with their fathers and girls in female ones with their mothers. Father-daughter and mother-son experiences are also important.

2. Work at gradually releasing the children into their own orbits by continuing to strengthen intimacy through a variety of experiences as man and wife as well as mother and father.

Stage 5: Parents of Adolescents (age thirteen to nineteen). The years when a couple's offspring are adolescents are, like the preteen stage, busy, hectic, and demanding on parents. Many pressures make it difficult for a couple to maintain an intimate marriage. For example, conflict between adolescents and parents easily raises barriers between parents. Parent-teen conflict frequently focuses on issues of how much freedom, responsibility, and discipline are appropriate—issues on which parents usually have strong feelings and sometimes a lack of agreement. Thus, latent conflict between spouses is stirred up by the necessity of deciding on what limits should be set and how to enforce them. Teenagers have become adept at exploiting disagreements between their parents, turning them to their own advantage, and increasing interparent conflict. They often become skillful at picking an area for rebelling in which the parents are least able to maintain a common position. They know "where parents tie their goat and how to get him."[16]

At each growth stage of children, parents tend to relive the comparable stage in their own earlier development. This unconscious reliving is particularly active when children are in their teens. Their sexual maturing and dating activities stir up old, unresolved conflicts and guilt feelings within the parents, which are projected onto the marriage relationship. Parents' control over their children is increasingly challenged as the young people become more independent, rely increasingly on their peers, and often rebel openly. Threats to the parents' sense of adequacy and worth can be severe when the maturing children reject their values, stimulating conflict in the marriage as well as with the youth.

Couples in the parents-of-teens category begin to feel the psychological impact of aging and the crisis of the middle years. In contrast to the vibrant youth and sexual attractiveness of blossoming adolescent children, they may feel like "has beens." Jealousy of their maturing children is often present, though usually unconscious.

If the marriage has been neglected in favor of the children during the previous fifteen or more years, it is faltering by this time and in no condition to provide the couple with resources for facing the empty nest years. Even relatively strong marriages may find the fifth stage rough going at times. Weak or malfunctioning marriages often experience further fragmentation and perhaps termination, partly as a result of the crises precipitated by the "adolescing" of the children.

Here are some of the tendencies of couples during these years, which contribute to nonrelating: The husband may get lost in his work and the wife in her children and outside activities. The frantic pace leaves little time for relating. Husband and wife tend to take each other and their marriage for granted. They are used to it, and no longer think in terms of the continuing need to invest themselves in deepening it. Both partners may become careless in personal grooming; this may reflect a depletion of self-esteem but it serves to further deplete feelings of self-worth, in a kind of vicious cycle. Loss of control of children may increase tendencies to try to control the spouse, with resentment resulting. Sources of mutual satisfaction, sexual and otherwise, tend to become constricted. Nagging and accusing increase, as appreciation decreases. Boredom and the feeling that life is passing them by may result in extramarital affairs. Infidelities on the part of one or both partners almost always are symptomatic of basic inadequacies in the relationship.

These are inevitably years of stress, but they need not be grim. They can be fulfilling for a couple, providing they have worked at their relationship through the years and continue to do so. It is even not too late to begin. Consistent investment in a marriage pays off during these years in deepening intimacy; consistent neglect pays off in widening separation. To meet the needs of their adolescent children, parents need solidarity and connectedness in their relating. The adolescent needs support and a sense of acceptance, often when he least deserves it. When he is glum, uncommunicative, and rebellious, because of his own anxieties and identity struggles, he needs to know that he can count on the love and trust of his parents. In his struggles toward adulthood, he needs a firm foundation under his feet—the foundation of a solid relationship between his parents which gives him the courage and the incentive to seek a comparable relationship with a girl of his own age group.

There are a number of things that can be done to strengthen marriage and guard against the hazards of these years:

1. Support each other's self-esteem at every opportunity. Make sure that you aren't neglecting to give such important gifts as appreciation, respect, concern, and courtesy.

2. Be aware of the particular pressures—external and internal —under which each partner is functioning. For the husband it may be worry about the responsibilities of his job, together with the feeling that younger men are passing him by. For the wife, the pressures may be anticipatory anxiety about what will happen to her life when the children are gone. Support through *mutual understanding*. As one wife put it, "To know that my husband cares about my fears helps take the edge off them."

3. Keep the lines of communication open by having definite times alone to talk. A regular Sunday afternoon walk in the park or a leisurely meal together at a local restaurant can give a couple a time to clear the channels, talk through problems or hurts before they accumulate and grow, and generally get reconnected.

4. Make every effort to keep conflicts with teenagers from

infecting marriage intimacy. Remember, couples either hang to-gether or they will hang separately on the problems of providing loving limits for an adolescent. When differences arise, a strategy conference may be helpful.

5. Plan a gradually increasing number of satisfying activities *without the children.* As they move more and more in their own peer circles, parents need to offset lost satisfaction by developing their own activities, alone and with other couples.

6. Attention to personal appearance is important. The tendency of middle-aged figures to develop their growing edges on the wrong side, to "go to pot," usually lowers morale and feelings of sexual adequacy as well as affects health adversely. Sports or exercise in which both participate can be rewarding and can keep muscles in good tone and figures from sagging.

7. Develop new hobbies, interests, and skills; keep growing as a person. This is important for both partners, but particularly so for the wife; the forthcoming exodus of the children will leave a larger void in her world of satisfactions than will be true of her husband, whose job demands and satisfactions will probably be at their peak during the child-leaving years. It may be that the wife should begin considering how she wishes to use the extra time she will have available after the children leave. Retooling for a second career may need to begin now. If the wife goes back to school or to work, this will put strains on her and on her husband, which must be faced and worked through. (We can say this with conviction and feeling!)

Feelings about aging will be dealt with in the discussion about the seventh stage, the stage during which these feelings usually become acute. Here it can be said, however, that the key to suc-cessful aging begins now, in working to deepen the marriage and to find inner values for coping creatively with the years of maturity.

Stage 6: Parents of Children Leaving Home. The child-leaving phase is a crucial one for the future quality of the marriage. At each of the child-rearing stages, the couple had to adapt to changing demands on them from the children and from each other. An even more dramatic shift occurs when the children begin to leave the nest. Further profound adjustments in parental and spouse roles must be made; for most it is a time of stress and testing. There are crises related to the distance-closeness adjustments of every stage, but the magnitude of the intimacy crisis of the emptying-nest stage is exceeded, if at all, only by that of the early years of marriage during young adulthood.

To understand the problems of this stage, it must be seen as the *crisis of the middle years.* Child-leaving itself often triggers the onset of the crisis and contributes to its severity. This is especially true in marriages in which the spouses have used the children as a primary way of relating or as a means of avoiding intimacy (by always having the children between them as a buffer). Excessive child-centeredness is often a *symptom* of an impoverished husband-wife relationship. In any case, excessive child-centeredness *contributes to* impoverishment of the marriage. The underlying marital weakness usually does not become apparent until the center is taken away (as the children leave) and the couple must relate to each other in a "psychologically naked" way, as one such couple expressed it. Some marriages survive at least formally, in spite of a vacuum at their centers, by both parties quickly becoming overinvolved in such things as their jobs, community service, and church activities, and eventually with grandchildren. All these can be escapes from facing the emptiness of the marriage.

In the early forties for most people problems of aging become unavoidably obvious. Repeated experiences of loss—hair, teeth, vitality, youthful appearance, rapid recuperative powers, etc.—bring mourning and the reminder of even larger losses in the future. Aging parents may put a strain on the emotional if not the financial resources of the family. Loss of parents usually takes place during this stage. The death of parents stirs up deep feelings from childhood including unresolved guilt toward them; it also reminds the couple that they are one step closer to death themselves. "Now, I am next in line," is the way one woman put it.

Fear of death, like other fears, may be transformed into anger and expressed in the marriage.

Decline in physical attractiveness and sex drive may reveal the poverty of the marriage in other areas. If sex has been the main cement that held the couple together, the diminishing intensity of this drive and the accumulation of hostility derived from the general emptiness of the marriage will contribute to fragmentation. If body narcissism (being enamored with one's physical attractiveness) is prominent, aging of oneself and one's partner will be profoundly threatening. The signs of aging in the partner will be hated because they are reminders of one's own aging. Attraction to younger persons, in such cases, is an attempt to find the fountain of youth for oneself.

Disappointments and losses become more difficult to reverse as the years pass. The unfulfilled dreams of youth become the disillusionment of the preretirement period. The husband's self-esteem is damaged by having to face the unhappy fact that he is not going to become president of the company. Anything that hurts self-esteem troubles a marriage. Each party tends to blame the other for things that are the result of circumstances beyond the control of both, including aging. For women, the leaving of children often represents a loss of the central source of meaning, satisfactions, and sense of worth in their lives. Furthermore, children-leaving often comes within the same period as menopause. For many women, this represents not only a loss of reproductive powers but of feelings of worthwhileness and sexual attractiveness. Menopausal distress may reduce the wife's frustration tolerance sharply, making her irritable, nervous, and perhaps suspicious. Many women, of course, take menopause in their stride with little or no emotional upheaval, and a considerable sense of relief that they no longer have to worry about unwanted pregnancies.

Couples in middle age are often confronted with their feelings of boredom and of being "fed up" with the frustrating aspects of the marriage. If there has been little caring and sharing for years, except in relation to the children, couples may have no desire to spend the rest of their lives together. In some cases, one partner wants to go on, but the other does not. After twenty-five years of "Parent-Child" games, one or both parties may say, "To hell with it!" One husband, after thirty years of submissiveness to his wife's controlling and nagging, rebelled and had an affair with his secretary. This was his first major act of self-assertion in all those years. It ruptured the marriage.

The intensity of the middle-age intimacy crisis depends on the need-satisfyingness of the relationship and particularly on the success achieved in the previous stages of intimacy. If the basic art of loving mutuality was learned during the young adult years, most couples take the middle-years crisis in their stride. There is some re-examination of their relationship and some shift in their patterns of connecting. But since they possess the basic skills required in relating, they know how to go about changing and deepening their marriage to meet the needs of the second half of life.

In an insightful paper on "The Middle Years of Marriage," Theodor Bovet declares:

> If it is true that marriage makes of husbands and wives a new being, the married person, these middle years bring out its full maturity, the prime of life when the personality of the couple grows stronger and deeper. Otherwise these years are the visible tokens of old age and decrepitude. Marriage is subject to the same law as all living being: those who are unable to ripen grow old.[17]

Underneath all the problems of the middle years is the anxiety related to aging—the anxiety of nonbeing, of dying and death. Physical decline gradually shatters the illusion of perpetual youth and faces one with the ultimate fact that all of us are mortal. To cope constructively with the existential anxiety aroused by the increasing proximity of "the end of the line," a viable philosophy of life, relationships of trust, and a religious life that has reality are essential.

Carl Jung described the developmental task of the second half of life as the need to develop neglected inner resources and enrich the inner life. The first half is often given to the outer world—making one's place in it, getting established in one's job, raising a family, being involved in the community. This outer focus may result in the impoverishment of the inner life—the world of feelings, values, and inner creativity. To meet the challenge of aging and eventual death, the inner springs must flow. So, each partner needs to work at rediscovering an appreciation for truth, beauty, and other time-transcending values. Growth in relationships and growth in the vertical or spiritual dimension are vital parts of this awakening of inner resources for the road ahead. Together a couple may embark on a joint search for those experiences of the spirit which will be most meaningful to them.

One couple joined a Great Books discussion group to find stimulation in the realm of big ideas. Another took up painting together—a hobby which they had always said they would like to try "when we have time." Another couple found help in a "spiritual search group" in their church—a group of persons who share an interest in deepening their devotional life. Still another couple found inner enrichment in rediscovering the world of great music. The point of all this is that what two partners have to give to each other and what internal resources they possess for coping with life's second half depend on the development of their inner potentialities.

At the same time, ongoing interest in the community and the world helps a couple to continue the satisfactions of generativity after the children have left home.

Husbands and wives can help each other through the child-leaving stage by recognizing, supporting, and sharing each other's need to mourn. The emptying nest brings genuine grief with its constellation of many feelings—sadness, resentment, guilt, emptiness, and depression. Each partner must do his "grief work"—the work of his personality in letting go of the children emotionally, accepting the reality of their leaving and dealing with the varied feelings these events bring.

Coping with the crisis of the middle years can be done in several ways.

1. Emphasize growth of the "marriage personality," the relationship. This means cooperating to revitalize and deepen the marriage. Increasing, or perhaps rediscovering, mutuality, sharing, and closeness is an urgent necessity during this period. Husbands and wives can support each other's egos in many of the same ways they always have—appreciation, gifts, wanting to spend time together.

2. Continue to deepen relationships with other couples of various ages. The goal is to develop a network of mutually supporting and nurturing relationships, which can help to replace those lost with the children's leaving.

3. Become involved in some activities which will help to develop the spiritual potentialities of the marriage.

Stage 7: Empty Nest to Retirement. The patterns of relating established in earlier stages tend to continue in the empty-nest years. If a couple has learned to communicate in some depth, the passing years usually increase the intimacy of the relationship. If, on the other hand, their relationship has been essentially barren, the childless years tend to make the marriage more and more empty—an emotional wasteland. Some such couples develop parallel lives, touching at fewer and fewer points. In some cases, this is symbolized by the two living in separate sections of the house. They stay married because it is too much trouble or too expensive to separate, or because they gain some neurotic satisfactions from the cold war between them. Like the city of Berlin, what should be one is split by a wall which permits relatively little interchange.

In contrast, the couple which has stayed connected through the previous stages or achieved reconnection during the child-leaving stage, finds that the empty nest offers them all sorts of new opportunities for enjoying their marriage. One husband exclaimed, "Empty nest? Once we got used to the idea, we discovered it has a lot of advantages. We're doing the things as a couple we've always said we wanted to do but thought we didn't have time to because of the kids." The years between the leaving of the last child and retirement are valuable years from many standpoints. They should be highly productive and creative years, in which each partner finds new stimulation in developing interests and activities. Some of the energy that was formerly invested in children usually goes into grandparenting; but this is relatively minor, in most cases. Most of the energy is available for reinvestment in a second career for the wife, new hobbies for the husband, and joint projects in which the couple finds new meanings by giving themselves to meet some need in society. Social action groups are excellent for couples in this stage, keeping them involved with problems and perspectives beyond themselves, while using their aggressive energy to help reduce a social evil and make it a better world. Most important, self-investment—in social action and service-to-others—extends the period of "generativity" for the couple, helping them avoid ingrownness and the stagnation of increasing self-absorption. By continuing to invest their lives in the stream of things, they stay in touch with the world of growth and challenge.

The suggestions for coping with the two previous stages continue to be relevant in this one.

Stage 8: Retirement to Death of One Spouse. The husband's retirement often produces a marital crisis—more or less severe. To the extent that he has derived his vital satisfactions from his work, retirement may be experienced as a deprivation and an attack on his self-esteem. Feeling "finished," so far as a useful life is concerned, makes him difficult to live with. Mourning the lost job satisfactions is frequently present. The wife, too, often finds that the balance of the marriage is disturbed by the husband's retirement. She may have derived satisfactions from his work. Both are dependent, in many cases, on his schedule of going to work and coming home. The wife needs to give him support in this crucial adjustment, but often she is in need of support and perspective herself.

The couple facing retirement does well to attempt to work through their feelings about it before it occurs, and to make plans for how they can use the new time they will have available. Instead of emptiness, the future can be seen in terms of *opportunities* to do the things they have wanted to do but could not because of work obligations—travel, reading, hobbies, involvement in community and church projects. If they have a sound relationship, this can be a season of richness and fulfillment—"the last of life for which the first was made."

Some couples become more and more possessive as they face aging and death. It is as if they are clutching the relationship too tightly as they anticipate its loss. The postretirement years should be years of beginning to prepare for constructive living without the other. Facing widowhood is not easy, but it is essential. It means enjoying the relationship for all it is worth, working through old problems and being close, yet encouraging each to lean on his own resources and to develop relationships which can help when one partner dies. As William R. Alger observed in 1867: "There is a deep loneliness too in all the preparatory steps and approaches to death. Who can fitly describe the solitude of extreme age?"[18] This is the problem with which partners can help each other.

Couples in the postretirement years can make them more constructive by continuing the steps of Stage 7. In addition, it is important for them to work toward these goals:

1. Make the most of every day, week, and month you have together. By now you know how precious they are.

2. Support each other in the adjustments to retirement.

3. Enjoy the new leisure retirement brings—use it constructively.

4. Help prepare each other to live as widow or widower by strengthening inner resources and outer relationships. Reflect on the passing years and the experiences of transcendence you have shared.

For many couples who have achieved a degree of contentment and intimacy, and for others who are still willing to cultivate intimacy, these years can be the most fulfilling of the entire marriage. External pressures have diminished so that both partners have more emotional energy for each other. Assuming that health and finances are satisfactory, opportunities for sharing together in many interests are greater than ever. A couple in their late sixties likened their current stage to their courtship days, but with the added joys of having learned to know each other fully through forty years of shared experiences. Their communication is so vital at so many levels that they frequently do not need words to communicate their deepest thoughts. Such a marital identity is the goal toward which all the former stages strive.

We have reviewed the stages of marriage and intimacy—each with its own problems and possibilities. The words of Robert MacIver are appropriate:

> Time is the greatest of all human mysteries. . . . The way we respond to the challenge of time is a test of what we are, of what we are becoming. We grow older day by day. . . . Does that fact disturb us greatly, little, sometimes, often? How else are we growing in the same time? . . . For life is—or has—this unique energy possessed of sensitivity and perceptiveness that makes for itself a web of relationships, thus binding its past to its future.[19]

TAKING ACTION

Consider the guidelines at the conclusion of the stage of marriage which applies to your current relationship. Decide which of the suggestions seem helpful to you and make plans for using them to develop more joy and closeness.

NOTES

1. Howard Whitman, *Philadelphia Sunday Bulletin,* January 15, 1967.
2. Otto Pollak, lecture, University of Pennsylvania, January 18, 1967.
3. Ernest Havemann, "The Intricate Balance of a Happy Marriage," *Life,* September 29, 1961, p. 122.

4. For a summary see, Evelyn M. Duvall, *Family Development* (Philadelphia: J. B. Lippincott Co., 1957), pp. 5–9. This is a slight modification of the 8-stage schema of E. Duvall, pp. 8–9, from the point of view of the marital partners.

5. "A developmental task is a task which arises at or about a certain period of the life of an individual, successful achievement of which leads to happiness and to success with later tasks, while failure leads to unhappiness in the individual, disapproval of society, and difficulty with later tasks" (Robert J. Havighurst, quoted by Duvall, *op. cit.,* pp. 98–99).

6. Eric Berne, *Games People Play* (New York: Grove Press, 1964).

7. Aaron Rutledge, *Pre-Marital Counseling* (Cambridge, Mass.: Schenkman Publishing Co., 1966), p. 20.

8. *Ibid.,* p. 18.

9. Otto Pollak, lecture, University of Pennsylvania, February 23, 1967; a number of insights in this section are from Pollak.

10. Mariam Jolesch, "Casework Treatment of Young Adult Couples," *Social Casework,* Vol. XLIII, No. 5 (May, 1962), p. 245.

11. Havemann, "The Intricate Balance of a Happy Marriage," *Life,* September 21, 1961. (Paraphrasing Levy and Monroe.)

12. Jolesch, *op. cit.,* p. 246.

13. Otto Pollak, "Sociological and Psychoanalytic Concepts in Family Diagnosis," *The Psychotherapy of Marital Disharmonies,* ed. B. L. Green (New York: The Free Press, 1965), p. 18.

14. Duvall, *op. cit.,* p. 271.

15. *Ibid.,* p. 276.

16. From a statement by Lorna Forbes.

17. Boret, "The Middle Years of Marriage" (Paris: International Union of Family Organizations, June 1962), p. 4.

18. Alger, *The Genius of Solitude* (Boston. Roberts Bros., 1867), p. 84.

19. R. M. MacIver, *The Challenge of the Passing Years, My Encounter with Time* (New York: Simon and Schuster, 1962), pp. 47, xxii, 14.

7 *Increasing Sexual Intimacy*

> I defined love, not as an emotion so much as freely expressed behavior, undertaken with the aim of fostering happiness and growth in the person loved. But there is something grim and joyless and even a sense of hard work implicit in that conception of love. I would like . . . to spice this conception with some laughter, some wholesome, lusty, fully expressed, mischievous, lecherous, saucy sex. Not sex as mere coupling, but sex as an expression of *joie-de-vivre*, of a sharing of the good things in life. Sex that is something deeply enjoyed, freely given and taken, with good, deep, soul-shaking climaxes, the kind that make a well-married couple look at each other from time to time, and either wink, or grin, or become humble at the remembrance of joys past and expectant of those yet to be enjoyed.
>
> Sidney M. Jourard, *The Transparent Self*[1]

Discussions of love often emphasize the hard work involved and miss the spice and joy. The same is true of intimacy, which if it is genuine is positive and pleasurable in its impact on a marriage. Even sexual intimacy, in some marriage manuals, is made so antiseptic and complicated that the essence of sexual enjoyment—spontaneity, playfulness, lusty experimentation—evaporates. The feeling tone which is sometimes communicated is like the mood of a cartoon showing a tired, bedraggled couple on a vacation. The husband is saying, "How many more happy carefree days do we have to go?" Intimacy does take effort but if it is a burden, then it isn't the real thing. Sex is the dimension of intimacy which is most fun-filled. When sex is good in a marriage, the pleasure side of all other dimensions is enriched and fed. "Sexual intimacy" is more than the mere physical familiarity of intercourse. Prostitutes have for centuries engaged in an impersonal profession. "Sexual intimacy" is meant here to encompass the *total* experience of man and woman loving each other.

THE CENTRAL PLACE OF SEX

Sex is a powerful, pervasive drive in human beings. It is a dynamic force in the will to relate. It colors everything else—a dull gray if it is poor, a passionate pink if it is rich. Some people seem to wish that sex were not such a prominent motivator in human relationships. Such people are something like the woman who greeted the news of Darwin's discoveries with, "Let's hope that it isn't true and if it is, that it won't become generally known." In any marriage, sexual feelings are intertwined with every aspect of the relationship. In a healthy marriage, sex is affirmed and enjoyed so that it gives the total relationship warmth, joy, and resiliency.

It helps the person who is uneasy about the prominence of sex in his thinking to know that nearly everyone is as interested in sex as he is, and many even more so.[2] In other words, it is utterly normal for both men and women to have a keen interest in sex and in sexual pleasure. Someone has remarked that there are two kinds of people, those who are interested in sex, and liars. Sex is here to stay—a fact for which we can all be immensely glad—and it must be integrated into the totality of the good life if that life is to be truly good.

In contrast to the left-over Victorian attitudes and feelings about sex still to be noted among some individuals and communities (attitudes toward sex education, for example), are the increasingly mechanized and exploitative and depersonalizing attitudes toward sex which are prevalent in our society. Television and magazine advertising, some film making, the Playboy philosophy and the overemphasis on techniques are good examples. It is easy for the wonder and mystery of the "man-woman thing" to get lost. In the midst of what sometimes seems to be a national obsession with sex, it is often difficult for a couple to discover and cultivate the power of sexual intimacy which is so vital a part of marriage. Nonetheless, as Rollo May writes:

However much sex may be banalized in our society, it remains the power of procreation, the drive that perpetuates the race, the source at once of man's most intense pleasure and his most pervasive anxiety. It can, in its daimonic form, hurl the individual into sloughs of despond, and, when allied with eros, it can lift him into orbits of ecstasy.[3]

The raw power of sex is inherent in the fabric of creation—its power is God-given. Regular enjoyment of this powerful source of unity and pleasure is one of the best things about a good marriage. In fact, marriage offers the ideal relationship in which sex can be enjoyed with depth, intensity, and continuity over the years. Marriage is by far the most dependable and fulfilling way of satisfying this basic physical and emotional need.

Sex fulfills four positive purposes in a healthy marriage. The first is *reproduction* or parenting—the need to complete oneself in one's children. As Paul Tillich once observed, the biblical idea that mates become "one flesh"* goes beyond intercourse in its full expression. Two persons *literally* become one flesh in the joining of genes in their children. Sexual intercourse, of course, only begins the reproductive process. It plays a crucial but minor role. Seen against the background of the life-long process of parenting (one is *always* a parent after the process is begun), intercourse plays a tiny role. Only 1/1000 or less of sexual relationships in marriage have to do with reproduction. Obviously sex needs to be understood in terms of its broader functions.

Second, there is the *unifying function* of sex. Max Lerner has described love as "whatever breaks and bridges the terrible pathos of separateness of human beings from each other."[4] Satisfying sex is one of those good bridging experiences! Not only is it a de-

---

* "Therefore a man leaves his father and mother and cleaves to his wife and they become one flesh" (Genesis 2:24).

liciously beautiful way of expressing emotional connectedness, it is a powerful means of strengthening a relationship. Sex feeds love and is fed by love. Everyone at times belongs to the "walled-off people," to use Dostoevski's phrase. The physical-emotional-spiritual joining of sex in marriage is a remarkable means of overcoming the walls and of merging two inner worlds. The joining of bodies and spirits is powerful therapy for our loneliness and inner isolation.

> I know that love is worth the time it takes to find.
> Think of that when all the world seems made of walk up rooms
>   and hands in empty pockets.[5]

As these lines of Rod McKuen affirm, the knowledge that love exists and is precious, brings light to dark days of aloneness.

The power of the desire for sexual union stems from a basic truth about the world of living things:

> The power of sex is due to the sexual division of virtually all of creation. Male and female were not created to exist separately. Woman was made to complete man; and man, woman—anatomically, biologically, emotionally, mentally and spiritually. The power of the sex drive springs from the longings of the incomplete being for completion. A divided creation consequently suffers, longing for union and fulfillment. . . . The union sought, however, is more than sexual. It is a longing for a *personal* union of which the sexual is but a part and not the whole.[6]

The third function of sex in marriage is to enhance the *enjoyment of life* together. A satisfying sex life releases tension, renews tired spirits, and offsets the heartaches and failures of human existence. As suggested earlier, sex is a favorite way to drop the load of adult responsibilities and parenting duties and to let one's inner Child play regularly. In the midst of the worries and pressures of daily life, satisfying sex gives wings to the hearts of the mates. Together they celebrate the pleasures of life expressed in sex.

As the sayings of many languages put it, love & sex make one look at the world with "new" eyes. A sexual experience resembles a short vacation trip. A lover comes back to everyday conditions as a traveler returns home. Like the returning traveler he reacts more vividly and sharply to the accustomed environment.[7]

It is not surprising that the writer of Proverbs included the last clause in this list of wonders: "There are three things which are too wonderful for me, yea four which I know not: the way of an eagle in the air; the way of a serpent upon a rock; the way of a ship in the midst of the sea; the way of a man with a maid" (30:18). The sense of mystery and glad wonder is familiar to couples who have learned to enjoy rich, full-bodied sexual intimacy.

There is a fourth function of sex in marriage—*to strengthen and complete one's identity*. When a person asks the big identity questions—Who am I? What am I worth?—he cannot answer them apart from another question: Who am I and how effective am I as a man (or a woman)? Personal identity always includes sexual identity at its center. The firm sense of personal identity which is a prerequisite for intimacy in marriage and sexual relationships, is also strengthened and affirmed by experiences of interacting constructively with a person of the complementary sex. The sharpness of definition of one's own sexual identity is increased by joining worlds with a person of the other gender. The femaleness in a wife brings out the maleness in a husband, and vice versa. It is this mutual heightening of femininity and masculinity that brings zest to a marriage!

Couples in search of greater closeness need to go far beyond merely satisfying each other's physical desires. Of course, it is a mistake to withhold sex because the relationship is conflicted, or to use sex to manipulate the other. But beyond satisfying each other's physical needs, there is the context of those needs, the sexuality of each person; the maleness and femaleness which colors one's whole being. But the goal is never completely achieved; each of us brings a degree of unfinished identity to marriage, each of us needs to have our sexuality affirmed and rejoiced in by our mates. We have everything to gain and nothing to lose by nurturing each other in this basic way. A well-fed mate (fed in terms of his hunger for feelings of sexual power and worth) is the only kind who can share in a sexual celebration in which one's own needs will also be satisfied.

Conflicts often occur among the various functions of sex in marriage and the roles which are related to them. As most couples who have children can document from their experiences, the demands of parenting, companionship, and sex sometimes run into head-on collisions. It is inevitable. Close, complicated relationships and conflict go together. But in healthy marriages the conflict accruing from these roles is more than balanced by the ways in which they are mutually reinforcing. The fact that two people like (as well as love) each other and therefore enjoy being together and communicating makes the sexual part of their relationship deeply gratifying. Sex without companionship in marriage is better than no sex at all; but its pleasure falls far short of sex within a relationship of loving and trusting. Furthermore, parents who enjoy their children, feel the fulfillment of participating in their growth, and share in the "one-flesh" unity of this ongoing experience have much going for the sexual and companionship sides of their marriage. The goal is to relate in such a way as to allow the power of sex to bring a glow to the totality of the relationship. As one mother of three teenagers put it, "The pain and the happiness of these years of raising kids together has given us hundreds of experiences of sharing; we feel joined in so many areas that sex is often like a feast."

DEEPENING SEXUAL INTIMACY

Sexual relationships are essentially human relationships. That sexual skills are interpersonal skills is a point often ignored, to the detriment of sexual fulfillment in marriage. What is the relationship between interpersonal needs, satisfactions, and conflicts, on the one hand, and sexual needs, satisfactions, and conflicts, on the other? This is a crucial question. There is powerful interaction between these two sides of a marriage. Thus, one guideline to increasing sexual intimacy and pleasure is to *improve the quality of the marriage as a whole.* In practical terms, this means increasing communication skills and the ability to satisfy each other's heart-hungers, while at the same time practicing new techniques and tenderness in sexual intercourse.

At Ohio University a marriage survey of several hundred couples was made. The majority reported that they had intercourse twice a week, on the average. This was true both of the couples who described their marriages as "satisfactory" and those who saw them as "unsatisfactory." The husbands of unhappy couples tended to say that twice a week was more than their wives wanted but was satisfactory to them; their wives tended to report that it was just right for them, but less than their husbands wanted. In contrast, the husbands and wives in happy marriages generally said that twice a week was satisfying to their spouses and themselves. The problem was not in the actual frequency of intercourse (as the unhappy couples might have described it to a marriage counselor) but in their inability to communicate.[8]

In another study, people were asked to describe their own and their partner's feelings regarding a variety of forms of foreplay (from kissing and caressing to oral-genital play). Successful couples reported identical feelings and/or described their partner's feelings accurately approximately twelve times as often as did seriously conflicted couples.[9]

In an insightful passage on satisfying sex, William Lederer and Donald Jackson state:

What is special about sexual intercourse, a highly-satisfying male-female symbiosis, is that it requires a higher degree of collaborative communication than any other kind of behavior exchanged between spouses. Sex is consequently precious, but also perilous. It is the only relationship act which must have mutual spontaneity for mutual satisfaction. It can only be a conjoint union, and it represents a common goal which is clear and understood by both.[10]

Sexual intimacy is rooted in a biological drive pushing toward the discharge of sexual tension. This is the physiological basis of sexual attraction in all animals. But in man there develops a unique blend of the physiological and the psychological. The physical need for release of sexual tension is intertwined with a variety of psychological needs: for the security and warmth of body-closeness and stroking; for feeling loved, nurtured, cared about; for affirmation of one's masculinity or femininity. Both the joys and the problems of sex center almost entirely in the psychological-emotional area of relationships. It is in this unique human dimension that increased sexual intimacy is found. Sex without relationship is shallow sex, lacking in depth pleasure. As Clark Ellzey says, "If sex is sought on the animal level, nothing but animal returns can be expected."[11] Deep soul- and body-satisfying sex is never simply physical.

To deepen sexual intimacy, a couple needs to enjoy sex in ways that will cause it to feed their love. A marriage is vital to the extent that there is a uniting of these two forms of intimacy—physical and psychological. Satisfaction of the personality hungers of one's mate, particularly his sexual ego needs, is extremely important. Each partner should test his behavior in the marriage in terms of how well he uses opportunities to make his mate feel more adequate, attractive, and lovable as a male or a female. To say by words and behavior, "You're terrific in bed," or "We make sweet music together," or "You made last night heavenly!" causes one to prize his or her sexuality, which makes it easier to be loving, passionate, and giving the next time. "Good sex interaction not only expresses one's own feelings, but . . . the partner needs to feel valued and felt as a person of worth, as a real live human being."[12] The wedding ceremony contains an implicit truth about relationships in the phrase, "love, honor and cherish." A man and woman cannot really love deeply unless they also honor (esteem, appreciate, respect) and cherish (nurture, prize, hold dear) each other. The total quality and value of the relationship affects the meaning and satisfaction derived from sexual intercourse.[13] There is a fundamental difference between alienated and intimate sex—the difference is love.

Cultivating the art of love-making is another way to increase sexual intimacy. Most couples, if they try, can enhance their repertory of sexual enjoyment; they can help make sex play better for themselves and each other. It takes time to improve sexual artistry, and that is often a problem in our frantic society. Setting aside time for regular "let's-enjoy-each-other" nights or days is a practice that pays big dividends. One couple near the termination of marriage counseling reported: "Up until we started having 'our nights,' sharing, including sex, got the tag ends of our time. We allowed other less important things to squeeze love-making into late, hurried moments which made it terribly mechanical. In the last months we've rediscovered what we've been missing. Wow!" A frustrated wife confronted her husband with her disappointment at the shallow, mechanical rut into which their sex life had slipped: "I get the 'now it's Friday night again' feeling about our love life. The long, lingering Sunday afternoon in the bedroom—what happened to that? Let's do something to get the life back into things."

Working hard to get the spontaneity back is something like relaxing as hard as possible. It's self-defeating. Setting aside regular times and protecting them from encroachment is a good place to begin. During that time, sharing is the key—talking, listening to the rain, or reading a sexy novel together, taking a walk along a stream, eating by candlelight—whatever both mates find relaxing, satisfying, and at least a little romantic. Each couple should discover what encourages spontaneity and playfulness. Having a number of paths to relaxed sharing is an advantage. Wives often find eating out particularly satisfying and romantic. "It gives us time to really talk and, what's more, *I* don't have to fix the meal! Being away from the kids lets me turn my parent side off for a while, which feels good." These words of a young wife could be duplicated by many other wives. Couples who love music may find their depth sharing in "listening together to the murmur of hidden meaning within music . . . until the harmonies of what it means to-be-human pulse also in you."[14]

Getting into the mood is much more than a prelude to intercourse. It is a delicious part of the process, of which intercourse is the climax. The same applies to so-called "foreplay"—a misleading label which suggests merely a warm up before the game starts. How unfortunate! Such a misunderstanding leads to feelings on the part of some husbands that "I'll have to work hard to get her ready." The sense of burden and duty takes the edge off what can be a mutually delightful experience of pleasure and shared tenderness.

Cultivating the art of love-making doesn't necessarily mean that a couple will increase the frequency of intercourse, although that may result from its becoming more enjoyable to both. On some occasions, sharing may be fulfilling and even delightful, without including intercourse. Those whose sex life is satisfying and beautiful may have intercourse with less frequency than unhappy couples who are frantically proving their sexuality or searching for a solution to their emotional pain.

There are times in a sex-enjoying marriage when the enjoyment is in quiet closeness. At other times, stormy, carefree passion meets the needs of both. Couples should be free to follow their own impulses sexually, to play and experiment with new positions, new settings, and new approaches to foreplay. Open communication about what gives each maximum pleasure is tremendously helpful in developing their unique style. Whatever gives both pleasure—this is the one criterion for deciding whether or not to engage in various forms of sex play. If a wife enjoys being kissed all over her body, she should say so. Overcoming embarrassment derived from left-over childhood feelings about sex helps free a couple to talk about and explore their mutual pleasure. Sex itself is a form of communication. Learning to read the nonverbal language is a part of the enjoyment of married sex—for example, recognizing the signals of heightened desire in one's mate or, during intercourse, when the other is ready for consummating that experience of loving passion. However, checking out ambiguous nonverbal messages by asking the other, helps sex to be mutually satisfying.

Freedom to enjoy their own style of sex is sometimes inhibited by the need to succeed according to some alleged standard of what success is. The need to succeed is one reason for failure because it imposes pressures on the sex act which take the fun out and put the demand quality in. The pressure to succeed was illustrated by one couple who devised a ten-point scale on which they each attempted to rate the intensity of their orgasms. Those approaching marriage may be captives of the illusion that they must measure up—"perform like everyone else." They may ask worried questions such as:

How often should we have sex? What is the best position? . . . Should we scratch and bite each other? What time of day should it be done? The questions sound like inquiries about the type of gymnastic procedures to be followed for attaining muscles like Mr. America's or a rear end or bust like Miss America's. Perhaps even worse off are the myriads of couples who don't dare ask questions and just assume they *must* be abnormal because their own practice differs from some so-called standard.[15]

"To decide where sex fits into their particular marriage, a couple must look inward at the marriage, not outward at the deceptive advice and make believe standards set by others."[16] There are as many different and satisfying sexual relationships as there are couples who enjoy sex. Criteria like simultaneous orgasm, multiple orgasm, frequency of intercourse, should never be used as mechanical standards which suggest sexual failure if they are not met. To the question, "What is the ideal sexual relationship?" the only valid answer is, "There is no such thing!" Each couple should aim at the unique pattern which gives them both the greatest fulfillment, recognizing as well that their own pattern is changeable from one day and one year to the next, and that the degree of tenderness and passion waxes and wanes continually in their relationship.

At the same time, the art of love-making for most couples can be continually developed. Skills do improve with practice and patience, and as skills improve and a feeling of greater unity develops, sex can become increasingly satisfying.

Understanding the differences as well as the likenesses in the sexual responses of men and women, and in the particular man or woman one is married to, stimulates the growth of intimacy. Many of the old generalizations about male-female differences no longer apply. It is probably true that the arousal of passion is more closely linked with emotional factors in many women than in many men. If this is true in a particular marriage, it is important for the husband to understand that his wife literally can't respond as she and he would like, when her feelings are hurt, the bedroom is cluttered, or the children are stirring in the next room. It is well worth the effort to create the needed atmosphere to allow her romantic side to flower. Many women experience sexual arousal more slowly than their husbands and respond to considerable tenderness, caressing, fondling, and reassurances of love in the full enjoyment of intercourse. What many men discover is that the total sexual experience is much more satisfying and pleasurable to them if they allow themselves to *enjoy* longer periods of play. The too-rapid sex act often leaves the wife tense, angry, and unsatisfied; it also short-changes the man, frequently without his knowing it.

Most women want lusty physical sex as intensely as men. Contrary to previous cultural myths, women can be aroused to a high, sustained level of sexual excitement. They may arouse more gradually but they can enjoy the full range of sex play including intercourse and orgasm, as fully as men. (One of the liberating findings, as long as it does not become standard setting, of the Masters and Johnson research is that many women are capable of multiple orgasms—a series of climaxes during the same experience of intercourse.)

It is important for the husband and wife to cooperate, if necessary, in helping her achieve a climax. It helps for the husband to discover the areas of her body which are particularly pleasurable to her. On the basis of their research, Masters and Johnson recommend:

> Rather than following any preconceived plan for stimulating his sexual partner, the male will be infinitely more effective if he encourages vocalization on her part. The individual woman knows best the areas of her strongest sensual focus and the rapidity and intensity of manipulative technique that provides her with the greatest degree of sexual stimulation.[17]

Manual manipulation of the clitoris up to and including orgasm may be a part of love-making which allows her to enjoy the full delights of the experience. The clitoris is the major center of sexual response in the woman's pelvic area and is the key to orgasm in many women.[18] The idea that a clitoral orgasm is somehow inferior to a vaginal orgasm has been exploded by the Masters and Johnson evidence that the distinction between these two types is a fiction. An orgasm, however induced, is experienced throughout the pelvic area (and the entire body, to some degree).[19]

The rejection of the Victorian idea that sex is man's privilege and woman's duty has freed woman to enjoy sex fully. It has also freed her to respond and relate to her husband in ways that make sex more fulfilling to him. The active, passionate wife is much more fun in bed than the passive, dutiful "object of a man's desire." Many men need and enjoy the affirmation of a wife who is seductive and enticing, who is able to show her interest in sex and, on occasion, to initiate sexual relations. This communicates a masculinity-enhancing message: "As your female, I find you attractive and desirable as a male." The mutuality of present-day marriage in which the sexual relationship can be one of joy both in satisfying the other and in receiving satisfaction from the other, can strengthen the maleness and femaleness of the partners, thereby strengthening the marriage. In "Lines to an Unhandy Man," Lois Wyse writes:

> You never made
> A lamp base out of a Cracker Jack box,
> An extra room out of an unused closet,

Or a garden out of a pile of clay.
All you ever made was
A woman out of me.[20]

One can be sure that in the interaction which made a woman out of her, her husband became more of a man.

In some marriages, sexual intimacy carries too much of the over-all human need for intimacy. It may even be the only form of sharing and closeness. This overloading of sex and lack of companionship tends to keep sex from finding its full flowering. It is well to remember that intimacy can exist in a relationship— for example, a friendship—without physical contact of any kind. When sex becomes a part of a relationship, as in marriage, a whole new set of possibilities and potential problems is introduced. Yet, the fundamental basis of interpersonal intimacy is the same, with or without the sexual factor. Marital intimacy is much broader than sex, though all facets are colored by the sexuality of the partners. Two astute observers of contemporary marriage conclude: "It can be a good marriage even if the partners don't find heaven in bed."[21] Most couples achieve something less than heaven in bed and yet value and cherish the pleasure they do enjoy together. The ability to relax and enjoy what they have often enables them to find more.

SEXUAL INTIMACY THROUGH THE YEARS

The challenge and opportunity of the sexual facet of intimacy is that it can stay robust and grow more satisfying through the years. Many people think of romance as the Hollywood-style, ecstatic rapture of adolescent love; they assume that romance must fade sometime after the honeymoon, or at least in the first years of marriage. Understood in those terms, it does. What this limited conception of the romantic aspect of male-female relationships misses is that there is a form of romance appropriate to and available in each age and stage of the marital cycle. (See Ellzey's book in the Bibliography.) Such romance and the sexual intimacy that is its driving force are changing, growing realities in good marriages. Romance continues in its varied expressions in a marriage where two people are maturing in their love for each other. Such love will grow only if it is nourished day-in and day-out as a couple makes an art of keeping their romance alive and healthy. They develop what has been called a "high monogamy"—"an intensified monogamy dedicated to honesty, loyalty and old-fashioned man and woman love."[22]

In the weeks and months after the wedding ceremony, the pink-cloud phase of romance may remain strong, but sexual adjustment problems are frequent. The "myth of sexual compatibility" with which young people grow up misleads many young couples into believing that because they are "in love," they can go to bed on the night of the wedding and have a glorious experience. Oscar Wilde once commented that Niagara Falls is the second greatest disappointment of an American bride's honeymoon. Contrary to the myth, learning the art of love-making takes time and practice within a secure relationship (which most premarital relationships are not). Therefore, sexual-adjustment difficulties are more the rule than the exception during the early years.[23] Guilt and embarrassment need to be worked through. It is important for the young couple to be released from the fear that if sex doesn't go well or isn't strikingly satisfying, it never will be. Getting off to a slow or frustrating start does not consign a couple to a lifetime of sexual incompatibility. By investing themselves in enhancing the general quality of their relationship and improving their communication skills, they will probably do more to increase intimacy than by pouring their worried attention onto their "sex problem." If sex relations have not become more mutually satisfying after a year or so, it is wise to seek the help of a marriage counselor. But time, patience, and practice usually suffice.

The period after the first child is born is filled with adjusting to the new parental roles. Housework increases substantially and fatigue plus the new responsibilities may cause problems in the husband-wife relationship. The wife's overinvestment in the baby may interfere, as may the husband's jealousy. When couples say, "The romance has evaporated," they usually mean that the courtship-honeymoon days are gone or at least diminished. A new, deeper romance is available, however, cemented by the bond of child-bearing and rearing. There is a lift and a thrill (as well as a lot of hard work) in building a loving home. The assumption that the romance of marriage naturally declines after advent of children is true only in those instances when a couple neglect themselves and their relationship, and fail to engage in continuing courtship. It is true, in Gibson Winter's words, that "marital intimacy has to find a deeper foundation if it is to continue at the heart of marriage."[24]

Sexual intimacy can be a reality in the middle and older years. If a relationship has achieved appreciable intimacy in the young-adult years, and deepened during the child-leaving years, it is likely that it will enjoy a continuing sense of sexual intimacy. In the years of uncertainty around the menopause, wives often need reassurance and reaffirmation of their sexual desirability and attractiveness. Husbands may be worried about slowing down in the sexual area and need the same kind of affirmation from their mates. It is significant that, in spite of the youth-orientation of our culture and the inherent problems of aging therein, Kinsey found an increasing percentage of marital coitus leading to orgasm for both parties, decade by decade. Certainly, if couples revitalize their relationship during the middle years, there is no reason for sexual intimacy to decline. In fact, it can become deeper and richer because it includes the joys and heartaches, the accomplishments and disappointments, the storms and the peace of years of sharing each other's worlds.

A man who had been married for thirty years said: " 'I still like to hold my wife's hand.' He did not get the same electric spark he received when he first held her hand, but holding it gave him a sense of security and strength. At times it gave promise of a more complete physical union. More often the touch of her hand said, 'I need you. I'm glad we have each other. I love you now as always.' This reaction he claimed was more thrilling, more satisfying than the exciting experiences of courtship."[25]

Two recent volumes, *Sex after Forty*[26] and *Sexual Life after Sixty*[27] make it clear that the spark can stay alive long, long after the early years of marriage. When sexual intimacy is lost it is usually because of unresolved emotional conflicts within and between the marital partners.

Masters' and Johnson's study of the human sexual response showed that "Many a woman develops renewed interest in her husband and in the physical maintenance of her own person, and has described a 'second honeymoon' during the early fifties." In their study of geriatric sexual responses and the problems of living within "our new found longevity," they reported: "There is no time limit drawn by the advancing years to female sexuality." Of husbands they said, "If elevated levels of sexual activity are maintained from earlier years and if neither acute nor chronic physical incapacity intervenes, aging males usually are able to continue some form of active sexual expression into the 70– and even 80– year age groups."[28] The general pattern of sexual intimacy established in the earlier years tend to be maintained in the advancing years.

A specialist on marriage, in speaking to a group of ministers about the crisis of middle age, referred to the shock of discovering one day that one is "married to a grandmother." A vigorous man, obviously in that age category, interrupted with the exclamation— "But man, what a grandmother!" It was apparent from the lift in his voice and the light in his eyes that they had discovered the deepening romance of the passing years.

COPING WITH SEXUAL PROBLEMS

It should be clear that, from the perspective of this book, sex is not a problem but a positive resource for relating. However, knowing how to deal with some of the problems that are associated with sex helps to keep it functioning as a positive resource.

Dorothy W. Baruch highlights the dual possibilities for pleasure and pain in sex:

Sex is man and woman, and all each contains, brought to the other. But sex can also be man and woman, each struggling alone and apart to get from the other what each feels has been missed.

Sex can be the highest and smoothest place of going, the utmost of being together, the least of loneliness any human can find. But sex can also be agony and wanting. Hurting and being hurt. And the endless waiting for what never is reached.

Sex can be warm and generous. But, in contrast, it can be drab and ugly, stingy little offering, faintly stretched forth, weakly proffered, fearingly begrudged.

Sex can be togetherness in love—or of hate that holds people attached.[29]

There are times, in most marriages, when sex does not go well. It has its ups and downs. Knowing what to do to improve this important aspect of marriage helps a couple to shorten these periods of sexual conflict or distancing.

Psychiatrist Martin Goldberg has suggested that there are six areas in which sexual problems occur:[30]

1. *Problems related to ignorance and naïveté:* Lack of knowledge of sexual anatomy and techniques of intercourse can contribute to lessening the mutual enjoyment of sex. Where this is a problem, reading a well-written sex manual such as John E. Eichenlaub, *The Marriage Art,*[31] is the place to begin. Discussing unanswered questions with a physician, clergyman, or marriage counselor is the other logical solution to this problem. Lack of information may be a symptom of emotional problems in the area of sex which prevents one from learning from readily available sources.

2. *Problems derived from sexual inhibitions and guilts:* Left-over attitudes and feelings from childhood are more frequent sex-spoilers than lack of information. Guilt and fear can cause lack of sexual warmth, enjoyment, and interest in both males and females. Ghosts from the past including parentifying one's spouse (Chapter 3) are sources of pleasure-blocking anxieties and guilt-

feelings. A psychotherapist described a woman who could not accept sexuality: "Her body said 'no' to almost everything."[32] Where guilts and inhibitions are not so severe, they may gradually be diminished by the corrective emotional experience of a marriage with an understanding mate who is more able to enjoy sex, and help his (or her) spouse to do so. In more severe cases, counseling or psychotherapy may be essential to help the person unlearn his archaic responses and learn how to say Yes to sexual enjoyment. If sexual prohibitions have been clothed in religious guises, a counseling clergyman who sees sex as God-given may be the one who can help release the person to affirm his sexuality.

3. *Problems resulting from specific fears:* Couples facing marriage may be afraid that their sexual organs, penis and vagina, respectively, are not large enough to enjoy sex fully. The findings of the Masters and Johnson research show that such fears are ungrounded. Almost any vagina can stretch to accommodate any penis and the size of the penis or clitoris has no correlation with degree of sexual pleasure attained. Sound counseling by a physision can allay many such fears; the fear of unwanted pregnancies can be reduced by using the most reliable contraceptives. The enlightened physician is best equipped to assist a couple in separating realistic from unrealistic fears.

The fear of failure to maintain an erection or have an orgasm is a specific cause of some sexual failure. One of the encouraging discoveries of the Masters and Johnson therapy is that many men who suffer from impotence or premature ejaculation, and many women who are sexually unresponsive, can be helped decisively by relatively short-term measures. This suggests that some such problems are *not* the result of deep personality problems requiring long-term therapy, as previously thought, but, rather, stem from faulty learning experiences. A husband attempts to have intercourse when he is very tired. He fails and he feels deeply chagrined, perhaps even unmanly. His fears of failing again increase the possibility that he will, in fact, have trouble the next time. Thus, a self-reinforcing cycle may be established. It is reassuring to know that an occasional inability to maintain an erection, particularly when one is fatigued, preoccupied, or has had too much to drink, is not a sign of abnormality. Reducing the "demand quality" of sex, as indicated earlier, can help in this area. The more a couple can accept the fact that their sex life will have its variations, and the less they have to prove their masculinity or femininity by performing successfully, the more they will be able to relax and enjoy love-making. The understanding of each partner for the other at such times is crucial. The wife who feels her femininity severely threatened or feels herself a failure because of her husband's temporary impotence, thus increases the tension and aggravates what might otherwise be a quickly passing phenomenon.

4. *Problems related to external factors:* A husband or wife who is working long hours or under heavy stress will usually have diminished sexual interest. Lack of privacy because of a too-small house or too-thin walls may interfere with a couple's ability to let go with glad abandon in their sexual play. An overworked mother of a covey of children under six may have little time or energy to take care of herself or get in the mood for love. The logical approach to such problems is to do something to change the external factors—cut down on one's work schedule (is it *really* necessary to work fourteen hours a day?) or get some help with the housework, perhaps from relatives or friends if money for hired help isn't available. Ingenuity can usually find some ways of freeing more time and energy for relating, *if the relationship is seen as important by the mates.* Overwork and overscheduling are often symptoms of a fear of intimacy (sexual and emotional); in such cases, the fear should be dealt with in counseling.

5. *Problems resulting from interpersonal difficulties:* As has been implied previously, it is erroneous to assume that sexual problems are the fundamental cause of marital conflict. Kinsey's studies showed that sexual problems were involved in three out of four divorces. It does not follow from this statistic that sexual problems *caused* all these divorces. In most cases, such problems begin

and remain the effects of general unhappiness in the marriage relationship. True, the sexual frustrations contribute to the vicious cycle of the disintegration of the marriage, but they usually begin as symptoms, not as causes.

Sex as a form of communication conveys many messages in addition to love, tenderness, and self-giving. In fact, the language of sex can be used to express any feeling and any facet of the relationship, including anger, the need to dominate, coerce, and hurt, or the need to suffer and be rejected. If a couple suspects that some negative, disguised feeling is expressing itself in and to the detriment of their sex life, it behooves them to obtain skilled counseling. This can help them to translate the message from the language of being acted out in hurting ways in their sexual behavior, to being expressed and worked through in verbal forms.

Unexpressed hostility is one contributor to poor sex. If this can be recognized and resolved (through expression on an inanimate object such as pounding a pillow, or talked out in counseling), it will no longer be a barrier to mutual sexual fulfillment. A husband, when asked by reporters on his fiftieth wedding anniversary if he had ever considered divorce, replied: "Never divorce. Murder many times, but never divorce." Many couples would not need to divorce, or to live in a *de facto* divorce of a dead relationship, if they could face and resolve their angers rather than let them accumulate.

Changes in the male/female roles may cause interpersonal conflict leading to sexual problems.[33] The emancipation of women in terms of outside employment, and the decline in the dual standard in the sexual area, threatens men whose self-esteem depended on perceiving women as submissive or second-class human beings. However, these changes and the peer-companionship model of marriage of which they are a part, also releases women to be both more satisfied and more satisfying to their sex partners. In discussing the way in which women have joined men on the last frontier—sex—David Riesman comments:

The very ability of women to respond in a way that only courtesans were supposed to in an earlier age means, moreover, that qualitative differences of sex experience—the impenetrable mystery—can be sought for night after night, and not only in periodic visits to a mistress or brothel.[34]

In other words, the same forces which create relationship-sexual problems in contemporary marriage also create exciting new possibilities.

6. *Problems caused by intra-psychic difficulties:* Some sexual problems are derived from deep, unconscious conflicts, the only effective treatment of which is intensive psychotherapy. It is a mistake to assume that this is the case without exhausting the possibilities that such problems fall into one or more of the previous categories. Often the guidance of a counselor or psychotherapist is needed in order to help an individual or a couple decide how deep the difficulty probably is and, therefore, what constitutes the appropriate therapy.

The problem of infidelity may or may not be the result of pronounced intra-psychic difficulties. The Don Juan or *femme fatale* who has repeated affairs is acting out deep problems such as anxiety about sexual adequacy or identity, hatred toward the opposite sex, or the unconscious search for the missing parent of the opposite sex. In contrast, the single episode may be a passing infatuation resulting from marital problems. Infidelity is always a sign that something has been missing from the marriage. When interpersonal intimacy is missing or in short supply, the partners are highly vulnerable to extra-marital affairs.

The best way to prevent infidelity is to achieve creative closeness in the marriage. Fidelity is essential to a growing relationship, to the realization of full sexual satisfaction, and to the security of children. Choosing the path of infidelity means choosing to miss these values in marriage. Approaching fidelity, not as a burdensome life sentence, but as a pathway—the only pathway—to a highly desirable set of goals, makes it a positive style of relating.

Erik Erikson describes these goals in discussing "genitality"—the capacity to function sexually in a full, adult fashion:

In order to be of lasting social significance, the utopia of genitality should include: 1. mutuality of orgasm, 2. with a loved partner, 3. of the opposite sex, 4. with whom one is able and willing to share a mutual trust, 5. and with whom one is able and willing to regulate the cycles of, a. work, b. procreation, c. recreation, 6. so as to secure to the offspring, too, a satisfactory development.[35]

To the degree that a couple achieves this integration of the sexual and the interpersonal, fidelity will be fulfilling. This is not to say that all temptation to stray will be eliminated; but, rather, that the positive values of fidelity will become so rich and obvious in the marriage that the partners will choose it as the more desirable way of life.

These suggested ways of approaching the various sexual difficulties may make it sound easy to overcome them. It is clear that even near-the-surface problems often take serious and determined struggle to find a solution that is effective. But the thrust of what we have been saying is that some sexual difficulties are not as deep as they may seem, and there is realistic hope for the vast majority of couples who approach their problems with the will to grow together and to get professional help in the process if that proves to be necessary.

The emphasis of this chapter has been that sexual intimacy can be both the spice which keeps the marriage joyful and the cement which can hold together the other facets of intimacy. As satisfying sex enhances other aspects of the relationship it is itself enhanced. Sex in marriage is not a matter of achievement or performance, but an expression of and a foundation for intimacy in marriage.

When we cut through all the rigmarole about roles and performance, the sheer fact of intimacy remains amazingly important in making a sexual encounter memorable—the meeting, the growing closeness, the excitement of not knowing where it will lead, the assertion of self, and the giving of self. Is it not this intimacy that makes us return to the event in memory again and again when we need to be warmed by whatever hearths life makes available?[36]

These words of Rollo May describe the element of mystery and wonder in sexual intimacy which in a good marriage pervades all facets of the relationship. By joining parts of their bodies, a husband and wife continue their family heritage, affirm their own individual and marital identity, and perpetuate the stream of life. In this deep sharing, they may experience a kind of intimacy which is closer than sex—a touching of souls.

TAKING ACTION

Discuss the things that each of you enjoys most when you make love, and the things that would make it better for each of you. What things are difficult to talk about? Share thoughts about these. Try changing the pattern of your sex life—vary the setting, the hour, the position. Try to find a place where you can make love outdoors. Take a weekend in a motel, in a cottage at the beach, or in a secluded spot. Make an effort to do and say the things that you know affirm your partner's sexuality, but which you each tend to neglect.

Obtain a copy of *Sense Relaxation* by Bernard Gunter (New York: Collier Books, 1968), and try some of the "intimate games" of touching and tapping, and feeling. Let go and have fun being more alive.

If either of you lacks knowledge of your own or your spouse's sexual potential, read a book like *The Marriage Art* by John H. Eichenlaub (New York: Dell Publishing Co., 1961) to increase your understanding and therefore your enjoyment of sexuality.

NOTES

1. Jourard, *The Transparent Self* (Princeton, N.J.: D. Van Nostrand Co., 1961, Insight Edition), p. 31.
2. Lecture by Joseph B. Trainer, Philadelphia, October 19, 1966.
3. Rollo May, *Love and Will* in *Psychology Today,* Vol. 3, No. 3, August 1969, p. 24.
4. *Woman's Day,* February 1968, p. R6.
5. Rod McKuen, *Stanyan Street and Other Sorrows* (New York: Random House, 1954), p. 41.

6. Reuel Howe, "The Pastor Speaks of Sex and Marriage," *Reader's Digest* (October, 1958), p. 78. The fact that the human female does not have limited periods of sexual desire and availability (although she does have times of heightened and diminished desire), is probably a major reason for the development of two-parent family life in the dim prehistory of human beings. Unlike most other animals, men and women enjoy sex regularly and frequently. This probably accounts for the early attachment of the male to the family.

7. Edrita Fried, *The Ego in Love and Sexuality* (New York: Grune and Stratton, 1960), p. 1.

8. William J. Lederer and Donald D. Jackson, *The Mirages of Marriage* (New York: W. W. Norton, 1968), pp. 116–117.

9. Emily H. Mudd, *et al., Success in Family Living* (New York: Association Press, 1965), p. 110.

10. Lederer and Jackson, *op. cit.,* pp. 117–118.

11. W. Clark Ellzey, *How to Keep Romance in Your Marriage* (New York: Association Press, 1951), p. 171. The weakness of the Kinsey reports is that they tend to ignore the uniquely human dimension of human sexuality, reducing it to "outlets" on an animal level. This ignores the fact that sex takes place between persons—each with a network of values, feelings, and conditionings which influence everything he does, including sex. The naïve physiological view and oversimplified hedonism of this approach prevent these studies from effectively influencing negative attitudes toward sex in religious circles. (See Reinhold Niebuhr, "Kinsey and the Moral Problems of Man's Sexual Life," in D. P. Geddes (ed.), *An Analysis of the Kinsey Reports* (New York: New American Library, 1954), pp. 62ff.

12. Sylvia R. Sacks, "Widening the Perspective on Adolescent Sex Problems," *Adolescence,* Vol. 1, No. 1 (Spring, 1966), p. 89.

13. As Clara Thompson once stated: "Most sexual relationships have meaning in interpersonal terms, in addition to satisfying physical drives. The relationship as a whole has significance. The value of the relationship in turn affects the satisfaction obtained from the sexual activity" (Nashville: Abingdon Press, 1968).

14. Ross Snyder, *Inscape* (Nashville: Abingdon Press, 1968), p. 16.

15. Lederer and Jackson, *op. cit.,* p. 118.

16. *Ibid.*

17. William H. Masters and Virginia E. Johnson, *Human Sexual Response* (Boston: Little, Brown and Co., 1966), p. 66.

18. Masters and Johnson state: "The primary focus for sexual response in the human female's pelvis is the clitoral body. The clitoris responds with equal facility to both somatogenic & psychogenic forms of stimulation, and is truly unique in the human organ system in that its only known function is that of serving as an erotic focus for both afferent and efferent forms of sexual stimulation" (*op. cit.,* pp. 60–61).

19. Here are some conclusions of the Masters and Johnson studies: "Are clitoral and vaginal orgasms truly separate anatomic entities? From a biologic point of view, the answer to this question is an unequivocal No. . . . From an anatomic point of view, there is absolutely no difference in the responses of the pelvic viscera to effective sexual stimulation, regardless of whether the stimulation occurs as a result of clitoral-body or mons area manipulation, . . . or, for that matter, specific stimulation of any other erogenous area of the female body.

"There may be great variation in duration and intensity of orgasmic experience, varying from individual to individual and within the same woman from time to time. However, when any woman experiences orgasmic response to effective sexual stimulation, the vagina and clitoris react in consistent physiologic patterns. Thus, clitoral and vaginal orgasms are not separate biologic entities" (*op. cit.*, pp. 66–67).

20. Wyse, *Love Poems for the Very Married* (Cleveland: World Publishing Co., 1967), p. 45.
21. Lederer and Jackson, *op. cit.*, p. 124.
22. George G. Leonard, "The Man and Woman Thing," *Look,* December 24, 1968, p. 62.
23. This discussion of the myth and the early adjustment is adapted from a lecture by Martin Goldberg, "Counseling in Sexual Incompatibilities," Philadelphia, October 19, 1966.
24. Gibson Winter, *Love and Conflict* (Garden City, N.Y.: Doubleday and Co., 1958), p. 101.
25. Mudd, *et al., op. cit.*, p. 123.
26. S. A. Lewin and John Gilmore, *Sex After Forty* (New York: Medical Research Press, 1952).
27. Isadore Rubin (New York: Basic Books, 1965).
28. Masters and Johnson, *op. cit.*, p. 263.
29. *New Ways in Sex Education* (New York: McGraw-Hill, 1959, pp. 9–10.
30. Lecture by Martin Goldberg, *supra.*
31. John Eichenlaub, *The Marriage Art* (New York: Dell Pub. Co., 1961).
32. Fried, *op. cit.*, p. 52.
33. See Vance Packard, *The Sexual Wilderness, the Contemporary Upheaval in Male-Female Relationships* (New York: McKurg, 1968).
34. David Riesman with Nathan Glazer and Reuel Denney, *The Lonely Crowd* (Garden City, N.Y.: Doubleday Anchor Books, 1954), pp. 174–175.
35. *Childhood and Society* (New York: W. W. Norton, 1950), pp. 230–231.
36. Rollo May, *Love and Will* in *Psychology Today,* Vol. 3, No. 3, August, 1969, p. 25.

8   *Developing Parent-Child Intimacy*

> Each of us is the product of what has happened in countless generations of families before us; each of us in turn will inevitably affect the lives of our children, grandchildren and great-grandchildren for as long as mankind exists.
>
> Clifford Kirkpatrick, *The Family*[1]

> . . . marriage begins in infancy.
>
> Levy and Monroe, *The Happy Family*[2]

The capacity for intimacy is catching. In the early days and weeks and months of a child's life, long before he is aware of himself as a separate person, he is absorbing fundamental patterns, *ways* of relating and *feelings about* relating, which will influence him throughout his life. Long before he can interpret the sights he sees or the sounds he hears, they are becoming part of his own way of being. Every child comes into the world with a unique heritage of humanness. The manner in which his parents and older siblings respond to his individuality helps to determine whether he will be a person who relates to others intimately or distantly. The family which provides an environment of healthy intimacy, an intimacy that includes respect for autonomy and distance, provides the child with a climate in which he can develop the strong sense of identity so basic to his own capacity for intimacy. The vital responsibility of the parents, then, is to create through their own relationship of intimacy an atmosphere which both envelops the child in its warmth, and progressively releases him to his own relationships of intimacy. Such intimacy is as rewarding to parents as it is to children, for it allows parents to share in the rich inner world of the children who by their very existence give parents the gift of immortality. Such sharing can help to reopen parents to their own inner worlds, past and present, thereby deepening marital intimacy.

Intimacy between parents and children is psychologically different from that between husband and wife. The latter is a peer relationship based on mutual dependence and mutual need-satisfaction. The full intimacy of the marriage relationship is one which grows deeper and richer as the years go by. It is a relationship possible only between equals. Parent-child intimacy, on the other hand, is based on the initial physical and emotional dependence of the child. The parents' need is satisfied by the child's response to their giving. Parent-child intimacy gradually diminishes as the child develops his own autonomy over the years. Parents can enjoy and treasure many moments of personal intimacy with their children, but they cannot count on the increasingly intimate relationship which they expect from each other. Parent-child intimacy prepares the child for future relationships with peers. Husband-wife intimacy strengthens their own ongoing relationship.

THE DEVELOPMENT OF PARENT-CHILD INTIMACY

The foundation of parent-child intimacy is laid even before the birth of the baby in the relationship of the parents. A husband and wife who have a mutually satisfying and growing relationship are more able to make the baby a part of their relationship instead of a divisive factor, than are couples who are distant or severely conflicted. Usually it is true, as well, that the more the husband is able to participate in the pregnancy and in the childbirth itself, the stronger will be his sense of mutuality with his wife in their new creation.

Never before have you had fully a chance to co-create a new world with another person—or to bring forth children who will take their place in the long, long pilgrimage of man down this earth valley.[3]

It is important to the coming father-child relationship for him to be able to take as much part in this co-creation as is possible. Many doctors and hospitals now allow and even encourage prospective fathers to be present during labor and delivery. If such an experience climaxes nine months of mutual awareness and involvement in the prenatal development of the baby, the husband is already included in the intimacy so often assumed to be only the mother's privilege and prerogative.

Once the baby is born and laid in his mother's arms (ideally in a rooming-in hospital where the father can also participate), the development of what Erik Erikson calls *basic trust*[4] already is in progress. The ways in which the baby is held and fed, bathed and dressed, convey the feelings in the family about his presence. Does the father also bathe and hold and feed him, so that he feels the strong, rough hands as well as the smooth, soft ones? What is the response to his crying, to his grasping for breast or bottle, to the mess in his diapers, to his first smile?

Thus the child's active grasping for mutuality will not do, if the reaching out is not met by a parallel enjoyment in the mother at being clung to; if the result is not a process of mutual interaction.[5]

All of this is not to say that the baby must experience *only* joy and peace. He is part of a real world, of its pain and anger as well as of its satisfactions. Plenty of that pain comes from his own body. If he gets, most of the time, loving response to his needs, he can take also the impatience at his dependence that comes when the mother is tired, the angry words between his parents when their own needs are not being met, the conflict that is inevitable in any family.

It is at this early time in the beginning of parent-child intimacy that the first danger may become apparent. Even in the strongest marriage relationships, the strength of the mother-baby bond is sometimes felt as a threat by the father. In severely conflicted marriages, this is often the point at which the destruction of the husband-wife intimacy begins and the unhealthy intimacy of the mother and child begins. The wife may begin to use the baby for the satisfaction of emotional needs which the marriage is not providing. The husband's jealousy may drive him further away. Even in healthy marriages, there is always some of this threat. It helps to be aware of it, so that the advent of children will contribute more to the uniting of parents than to the dividing of them. "No matter how going a concern a marriage may be, the advent of children causes severe strain between parents. Newborn babies cannot be taken in their stride."[6]

Awareness of the problem is often all that is needed to cope with it. Certainly, for the father to participate as much as possible in the care of the baby, and the parents' constant affirmation of each other as parents and as husband and wife are important. The father who will gaze with pride and joy and a sense of involvement, as well as with a twinge of jealousy, upon his wife as she nurses their child can feel the child as a bond which connects them. Some of the suggestions in Chapter 6 encouraging the new parents to make special efforts to be alone together regularly are important. For subsequent babies, as well as for the first, all that we have been saying here holds true.

Parent-child intimacy begins then, with the parents' response to the baby's almost complete dependence. Feelings are more important than techniques at this stage (or at any other). The baby whose needs are met *most of the time,* whose body is handled *most of the time* with tenderness and pleasure, who has *frequent* experiences of closeness and warmth from both parents, will respond to them in ways that satisfy their needs as successful, life-giving parents. On the other hand, parents who because of their own unmet needs can respond only with impatience to their child's crying and with disgust to the requirements of his body, will be unable to encourage the sense of basic trust so necessary if the growing child is to relate warmly to his parents or to anyone else.

In the early weeks and months of a child's life, parent-child intimacy means for the child the satisfaction of his needs for comfort, warmth, closeness, and peace. For the parent it means the joy of having met these needs and the warm response of a baby who is for the most part content. But even in the midst of this warm closeness, the ebb and flow of intimacy which are part of any relationship prevail. Even for a baby, life is hard and needs cannot always be met, no matter how perceptive the parents. Thus even as life begins, the seeds of autonomy are sown. Growth is struggle.

The intimate closeness of mother and child, however healthy, cannot continue. The necessity for weaning becomes a fact of life for the baby. As he grows older he must grow more distant from the mother. He cannot always have the breast or bottle, or the arms of his mother and father. Before long the word "no" enters his life. He learns that the world has limits and that he is a person separate from his parents and sometimes in conflict with them. Presently even the products of his body are no longer his. He must accept toilet-training in one form or another as one of his first concessions to the expectations of society and the family. All of these confrontations with the reality of life mean that the small child is increasingly required to give up the complete dependence which he enjoyed in babyhood and to begin to establish himself as a responsible human being. Thus the quality of parent-child intimacy is also required to change. With the making of demands and the setting of limits, the parents become different kinds of need-satisfiers. If the basic trust is strong in the child, and if the parents are secure in their own relationship and not too threatened by the child's budding autonomy which at times makes him resist the demands of the parents, a new dimension of parent-child intimacy can develop.

In the learning to walk and talk, to use the bathroom and to accept limits, parent-child intimacy revolves around the setting of these limits and the acceptance of feelings about them. Can the parents say "No" when the child runs into the street, and prevent him from doing it, while at the same time accepting his feeling of anger and frustration at being thus limited. Can they prevent his impulse to drop a wooden block on his new baby brother's head, while at the same time letting him know that his feeling of jealousy and rage is not bad in itself and that he is not a bad person for having it? Can they encourage him to use the potty to defecate without punishing him for his failures or making him feel that his body and its products are bad?

In short, parent-child intimacy at the toddler and young-child stage is closely related to the child's growing autonomy and sense of himself as a separate person. It is a difficult period, for the child's love-hate ambivalence is very strong. He both fears and wants to grow up. He both needs his parents desperately, and needs desperately to establish himself as an important person in his own right. His parents must allow him the distance he needs to become himself, with a growing sense that he is worthwhile and has some control over his own destiny. At the same time they need to derive satisfaction from being with him in feeling, and taking pride in his achievements. Continued unequivocal love within the necessary setting of limits is important.

Parents who are too threatened by their child's angry, "I hate you!" when he is frustrated are unable to accept his feeling. Usually such parents have not been able to admit to or accept strong negative feelings in themselves, and thus project onto the child their own feelings of badness. The child may then accept his parents' label, "I'm bad" and either withhold his deepest feelings in the future, or lash out more violently at his surroundings, thus becoming a "behavior problem." Either way, parent-child intimacy is blocked. The mother and father who are open to and accepting of their own negative feelings are far more able to tolerate their child when behavior is difficult and angry feelings run high. The child's emotional demands at this stage are excessive. "For this reason, parents need a strong love for each other if the trinity of father-mother-child, is to grow on a positive emotional basis."[7]

An intimate marital relationship which rejoices in the wide range of human feeling, which includes anger in its definition of love, can include the child in the "freedom to feel."

Four-year-old Billy was brought to a child guidance clinic at the suggestion of his nursery school teacher. She felt that he was angry most of the time, for he lashed out physically at the other children and regularly destroyed the toys and equipment of the school. His parents described him as unmanageable at home, always trying to hurt his little sister, smashing his toys and refusing to obey.

During many weeks of play therapy sessions Billy seemed chiefly to want to play in the water. He floated the boats and then sank them. He caused tidal waves which washed the cars and trucks into the water and drowned the people. He threw the cowboys and Indians into the water and drowned them. All the while he talked quietly to himself about what he was doing, but loud enough so that the therapist could hear him. The therapist consistently repeated back to him what he said he was doing, with acceptance but no approval or disapproval in her voice.

One day Billy said to her, "I wonder why I come here. Maybe it's because I'm unhappy." With a quizzical look at the therapist he picked up the baby doll which he had never before touched, put it in the water and held it under for a long, silent moment. Then with an audible sigh of relief he took the doll out, dried it off, and dressed it. He never played with the water again, nor with the doll. In subsequent sessions he played in a variety of ways and with a good deal of relaxed spontaneity. Meantime his behavior at home and at school had modified. His parents had been getting help, too, and were more aware of their own feelings and of Billy's. They had begun to accept his anger at the little sister verbally, while at the same time letting him know he couldn't hurt her. They had got him a pounding bench and encouraged him to use it when he was angry.

It seemed as though Billy had at last been able to express the feelings he had stored up from the time of his sister's birth. His parents previously had not allowed him to express any negative feelings about her. When he and they could feel and accept the ambivalence that characterizes all close relationships,

Billy was gradually able to channel his anger more appropriately. This experience was the beginning of both parent-child and marital intimacy for Billy and his family.

During the period from about three to six years, children normally establish an especially warm, close relationship with the parent of the other sex. Through this bond, a child is awakened to the basic goodness of male-female relationships. This closeness is one of the crucial roots of all future intimacy across sex lines. It is one foundation stone for adult heterosexual relationships.

For the growth of the preschooler to be complete, the child needs a loving, caring relationship with his same-sexed parent, too. Normally, the child feels jealousy toward this parent; he also needs to have feelings of love and acceptance from the parent. These feelings give balance to his attachment to the parent of the other sex, and help him move beyond this attachment in the next period of his growth. It is particularly important that the husband-wife rapport be steady and strong during the child's preschool development. This often is difficult because the husband is preoccupied with getting established in his work. If this is the case, his daughter will have difficulty finding the warm closeness she needs with him. When a strong father-daughter bond is established, the wife may be threatened because of her unmet hungers in the marriage. Where marital intimacy is robust, on the other hand, the balance of good relationships with *both* parents during these years in a child's life will usually be present automatically.

If, during the toddler and young-child stage, parents are sensitive and accepting enough to help the child to understand how he feels, and to put their understanding into words and actions, they and the child are well prepared for the next stage of parent-child intimacy. When the child goes to school he is taking another big step along his road to autonomy and identity. In the physical sense, he needs his parents less and less. But he is still very much dependent on them for emotional support in coping with the many new involvements which he experiences outside the home. Now that he is more able to put his feelings into words, is he free, from his parents' point of view, to share with them the hurts and joys and frustrations which he is bound to experience in the outside world? Correcting behavior without condemning feeling, listening to and accepting fears and worries without taking charge in an overprotective way, allowing free rein to the developing need for freedom while at the same time holding fast to the limits appropriate to his age—these are the continuing bases of parent-child intimacy. As in earlier years, acceptance and reflection of feeling, so that the child feels that there is *no feeling* he cannot express, however bad, however frightening, is the essence of intimacy. When children are free to share their fear and rage with their parents, they are eager to share their joys and loves.

The early school years are foundational for a child's growth in the ability to relate trustfully with his own sex. A strong identification with his same-sexed parent is normal and necessary. Through a close relationship with his dad (or a father substitute), a boy learns to belong to the male world—to think, feel, and act like a male in his culture. He moves from this to close relations with boys his own age. A parallel process occurs in the normal growth of a girl.

During the years of childhood with its increasing autonomy, the closeness-distance cycle between parents and children is in constant motion. There are times when the child seems free and happy and little in need of mothering and fathering. If his parents can accept his freedom without being threatened by not being needed, the child will return for the sustenance he needs when things go wrong and he needs temporarily to regress. Letting the child set the pace of intimacy—being there when they are needed and not pushing when they are not needed—this is the parents' job. Parents need each other in a steadier relationship of intimacy and a sharing which allows them together to move with the ebb and flow of their children's closeness and distance. The changing needs of the child require ever new and different patterns of response and need-satisfaction from the parents.

As adolescence approaches, the child is more and more finding his intimate satisfactions away from his parents. In preadolescence and early adolescence the intimate relationships are with persons of the same sex. As adolescence advances, the transfer is made to persons of the other sex as the inner preparation for a life of intimacy with a marriage partner continues. Parent-child intimacy during adolescence often seems to parents to be a one-way street. The adolescent is intimate when he wants something and far away emotionally at all other times! But this is only a part of the story. The adolescent still needs from his parents the same feeling of affirmation that he has always needed, but in different ways. At this stage as in the previous one, the parent who is open and ready when the young person needs him is often able to share in his almost-adult children's struggle for identity. This can be among the most rewarding experiences of parenthood. Like the moments of intimacy at other times in the child's life, the rare moments of sharing with adolescent children can also help the parent to reopen and relive some of his own youth by sharing in his children's growth.

Here are the words of Jeeney Ray,[8] a spastic girl who is an orphan and who has had few experiences of intimacy in her lifetime. Then along comes an adult who cares:

> I study him well and receive the kindred of one to another. . . . I reach as far into his eyes as I can to understand the fullness of what he says and the way he looks me over; puzzled back in thinking is how he is, and grinning and frowning, then going way down to pierce darkness. . . . It is when thinking is coming from the other person into yourself and touching the same thinking as the other person; it is quiet then, and words come from their hiding hearts.

Such moments of parent-child intimacy in adolescence are rare, but they are possible. It is also true that the withdrawal of the child during adolescence can provide the parents with new opportunities for self-understanding and for renewal of the intimacy between them. Karen's parents had been in a therapy group of couples who were also parents of disturbed adolescents. The experience had opened for them a whole new world of understanding between themselves and within the family. Here are the words which Karen's mother wrote at one point in their struggle:

> Our daughter the Rebel—
>   is the nicest thing that's happened to us—
> She has made us *see* her for the first time
> She has made us *feel her* feelings and
>   *understand* her troubled feelings and ours.
> She has made us *aware,* aware of *so* many
>   new feelings and sights
> Our daughter the Rebel, so *sensitive* but so
>   full of *courage* has filled our hearts with a new love.
> We thank God for our *honest* daughter, the Rebel.

After an adolescent has successfully separated himself from his parents and found both his own identity and a place for himself in intimate relationships with young-adult peers, he may be able to establish a new kind of mature closeness with his parents. This adult-to-adult intimacy is possible only if the parents can let go of their need to treat their offspring as a dependent child. The intimacy between adult child and parents, when it develops, can have a special quality of closeness not present in other adult relationships.

WHAT PARENT-CHILD INTIMACY IS NOT

There are several kinds of parent-child relationships which are often mistaken for parent-child intimacy. Parent-child intimacy does not include making the child a substitute spouse. For this reason a reasonably need-satisfying marital (or other adult-to-adult) relationship is a prerequisite for healthy parent-child intimacy. The mother who is having all her emotional needs met through her relationships with her children is unable to grant them the autonomy they need in order to grow up. Her own need to be needed causes her to be overprotective and forces the children to become too dependent on her. This is not intimacy; it is smothering. The children are never free to grow up and establish peer relationships of intimacy on their own. The importance of cultivating a good marital relationship, utilizing professional help if necessary, cannot be overemphasized. In one study[9] of disturbed children, it was discovered that when parents became more invested in each other than either was in the child, the child improved regardless of what either parent did. When either parent became more emotionally invested in the child than in the marital partner, the child immediately regressed. Nothing is more devastating to a child than to find that he can come between his parents. When a parent is too dependent on the child for his own need-satisfaction, the child is heavily burdened and unable to separate from the parent. Parents must lean on each other, not on their children.

Parent-child intimacy also is not a matter of the parents living out their unfulfilled lives through their children. The father who, upon the birth of his first son, buys a room full of balls and bats and weights and punching bags had better examine his own sense of identity. The mother who pushes her daughter into early dating and an extensive social life may need to do the same. Otto Pollak says that throughout the child-rearing stage of marriage, spouses should each protect the children from the other spouse's unfinished identity.[10] For all of us as parents the temptation is to put our unfinished identity on our children. Such relating is not intimacy because it is stifling, not growth-stimulating. It burdens the child with responsibility for his parents' fulfillment as well as his own. Parents can help each other with unfinished identity. But children cannot be expected to do the same for their parents. Sometimes the simple awareness that such a tendency exists is enough to keep parents alert to the dangers.

"How can a child be himself and at the same time be what his parents want him to be? For the parents, how can they have a child whom they love while helping him to be an individual different from them?[11] Psychiatrist Frederick Allen's questions are crucial ones for families. Again, a large part of the answer lies in the strength of the marital relationship which makes the child's self-fulfillment in *his own unique way* the fulfillment of the parents' needs too.

Parent-child intimacy is not meant to be "sacrifice." Some mothers, especially, pride themselves on the feeling that they will give up anything for the sake of their children. A certain amount of self-sacrifice is a requisite to any relationship of mutuality. But sacrifice is not sound if it means neglect of the satisfactions of adult needs. The wife who cannot ever go out with her husband because she cannot leave her children is hurting them as well as the marriage relationship. The children will be required to pay for their mother's sacrifice with guilt and success. Similarly, the father who spends all his time working sacrificially so that his children will have things better than he did as a boy is sacrificing for them from his point of view. But he is also sacrificing both the parent-child and the marital relationship. What a father gives of *himself* to his children is more important than what he provides for them financially. (Adequate economic support *is* a form of self-giving, of course.)

Another misinterpretation of parent-child intimacy is that such intimacy is a relationship of equality. Some parents mistake peership for intimacy. At any stage of the child's growth, from babyhood to adulthood, the generation gap is a necessary and vital phenomenon. Children and adolescents need parents to be parents. They need the freedom to express negative feelings from time to time and to rebel occasionally, but they need the parents to be in charge in the long run. Thomas J. Cottle has remarked:

When a small child orders his parent out of his bedroom he necessarily fears the enormity of the act. In a tearful rage, he can only pray that the parent will go no farther than the living room. There is, then, a primitive core, developing first in interactions with parents, that pleads for the overthrow of authority, yet simultaneously for the inability to do it by nature of the superordinate's strength in resisting. Parents simply cannot break down or retreat. They must prevail, and no one wants this more than the child. . . . Relationships with them preclude both equality and peership.[12]

Parents are often most strongly tempted to close the generation gap when their children are in adolescence. This is particularly true when the parents themselves feel their own adolescence unfinished, as all of us do to some degree. But again, parent-child intimacy in adolescence is dependent on the separation of the generations. "For some young people, a quiet inner strength vanishes when their parents trespass on the property of time and destroy the very same asymmetry that they themselves once wished to destroy."[13]

The opposite of a peer relationship between parents and children is the authoritarian relationship which demands that the children become not only unquestioningly obedient, but that they never express any negative feelings toward or about their parents. Such a relationship makes parent-child intimacy impossible. It precludes the *gradual* development of autonomy which is basic to relationships of intimacy at any level. Intimacy is a two-way street. Authoritarianism is a one-way street.

IS IT EVER TOO LATE?

As with marital intimacy, the development of parent-child intimacy can be cultivated at any stage of family life, if there is a *reasonably* good family identity. Within certain basic limits, parents can make many mistakes without damaging their children or stunting the capacity for intimacy. Erik Erikson writes:

> Now, while it is quite clear what *must* happen to keep a baby alive (the minimum supply necessary) and what *must not* happen, lest he be physically damaged or chronically upset (the maximum early frustration tolerable), there is a certain leeway in regard to what *may* happen; and different cultures make extensive use of their prerogatives to decide what they consider workable and insist upon calling necessary.[14]

The basic requirements of food and shelter and clothing are among the musts. Emotional satisfactions are also among the musts. The studies reported in *Infants in Institutions*[15] make it clear that simply providing good physical care without opportunities for strong emotional attachments to meaningful adults permanently cripples the child in his ability to establish relationships of intimacy and trust. Physical and emotional abuse and brutality are among the must nots. Some of these have been described in the foregoing section. But it is comforting to realize that the techniques of child-raising once thought to be crucial—breast or bottle feeding, time of weaning or toilet training, spanking or not spanking—are insufficient criteria for explaining behavioral and emotional reactions of children. Someone has said that it is not so much *how* you raise your children as how you *feel* about them. Ben is a child of the London blitz in a novel called *London Pride.* His mother "was often irritable and sometimes violent, but it didn't mean anything to Ben because of her more constant kindness. In a tough and dangerous world, his mother's kindness was the one thing Ben had learned to believe in."[16]

For most of us it is not so much that we have *failed* in our parent-child relationships, as that we have not developed them to the limits of their potentialities. Just as it is possible, given a certain basic strength in a marriage to deepen and broaden its intimacy, so in the parent-child relationship the potential is always present.

We have been saying that parent-child intimacy develops in the process of teaching the child to prize his own body and bodily experiences, his own senses and sensations, his own feelings, both good and bad. We have mentioned some of the misuses of the parent-child relationship which can cause the child to fear closeness because of the painful experiences which made closeness too threatening. Helping the child to discover his capacity for intimacy, for closeness with autonomy has been the focus of this chapter.

As a husband and wife in their own struggle for intimacy become open to their own feelings, and their relationship deepens, the children will automatically be affected by it. A good relationship in marriage automatically produces good relationships beyond itself.[17] But there are some conscious steps that parents can take to stimulate the development of intimacy with children.

A first step would be to become consciously aware of the ways in which their children express their feelings, and to let them know verbally that these feelings are accepted. When a nine-year-old boy comes storming in from school, throws his things around in defiance of all the rules of the household and makes a defiant remark to his mother besides, she can say, "Jerry, I see that you're angry and unhappy. Do you want to tell me about it?" Maybe he does and maybe he doesn't, but at least he knows that she understands and accepts his feeling. Maybe when he is ready he can talk about it. The important part is that somebody understands. This does not suggest that parents accept any action the child chooses for expression of his feelings. Jerry's mother may need to require him to pick up his things. Destructive and hurting behavior has always to be prevented or stopped. But usually it stops of its own accord when feelings are honestly accepted. The learning-to-listen discussed in Chapter 5 becomes important in parent-child intimacy. Ben's mother, when he needed her, ". . . emptied [her] mind to listen so that whatever you said had room to be at home in it."[18]

A second step that parents can take is to let their children in on their own feelings, both positive and negative. Some parents protect their children from parental emotions in the belief that these will somehow be damaging to the child. Feelings imagined can be much more damaging than those freely expressed. The child who sees his father pat his mother on the "fanny" as he goes by her standing at the kitchen sink is picking up some good feelings about sexual intimacy. Children who see a certain amount of honest argument between their parents, followed by friendly relations within a short time, are learning that anger is not necessarily destructive to a relationship but can be a positive force. Tears of pain and joy openly and unashamedly accepted from time to time, in parents as well as in children, teach a child the value of deep feeling in experiencing life to its fullest. All this does not say that the display of feelings by parents cannot be overdone. Certainly, destructive anger between parents will hurt the children. The parent who makes a confidant of the child because there is not a good spouse relationship in which feelings can be expressed is hurting the child. Excessive and chronic display of grief and sadness by the parent can be damaging to children as well. But a freedom and openness about the existence of feelings in parents helps children to be able to own their own feelings and increases parent-child intimacy.

Dorothy Walter Baruch writing about *One Little Boy,* says:

> I wondered when we would know better how to help children more widely in schools and homes to understand their feelings, and when we would be able to help parents understand theirs, so that the boys and girls now growing up might know not only about tanks and bullets but about the most powerful of all weapons for both good and evil—the human feelings that propel us, if we do not understand them, into hating in place of loving, into killing instead of creation.[19]

If parents treat their children in such a way that a conflict develops between the wish to be loved and cared for, and the wish to assert themselves, they will carry the conflict into their own marriages. The capacity for intimacy grows in a child as he experiences a sense of being wanted and approved, of belonging, of emotional warmth, of acceptance, of nearness and relatedness to security-giving adults, without feeling deprived of his need for autonomy, self-direction and self-fulfillment. Healthy parent-child intimacy at any stage of the family cycle frees the child for autonomy even as it pulls the parents closer together. When this happens the child learns that although things outside ourselves change, "if we learn to utilize our inner resources, we carry our security around with us."[20] Parents and children together can develop the quality of intimacy required for such a covenant.

TAKING ACTION

1. Read Chapter 15 in *New Ways of Discipline* by Baruch (New York: McGraw-Hill Book Co., 1949).
Practice listening to your children and encouraging them to pour

out their feelings. Your way of handling this will depend on their ages.

2. Practice repeating back to your children what you think their feelings are in a given situation. Ask them to correct you if you misinterpret them. Again, their ages will determine to what extent they can respond to this sort of game.

3. Look over the suggestions in Chapter 6 which fit the ages of your children and continue to cultivate the intimacy developing between you and your spouse.

4. Talk over with your spouse the ways you feel about each of your children and the ways you think they feel about you. Help each other to see how you are using your children to meet your own unmet needs.

5. Read *Between Parent and Child* or *Between Parent and Teenager* by Haim Ginot (New York: The Macmillan Co., 1965 and 1969) for concrete help in learning how to relate intimately with your children. Read some of the books cited in notes 2, 4, 7, 8, 16, 19, and 20, below.

NOTES

1. Clifford Kirkpatrick, *The Family* (New York: Ronald Press Co., 1963), p. 4.
2. Levy and Monroe, *The Happy Family* (New York: Alfred A. Knopf, 1938), p. 123.
3. Ross Snyder, *Inscape* (Nashville: Abingdon Press, 1968), p. 20.
4. Erik Erikson, *Childhood and Society* (New York: W. W. Norton, 1963).
5. Bruno Bettelheim, *The Empty Fortress* (New York: Free Press, 1967), p. 32.
6. Levy and Monroe, *op. cit.*, p. 243.
7. Margaret Ribble, *The Personality of the Young Child* (New York: Columbia University Press, 1955).
8. Iris Dornfield, *Jeeney Ray* (New York: The Viking Press, 1962), pp. 44, 50.
9. Virginia Satir, *Conjoint Family Therapy* (Palo Alto, Calif.: Science & Behavior Books, 1964), p. 4.
10. Otto Pollak, lecture, University of Pennsylvania, January 18, 1967.

11. Frederick H. Allen, *Positive Aspects of Child Psychiatry* (New York: W. W. Norton, 1963).
12. Thomas J. Cottle, "Parent and Child—The Hazards of Equality," *Saturday Review,* February 1, 1969, p. 17.
13. *Ibid.,* p. 16.
14. Erik Erikson, *Identity and the Life Cycle* (New York: International Universities Press, Inc., 1959), p. 57.
15. See Provence and Lipton, *Infants in Institutions* (New York: International Universities Press, 1962).
16. Phyllis Bottome, *London Pride* (Boston: Little Brown and Co., 1941), p. 8.
17. This point is basic to the upreach and outreach of marriages (see chapters 9 and 10).
18. Phyllis Bottome, *op. cit.,* p. 225.
19. Dorothy Walter Baruch, *One Little Boy* (New York: Julian Press, 1952), p. 236.
20. Virginia Axline, *Dibs, In Search of Self* (Boston: Houghton Mifflin, 1965), p. 51.

9 *The Spiritual Dimension of Marriage*

> Trust, trust in the world, because this human being exists. . . .
> Because this human being exists, meaninglessness, however hard
> pressed you are by it, cannot be the real truth. Because this human
> being exists, in the darkness the light lies hidden, in fear salvation,
> and in the callousness of one's fellow-men, the great Love.
>
> Martin Buber, *Between Man and Man*[1]

Intimacy is the interlocking of two individual persons joined by a
bond which partially overcomes their separateness. In the fullest
expression of intimacy there is a vertical dimension, a sense of
relatedness to the universe which both strengthens the marital relationship and is strengthened by it. Quite apart from any churchy
or churchly considerations, the spiritual dimension of marriage is
a practical source of food for marital growth and health. No single
factor does more to give a marriage joy or to keep it both a
venture and an adventure in mutual fulfillment than shared commitment to spiritual discovery. The life of the spirit is deeply
personal, so that moments of sharing on the spiritual level are
tender, precious moments in a relationship.

SPIRITUAL INTIMACY STRENGTHENS A MARRIAGE

By spiritual intimacy is meant the sense of a vital relationship
with that which transcends our brief, fragile existence—a relationship with the realm of values and meanings, with the flow of

history and life about us, and with that "ultimate concern" (Tillich) which we call God. The need for a sense of spiritual intimacy includes the need for a sense of "at-homeness" in the universe, and a deeply experienced feeling of what Erik Erikson calls "basic trust." The need for this kind of intimacy is a fundamental one, both for the individual and for his marriage. St. Augustine's well-known words, "Thou hast made us for Thyself and our hearts are restless till they rest in Thee,"[2] emphasize the fact that the *will to relate* to the Spirit of life is an inescapable part of man's hunger for depth relationships.

Intimacy on the horizontal, person-to-person plane and intimacy on the vertical or spiritual plane complement and reinforce each other. A person who feels himself to be an emotional isolate in his human relationships usually also feels himself to be a spiritual orphan in the universe, whatever his head-level religious beliefs may be. Conversely, one who feels a strong bond with all other human beings usually has a sense of connection with nature and with all of life, whether or not it is expressed in conventional religious forms. The ability to establish, nurture, and sustain an intimate human relationship, and the ability to commune vitally with nature, the universe, and God, are closely connected. Furthermore, each of these kinds of relatedness profoundly influences the other. He who loves his spouse, whom he has seen, is better able to love God, whom he has not seen, and vice versa.

The interconnectedness of interpersonal and spiritual intimacy is seen clearly in the area of trustfulness. The capacity to form a human relationship of mutual trust—a relationship in which one feels accepted, able to relinquish his struggle to prove his worth, and safe to be himself—springs from the same well as the capacity to trust Life. "To let go of the image which, in the eyes of this world, bears your name, the image in your consciousness of social ambition and sheer force of will. To let go and fall, fall—in trust and blind devotion. Toward another, another . . . ."[3] These words of Dag Hammarskjöld describe the experience of trust which removes the heavy burden of always being on trial. It is the fresh air of grace flowing into the stifling atmosphere of legalism. The person who knows this reality in his marriage is better equipped to experience it in life generally. Conversely, having a source of regular trust renewal in one's spiritual life provides a steady foundation for trustful human relationships. Vertical trust is particularly helpful in periods of marital stress when horizontal trust is weakened; the same is true in other crises when fragile human trust is not enough to sustain hope and courage. Having a sense that one can depend on life reduces the vulnerability that results from attempting to satisfy all one's trust needs in marriage. A couple which shares a robust spiritual vitality feels undergirded by life; this stabilizes their relationship when it is buffeted by fate and tragedy. There is usable wisdom in the words from *The Prophet:* "Give your hearts, but not into each other's keeping. For only the hand of Life can contain your hearts."[4] No human being can alone satisfy the spiritual hungers of his companion's heart.

Thus growth-producing intimacy is difficult if not impossible without a spiritual center and source. Intimacy reaches full flower for a couple only when they have found in, through, and beyond their marriage, a rich measure of those gifts which the great religions of the world have made available to men. There are at least three aspects to the fundamental religious needs of persons:

(1) *The need for an experience of the numinous and the transcendent.* Ruth Benedict has referred in her anthropological writings to the belief in "wonderful power" which was ubiquitous among the cultures she studied. This need to feel that there is something wonderful, transcending the mundaneness of life, is what is meant by the "vertical dimension." (2) *The need for a sense of meaning, purpose and values in one's existence.* . . . (3) *The need for a feeling of deep trust and relatedness to life.* Maslow uses the phrase "oceanic feeling," in his discussion of the self-actualized person, to describe the experience of being a part of the whole universe.[5]

In discussing the mature personality, Gordon Allport emphasizes the need for an adequate philosophy of life: "Maturity requires . . . a clear comprehension of life's purpose in terms of an intelligible theory. Or, in brief, some form of unifying philosophy of life."[6]

To be able to cultivate an intimate, long-term relationship, one needs sturdy self-esteem. He needs to feel and stand tall psychologically. Religion in the Hebrew-Christian tradition aims at helping persons to stand tall, with their heads spiritually erect as children of God, created in his image. Self-esteem is found and maintained only in relationships, horizontal and vertical. Pride or narcissism is the attempt, always foredoomed, to maintain a sense of worth apart from or even at the expense of others. To know that one is related to and accepted by the Spirit of the universe is a continued source of feelings of worth.

Psychiatrist Earl A. Loomis, Jr., has observed that "Man's image of God and his image of himself are somehow always linked together."[7] In a similar way, a man's style of emotionally significant relationships is always linked to his way of relating with the trans-human. Man creates his philosophy of life from the resources of his basic relationships; these relationships, in turn, are remolded by the influence of his faith, his values, his dedications, and his beliefs about life.

Shared meanings feed intimacy in a relationship; major differences in philosophies of life tend to lessen closeness. Couples with contradictory visions of life must cope with this conflict as well as learn how to compensate for the lack of sharing in the philosophical-religious area. All marriages are "mixed marriages" (in that all couples come from differing family backgrounds and world-views); but when there are deep disagreements about the core meanings of existence, a couple must work doubly hard to establish creative closeness. Religion is the celebration of life, and fortunate is the couple who can celebrate together. Those who cannot do so, because of religious conflicts, need to find alternative patterns of shared celebration of life's mystery and wonder.

Some couples from sharply mixed backgrounds avoid overt conflict by a tacit understanding that religious issues are off limits for discussion. This may be necessary to gain reduction of unconstructive conflict, but the price of peace is high. It is much better if they *can* learn to communicate on religious, philosophical, and value issues. Communication is the instrument by which they can compromise and resolve differences on such matters as in which tradition the children shall be raised. Cultivating the capacity to *respect* each other's religious convictions and abandoning the futile attempt to force the other to agree helps to keep differing religious backgrounds from blocking intimacy.

A considerable degree of emotional maturity is required to maintain a close relationship in spite of deep differences. (The ability to respect and not be threatened by differences is one of the hallmarks of maturity.) Couples with a high degree of self-esteem and maturity often discover positive resources in their differences. It can make marriage more interesting to have a variety of religious ideas, traditions, and customs from which to draw in creating the family's own style of belief and practice. (The same is true of cross-cultural marriages.)

A couple from mixed religious backgrounds is confronted by a challenge which can lead to spiritual growth for them and their children. This is the need to search for and find a core of shared meanings which transcend their differences and give them a basis for spiritual closeness. This challenge is present in every marriage, but acutely so in a mixed marriage. If a couple finds a common spiritual ground on which they can stand, it is *their* ground. In some cases, the discovery of this core of shared meanings is facilitated by searching out and participating in a lively church fellowship where the search for life-meanings is a central activity. This may be a church in the tradition of one or the other partner; more often, it is one which is somewhere between their childhood traditions. The willingness to compromise, that is, for each to give up something which he finds desirable for the greater good of the relationship is an essential factor in the growth of spiritual crea-tivity in mixed marriages.

A couple which is deprived of the cohesion of shared religion in their early marriage should not give up. Working through to a new level of shared meanings is usually a tough struggle, but the enrichment which results makes it more than worth the effort. It is important to remember that nonrelating or conflict in the spiritual area frequently occurs even between spouses from the same religious tradition, but who have basically different value systems and world-views derived from their respective families-of-origin.

Religious differences may be simply the battleground for psychological problems. One submissive wife finally rebelled after ten years of marriage by joining a sectarian group which believes that other denominations are not legitimate forms of Christianity. Her passionate participation in this group was an act of self-assertion against her husband's domination. But instead of producing healthy self-affirmation and constructive autonomy, her behavior had an angry, rebellious quality which resulted in chronic conflict and deterioration of the marriage. The husband, still a member of a middle-of-the-road Protestant group, felt the constant sting of her new affiliation and beliefs. In this case, what looked on the surface like a "religious problem" was actually a long-standing, hidden dominance-submission struggle in the marriage. In such cases, it is essential to deal with the destructive "game" the couple is playing, using religion as the playing board. Help from a skilled pastoral counselor may be necessary to distinguish genuinely religious problems from such pseudo-religious difficulties.

Religious one-up-man-ship is frequent in both of these kinds of marital conflict. It is based on the element of *exclusivism* in the religious traditions of the partners. Exclusivism is the belief that one's own position is the only right (true, Christian, road to salvation, etc.) approach or the "obviously superior" approach. Such attitudes create conflict by putting the other's tradition "one-down." Overcoming the elements of exclusivism in one's attitudes and feelings toward one's tradition contributes to spiritual intimacy.

That shared religion can be a strengthening factor in marriage is suggested by numerous studies which reveal a correlation between church attendance and greater marital stability.[8] There is no doubt that many families find positive resources in participating in a vital church or temple program. Worship is a nurturing, trust-restoring experience for many people, particularly when it takes place in a supportive network of meaningful relationships.[9] The lift of sharing in an experience of inspiring music and security-giving words can help a couple to mobilize inner resources for coping with the heavy demands of their day-to-day existence. The undergirding relationships of like-minded friends in a church fellowship are of major value to a family, particularly if they are separated by the generation gap and/or geography from their clan. Horizontal person-to-person relationships are supported by a shared view of reality, within the religious community of a church.

MARRIAGE AS A PATH TO SPIRITUAL REALITY

A shared spiritual life strengthens a marriage; conversely, a good marriage strengthens the spiritual life of the couple. Spiritual growth takes place best in a relationship in which religious values are experienced. A growing marriage provides just such a relationship.

Franz Rosenzweig once stated, "When pressed to its limits every psychological question becomes a theological one and every theological question a psychological one."[10] The truth of the assertion is illustrated throughout our discussion in this book, which deals with the issues and relationships that also are central in religion. George Albert Coe described religion as "the discovery of persons." Another way of putting it is that religion is the discovery of persons *in relationships.* A good marriage offers an ideal opportunity to discover each other in depth; in this encounter, many couples experience the central realities of religion. Their marriages become pathways to those spiritual experiences which transcend the marriage relationship. In biblical terms, they discover in marriage that "God is love, and he who abides in love abides in God and God abides in him" (I John 4:16*b*).

The "good news" is that love is supreme and is available in relationships, including our relationship with God. Our discussion of intimacy in marriage is an effort to explore the ways in which

the good news can come alive in a vital human relationship—
marriage. Its purpose is to illumine the ways in which the channels
of the relationship can be deepened and broadened so that the
love which is available in persons and in the universe can flow
more fully. Movement toward a more joyful marriage illuminates
the process by which the wholeness of persons is increased. Alienation and reconciliation are repeated realities in the periodic
estrangement/reconciliation experiences of marriage. Fortunate
is the couple in whose relationship there is something which allows
them both to experience grace—the accepting love which one does
not need to earn because it is present as a spontaneous expression
of the relationship.

Dostoevski once declared, "I ponder, 'What is hell?' I maintain it is the suffering of being unable to love."[11] The times when
couples yearn for love but are unable to relate in loving ways are
times when they experience the agonies of a hell-on-earth. Conversely, moments of loving connectedness which approach a communion of souls are moments which make the concept of heaven
very much alive in the here and now.

In the wonder and ultimate mystery of love, spiritual truths
come alive; they take on flesh-and-blood reality by being in-
carnated in persons. Encountering the being of one's partner—
really seeing and experiencing that unique person—is a deeply
moving spiritual meeting, spirit with spirit.

When couples achieve mutual understanding that goes beyond
understanding *about* the person, to understanding *the person in his
being,* they do so through what is essentially a spiritual experience.
Paul Tournier catches this truth:

To find the key to understanding, the secret of living—this is an
inner experience, a discovery, a conversion, and not simply an acquisition of new knowledge. It may happen at the very time when a
person feels most disheartened; it generally takes place in a way
which he could not have imagined. He may have read many books,
heard many sermons, accumulated much knowledge. And yet suddenly,
it is a rather insignificant happening that strikes him, a word, an

encounter, a death, a recovery, a look, or a natural event. God uses such to reach a man.[12]

Someone has described a wedding ring as "a small gold band that cuts off your circulation." For those in an unsatisfying relationship, marriage seems like a life sentence to the prison of boredom. Fidelity, if it exists at all, has the feel of a heavy weight. In contrast, fidelity in a healthy marriage, though perhaps strained at times, includes a feeling of opportunity for experimenting with more exciting forms of relating. Such fidelity is motivated by more than just the decision to be faithful in the formal sense, i.e., by not "cheating" on one's mate. It goes beyond this to the moving force of what in religious terms is called a "covenant." A covenant is more than a pledge of reciprocal faithfulness; it *is* such a pledge, but within the context of a wider framework of meaning for the couple, some wider context that includes but transcends the one-to-one relationship. This wider context usually includes some supportive community—a community of shared values such as a church or temple fellowship. The wider context includes the couple's awareness of their relatedness to the "ground of being." Faithfulness to this wider context of meaning is the foundation of their fidelity. Horizontal fidelity is incomplete and fragile without the vertical context of meaning. One wife put it this way: "There's something beyond us that we experience in our marriage —a kind of awareness of our place in the bigger picture. It's more than that, though. At times we feel a warm uniting presence which is in our being together. We usually don't call this God, but if we had to label it, I believe that would come closest to conveying the meaning it has for us."

In reflecting on the goals of his life, Bertrand Russell declared:

"I have sought love first because it brings ecstasy—ecstasy so great that I would often have sacrificed all the rest of my life for a few hours of this joy. I have sought it, next, because it relieves loneliness —that terrible loneliness in which one shivering consciousness looks over the rim of the world into the cold unfathomable lifeless abyss. I have sought it, finally, because in the union of love, I have seen, in a mystic miniature, the prefiguring vision of the heaven that saints and poets have imagined."[13]

The experience of loving intimacy is a pathway to those spiritual realities which give ultimate significance to our relationships and to our existence. No formal philosophy or theology of intimacy has been articulated in these pages, but all the issues which we have been discussing are ultimately matters of the spirit; they are potential paths to the Spirit of the universe.

SPIRITUAL NEEDS AND EXISTENTIAL ANXIETY

One of the roots of the need for spiritual relatedness is the experience of man as the animal who knows he will die. How can one cope constructively with the dizzy flight of the years, with the knowledge that every tick of the clock brings death closer? How can one confront the brevity of one's membership in the human family? How can one deal constructively with the ultimate threat of nonexistence? The fact that a man knows he will die colors all of his life. As noted in Chapter 1, behind the will to relate is man's existential loneliness and anxiety—the normal, nonpathological anxiety which is a part of what Paul Tillich once called man's "heritage of finitude." Erikson calls this form of anxiety the "ego chill." It slips up on a self-aware human being whenever he becomes conscious of his fragile position in the face of sickness, nature, fate and, ultimately, death.

There are echoes of such anxiety in any depth study of life or time. Consider this line from R. M. MacIver's *The Challenge of the Passing Years, My Encounter with Time:* "The deeds of men sink into the melting pot of time, with countless ripples that quickly disappear."[14] The impact of existential anxiety has had many effects in the life of mankind, including his long pilgrimage in every known culture toward understanding the nature of existence. This pilgrimage is man's religion. Existential anxiety drives man to seek a relationship beyond the limitations of human ties.

Unlike neurotic anxiety, there is no psychotherapeutic answer to existential anxiety. It is existential in that it is an inescapable part of existence—a normal response to man's awareness of his own mortality. *But,* the way a man handles his existential anxiety makes it either a stimulus to creativity or a paralyzing force which dulls his vitality and self-awareness. As Tillich made clear, it becomes a stimulus to creativity only if a man confronts it and incorporates it within his self-image. The courage to do this can come only from *facing existential anxiety within a relationship of trust and a philosophy of life which gives meaning to existence.*

Awareness of the need for a sense of connectedness with something that transcends human intimacy grows stronger as the years fly by. It is strong in all those periods when existential anxiety is the most activated and pressing—e.g., late adolescence, the crisis of the middle years, the retirement years, and in periods of sickness and bereavement. In these times, human and transhuman relationships of trust are needed as sources of that courage within which ultimate anxiety can be confronted and integrated into one's philosophy of life. The reciprocity of horizontal and vertical intimacy is seen in the fact that a person who comes into these periods possessing a sense of spiritual intimacy finds that his human relations are strengthened thereby, and vice versa.

As indicated earlier, a vacuous marriage becomes more and more painful as the couple approaches the middle years. If intimacy has not been achieved, a spirit of quiet desperation descends on the marriage in the mid-forties. The effects of the empty nest, the menopause, the death of parents, and the unavoidable evidence of one's own aging combine to produce the crisis of the middle years. The marriage problems of middle-aged couples cannot be understood fully unless one remembers the spiritual problem which is the context within which they occur.

Some couples try to deny their fear of aging by going to absurd extremes to stay young looking. The title of a recent paperback suggests the intensity of the pressure to escape from the reality of aging; it was, *How to be Thirty for Forty Years.* Sound ways of coping with aging focus on finding inner richness, making peace with existence and working to deepen one's relationships—with oneself, other people, and God. Such approaches do not eliminate existential anxiety, but they do make it possible to live with it, without panic or paralysis. The person who jokingly says, "I'm approaching forty—I won't say from which direction" probably is expressing both his continuing anxiety and his transcendence of it so that it does not interfere with his need-satisfying relationships.

The need for a trustful relationship with life, the universe, with God—is insistent in the so-called "golden years" (which actually are more like lead than gold for some people). What Erikson calls "ego integrity" is the way of coping constructively with existential anxiety in this period. Ego integrity is the product of having accomplished the tasks of the ego in the previous stages of the life journey; it is the positive acceptance of the one and only life on earth one has been given. It allows an aging person to face his dying without panic and with determination to "die living rather than to live dying."[15]

Through relationships of trust—both with persons and with a Higher Power—existential anxiety becomes, in Kierkegaard's words, a "school." The trustful relationships allow one to face the anxiety rather than run from it, and to use it to enrich rather than diminish life.[16]

An awareness of belonging to the human race and to life, makes it easier to maintain a sense of belonging in one's intimate relationships. In his prologue to *The Family of Man,* Carl Sandburg wrote: "The first cry of a newborn baby in Chicago or Zamboango, in Amsterdam or Rangoon, has the same pitch and key, each saying, 'I am! I have come through! I belong! I am a member of the Family.' "[17] The awareness that one *does* belong and *is* related in a deep mysterious way to life, humanity, and God makes it easier to resist the centrifugal forces which threaten to pull us away from the human family, especially from those who mean the most to us.

Coping with the fact of the transitoriness of existence releases a couple to mourn real losses and then to return to live fully the years and days which are their gifts from Life.[18] A functional religious faith and their awareness of the power of love free them to cope with losses and the anxiety they produce, and to continue to rejoice in the goodness of their life together.

Set me as a seal upon your heart . . . for love is strong as death. . . . Many waters cannot quench love, neither can floods drown it.

Song of Solomon 8:6–7

The trust and responsiveness that make intimacy flower often make life exciting. "The aware person is alive because he knows how he feels, where he is and when it is. He knows that after he dies the trees will still be there, but he will not be there to look at them again, so he wants to see them now with as much poignancy as possible."[19] Vital religion helps people to find this quality of aliveness in their interpersonal relationships, their interaction with nature, and their communion with God. Erich Fromm and his colleagues declare:

The aim of life is to be fully born, though its tragedy is that most of us die before we are thus born. . . . The answer is . . . to develop one's awareness, one's reason, one's capacity to love, to such a point that one transcends one's own egocentric involvement and arises at a new harmony and new wonder with the world.[20]

Healthy religion has this pro-life thrust and goal. Many centuries ago a young carpenter reminded his hearers of the necessity of spiritual rebirth; he stated "I have come that men may have life in all its fullness" (John 10:10). Sound religion can help a marriage to become a place where persons find this fullness in their lives together.

INCREASING SPIRITUAL INTIMACY

How can a couple strengthen the spiritual side of their marriage? Here are some approaches which are helpful in increasing vertical intimacy.

Central in this process is *discovering ways of "communion with the timeless."*[21] Each couple needs to find ways of connecting with time-transcending experiences in which they can find spiritual meanings together. Marital partners are blessed if they have discovered how to share in a wide variety of such experiences. For each couple, the things that are so experienced are different. One couple told of standing together high on a hill in November listening in silence to the far-away honking of wild geese as they made a jagged V lumbering across the sky. Another couple found time-transcendence in hearing unexpectedly a half-forgotten melody filled for them with memories of sadness and quiet joy. For many couples it is a full, throbbing consummation of sexual union, when time stands still and two lives are fused in shared ecstasy.

> We live our life when we exchange it for worthwhile experience, for experience that absorbs and satisfies. . . . There are high moments . . . when the life spirit takes full possession of us. It is as though all unknowingly we had reached a mountain top and see below us the wonder of the earth, as it never appears to our ordinary sight. And when we have descended, we say in effect: It was good for us to have been there. And memory bequeaths something to many quiet hours, conveying the sense that our time is no longer being lived through but being lived.[22]

Each couple must find its own style of intimacy with the unchangable in the midst of time—a style which satisfies their spiritual hungers. For some it involves connecting with values or causes which will live after them, and which are "bigger than my little world." Sharing in such experiences of meaning and dedication adds a dimension of height and breadth to the intimacy of marriage. The outreach dimension of intimacy will be explored more fully in the next chapter.

Time-transcending experiences are available all around us in nature and in science. In his beautiful account of his own interaction with nature, Loren Eiseley declares: "I can at best report only from my own wilderness. The important thing is that each man possess such a wilderness and that he consider what marvels are to be observed there."[23] Possessing one's own wilderness allows one "to understand and enjoy the miracles of this world,"[24] —for example, to see in an orb-weaving spider on a street lamp post, "a great black and yellow embodiment of the life force."[25] The pity is that so few persons have eyes which *see* such omnipresent miracles. The more one knows about the world of nature, the more likely that one's eyes will be opened to these wonders. Mankind is a part of an "immense journey." He was there three hundred million years ago when a fish emerged from the water and hobbled along on fins, gasping for oxygen with primitive lungs. He was there, for that was the beginning of a long line that led eventually to man.

The wider perspective which comes from possessing one's wilderness provides time-transcending experiences that help to reduce the grandiose need to play God. Oliver Wendell Holmes once observed: "The first step toward a truer faith is the recognition that *I,* at any rate, am *not* God."[26] When one considers the immensities of the universe and of geological time, it is difficult to keep "I-ism" intact. Surrendering this defensive pride opens an individual to real communion with other people and with the Power of the universe.

A couple can enhance the vertical dimension of their marriage by working together toward spiritual growth goals. This includes developing religious concepts and values which are meaningful to them at their present stage in adulthood. As they move along the marriage journey, it may be necessary periodically to revise their understanding of religion, to keep it in touch with their changing experiences, views of life, and spiritual needs.

Many couples find spiritual intimacy in sharing experiences which are mediated through religious images. Unfortunately, some adults are restricted by childhood ideas and feelings about religion— beliefs they can no longer accept as adults. They are ashamed to admit that they do not believe, even to each other, although neither of them still holds to the old beliefs. They are stuck with their minds full of dead symbols. Some still have mental images of God as a "resident policeman" or "parental hangover." In J. B. Phillips' phrase, their God is "too small."[27] Such persons need to realize that all our religious ideas and symbols are "at best only echoes of meanings we cannot reach."[28] Couples who realize this may break through to new freedom which allows them to talk together about the meaning of life and death; they may experience the satisfactions of discussing their own inner quest for purpose and their lonely longing for the most real.

Spiritual intimacy requires spiritual growth. A couple has the opportunity to develop together a style of religious belief and practice which satisfies their needs and the needs of their children. Chuck, a father in his twenties, reported:

> It opened up a whole new way of understanding the ideas of my childhood religious training when I saw that I could reinterpret them, evaluate them, accept or reject them in the light of my adult experience. Salvation by grace never made any sense to me until one time in a child-study group, when grace was presented as the unearned love that's present in every good home.

Some couples are released to grow spiritually when they stop confusing moralism (the "thou shalt nots") with religion. Healthy religion has a great deal to do with core values such as justice, brotherhood, mercy, integrity; it has nothing to do with what young people call "Mickey Mouse morals"—ethical trivia which unfortunately have occupied a prominent place in some expressions of Protestantism. H. L. Mencken once humorously defined a puritan as a person who lives in mortal fear that somewhere, sometime, someone is enjoying himself. The perspective which rejects enjoyment of life is not the viewpoint which leads to zest, joy, or fulfilling intimacy in marriage.

At the same time, as Erikson makes clear, sound values are essential ingredients in personality health and strength.[29] Shared values can increase the spiritual intimacy of a marriage. Human beings live in their values. What a person considers important—important enough to give his precious hours and days to—these values will have a deep influence on his marriage. Conflict concerning values occurs in all marriages to some degree, simply because any two persons have some differences in their philosophy of life and value hierarchy. But understanding of each other's values, and basic rapport in this area in spite of inevitable differences, are valuable ingredients in intimacy.

A couple can test the adequacy of the values by which they are currently living by this simple exercise: *Imagine that you are near the end of the road of your life and are looking back down the path along which you have come together. From that point of view, how do you feel about the way you are living now? Are the things that are consuming your time and energy the most important things? What changes in your present pattern of relating are indicated by your perspective?*[30]

What counts most in human relations and life generally is the question of one's destiny. It is a question with which it behooves each couple to wrestle until they find an answer that satisfies them. The answers will change as the years pass. One of the deep satisfactions of some marriages is that the couples change together in their philosophies of life and values. One couple in their forties agreed: "We've changed radically in our theological ideas, since the early days of our marriage. We're thankful that we've changed in the same general direction and that we've changed in a way that makes us feel freer and more open to life." In order for growth to occur in the spiritual area of a relationship, a couple must be able to discuss their deep concerns, their doubts, and their convictions with each other. This is difficult but rewarding.

It behooves married couples who no longer find their childhood tradition satisfying to search until they find a church or temple which does satisfy their spiritual needs and those of their children. A young couple in a marital growth group paid this tribute to their church: "Having an opportunity to participate together in various groups in our church has done a great deal for our marriage. Just sitting together for an hour each week, sharing in the worship service, and having our thinking stimulated about important issues gives us a weekly re-fueling." There are all kinds of churches. Some are narrow and constricted in their approach to religion. Others are open to personal searching and dedicated to social change. A church or temple in which the whole family feels at home and is spiritually fed, provides invaluable resources for their growth.

Spiritual maturing occurs when a couple *lives their religion;* that is, when they relate so that realities like faith, hope, and love come alive in their relationship. William Genné defines love as "the overwhelming desire and persistent effort of two persons to create for each other the conditions under which each can become the person God meant him to be."[31] Couples who even approximate this quality of loving discover the truths of religion in the fabric of their relationships.

The meaning which is discoverable in the everydayness of marriage and family life should be sought by a couple throughout their experience. As Erikson declares: "Any span of the cycle lived without vigorous meaning, at the beginning, in the middle, or at the end, endangers the sense of life and the meaning of death in all whose life stages are intertwined."[32] Starting with the rich meanings in the human dramas of courting, marriage, having children, living through the vicissitudes of the years together, a couple can build on these and glimpse those meanings which are greater even than those within their family—the meanings which are in the experiences of the family of man.

Marriage partners live their religion when they are sensitive and responsive to each other's pains and hopes, fears and longings. To sense that the other is struggling with hidden feelings of self-doubt, that he is wrestling with inner conflicts and tough problems, that he is watching for a gesture of affirmation from another—this is communion that brings spiritual aliveness within a marriage. One who is aware knows experiences such as this:

> The person sitting next to you is a thin darting line of awareness, playing peekaboo with the world, and run-sheep-run with eternal sleep—and ultimately losing. And knowing that he will lose. So all the time he is quivering sensitivity.[33]

When one knows and cares, this caring becomes the channel for the healing power of the universe to move through the relationship. "Deep within us is love—the throbbing life of the ages, . . ."[34] and this love means that fear and frustration and crushing failure are not the last word. In a growing marriage the experience of spiritual renewal occurs repeatedly. "As you relate to each other, each of you will again and again be reborn into present *spirit*."[35]

This is the day when theological truths, to be meaningful to most people, must be experienced in relationships. Marriage is the place where this can occur most frequently and powerfully. Here in the relationship where most people live and move and have their being, year after year, the good news must come alive or it will remain a dead abstraction for them.

Spiritual growth in marriage occurs as the couple become co-creators of newness—in themselves, their children, and in broader areas and relationships. Participation in constructing and creating is at the same time a spontaneous expression of man's inherent creativity and a positive way of coping with existential anxiety. Making something that will live after him is one of man's responses to the knowledge of his mortality. In his insightful discussion of married love, Reuel Howe states:

> By the discipline of creativity, I mean the discipline of learning and perfecting some skill in art or music or handicraft or sport in which there is opportunity to co-ordinate motor and mental power and to gain therefrom some sense of achievement. A creative approach to life, of course, is a part of a life of devotion. Creative activity is indispensable to the health of the human soul. . . .[36]

This approach to life and to marriage opens wide possibilities for shared creativity. Rearing children is a profound opportunity for participating in continuing creation. What could be more creative or more full of wonder than bringing a new person into being and helping to shape the direction of his development? Those who experience raising children as sharing in creation discover that it brings a new depth to a marital relationship.

The possibilities for marital creativity are almost limitless: sharing in helping to create a much-needed community service, a new approach to civil rights, a more humane approach to divorce laws, a new park, a group for intellectual enjoyment and serious study, a better mousetrap, a plan for increasing person-to-person relating across ethnic, racial and national boundaries, a program for helping eligible young adults to meet potential marriage partners; a new way of approaching disciplining one's children, celebrating holidays, taking trips, getting the household chores done efficiently, enjoying sex, participating in church, creating opportunities for fun in the family, and so on *ad infinitum*. "And without creation, love is an abstraction—a mere puff of wind . . . a gust of emotion."[37]

Teilhard de Chardin, the French paleontologist-theologian, has opened up for many people new understanding of the creative order of man. By his correlating of science and theology, he has disclosed fresh possibilities of man's participating in the new creation. The thrust that Teilhard represents is the awareness that the next great phase in man's evolution will be growth in the ethical, spiritual, and interpersonal realm and that man must participate actively in this process. This can provide a vigorous stimulus to thoughtful couples searching for a more creative style of married living. In "creating their own culture" (Snyder), as in all acts of deep sharing, a couple can experience a sense of communion.

MacIver, at the close of his book, poses the question of the ages—a question which every married couple should raise together:

What makes life worthwhile?
The answers offered have been themselves various and conflicting. But whatever they are, whether they find salvation through a way of believing, a way of doing or a way of feeling, they have all had at their base a common element. *The way they prescribe must enlist the personality in wholehearted unison with some reality that absorbs and fulfills the being.* The fulfillment of personality is thus a form of communion, whether it be with the God a man worships; or with nature under some aspect; or through intimate communication with ideal things, the inexhaustible quality of beauty or truth that pervades the universe; or with some cause that calls into action all one's powers; or

even with things of lesser significance so long as they satisfy the human craving for union.[38]

One of the mysteries and marvels of intimacy in marriage is that it offers so many opportunities to find those shared transcendent meanings that ultimately make life worthwhile.

TAKING ACTION

Find a quiet time and place and try to tell each other how you feel about several of the following:

1. What you believe to be worth living for.
2. What experiences give you a sense of time-transcendence.
3. What ideas seem to make the most sense to you, so far as the meaning of life is concerned.
4. How you feel and how you believe with respect to "religion."
5. How your feelings and beliefs have changed since you were married.
6. What you would like to see changed in your marriage and family, in the area of values, spiritual realities, religious practices.
7. How you will feel about the present way of investing your minutes, hours, and days, when you stand near the end of life looking back at your marriage and family.

Communication in this area is difficult for many husbands and wives; it is also rewarding. *Understanding* and *acceptance* are the bridges which join differing world-views, philosophies of life and values between spouses. They make spiritual intimacy possible—an intimacy that is at a deeper level than beliefs, even very personal beliefs.

NOTES

1. Buber, *Between Man and Man,* trans. Ronald Gregor Smith (Boston: Beacon Press, 1947), p. 98.

2. *Confessions of St. Augustine* (New York: Sheed & Ward, 1942), Book I, p. 3. (Translated by F. J. Sheed.)
3. Dag Hammarskjöld, *Markings,* trans. Lief Sjöberg and W. H. Auden (New York: Alfred A. Knopf, 1964), p. 24.
4. Kahlil Gibran, *The Prophet* (New York: Alfred A. Knopf, 1923), p. 20.
5. H. J. Clinebell, Jr., "Philosophical-Religious Factors in the Etiology and Treatment of Alcoholism," *Quarterly Journal of Studies on Alcohol,* Vol. 24, No. 3 (September, 1963), p. 477.
6. Gordon W. Allport, *Pattern and Growth in Personality* (New York: Holt, Rinehart and Winston, 1961), p. 294.
7. Loomis, *The Self in Pilgrimage* (New York: Harper & Row, 1960), p. 13.
8. Gurin, Gerald, et al., *Americans View Their Mental Health* (New York: Basic Books, 1960), p. 63.
9. For a discussion of the need-satisfying role of worship see H. J. Clinebell, Jr., *Mental Health through Christian Community* (Nashville: Abingdon Press, 1965), Chapter 3.
10. Rosenzweig, *Academy Reporter,* Vol. 11, No. 6 (June, 1966), p. 1, editorial.
11. Quoted in the journal *Marriage,* Vol. 49, No. 1 (January, 1967), p. 37.
12. Paul Tournier, *To Understand Each Other* (Richmond, Va.: John Knox Press, 1962), p. 59.
13. Bertrand Russell, quoted in *Life,* March 17, 1967, p. 37.
14. MacIver, Robert, *The Challenge of the Passing Years* (New York: Simon and Schuster, 1962), p. 81.
15. I am indebted to a counselee for this apt statement. Sharing mountain-peak experiences allows a couple to acquire resources for coping with existential anxiety. If one can face his finitude, it can enrich his life in many ways. He can gain satisfaction from his place in the stream of history. During her husband's terminal illness, Anne Philipe became keenly aware of his and her finitude; and yet there was an undergirding sense of being a part of a larger reality—the ongoing family of mankind. "What are our lives in the world's course? No longer than a sigh. And yet it is the sum of all those existences placed side by side, starting with that ancestor in the caves, that has made the history of humanity. You would die, and I would die a little later. We will have been one link in that chain" (Philipe, *No Longer than a Sigh,* p. 41).
16. In *The Concept of Dread* (Princeton: Princeton University Press, 1944), Kierkegaard observed that in the very experience of facing anxiety one is educated to inner certitude of faith. This gives him the "courage to renounce anxiety . . . which only faith is capable of—not that it annihilates anxiety, but remaining ever young, it is continually developing itself out of the death throes of anxiety" (p. 104).

17. *The Family of Man* (New York: The Museum of Modern Art, 1955), Prologue.

18. The ability to mourn and to accept the transitoriness of life permits one to enjoy beauty, nature, relationships—all of which are transitory. In an insightful comment on the problem of two individuals who were unable to enjoy the beauties of nature, Sigmund Freud stated: "What spoilt their enjoyment of beauty must have been a revolt in their minds against mourning. The idea that all this beauty was transient was giving these two sensitive minds a foretaste of mourning over its decease; and, since the mind instinctively recoils from anything that is painful, they felt their enjoyment of beauty interfered with by thoughts of its transience" ("On Transience," pp. 80–81; in *Collected Papers, Vol. V* [The Hogarth Press, The International Psycho-analytic Library, No. 37], ed. J. D. Sutherland, M.D.)

19. Eric Berne, *Games People Play* (New York: Grove Press, 1964), p. 180.

20. D. T. Suzuki, Erich Fromm, and Richard DeMartino, *Zen Buddhism and Psychoanalysis* (New York: Harper & Row, 1960), pp. 87–88.

21. MacIver, *op. cit.*, p. 129.

22. *Ibid.*, p. 126.

23. Loren Eiseley, *The Immense Journey* (New York: Vintage Books, 1957), p. 13.

24. *Ibid.*, p. 12.

25. *Ibid.*, p. 176.

26. Quoted in Erikson, *Insight and Responsibility* (New York: W. W. Norton, 1964), p. 30.

27. J. B. Phillips, *Your God Is Too Small* (New York: The Macmillan Co., 1961), pp. 12–29. Gordon Allport's thought provided a useful distinction between *extrinsic* and *intrinsic* religion. He stated "The religious sentiments of many people—perhaps most people—are decidedly immature. Often they are holdovers from childhood. They are self-centered constructions in which a deity is adopted who favors the immediate interests of the individual, like a Santa Claus or an overindulgent father. Or the sentiment may be of a tribal sort: 'My church is better than your church. God prefers my people to your people.' In cases of this sort religion . . . is utilitarian and incidental in the life. It is a defense mechanism (often an escape mechanism) and does not embrace and guide the life as a whole. It is an 'extrinsic' value in the sense that the person finds it 'useful' in serving his immediate ends.

"Studies show that ethnic prejudice is more common among churchgoers than among nonchurchgoers. This fact alone shows that religion is often divisive rather than unifying. Extrinsic religion lends support to exclusions, prejudices, hatreds that negate all our criteria of maturity. The self is not extended; there is no warm relating of self to others, no emotional security, no realistic perception, no self-insight or humor.

"At the same time the religious sentiment may be of such an order that it does provide an inclusive solution to life's puzzles in the light of an intelligible theory. It can do so if the religious quest is regarded as an end-in-itself, as the value underlying all things and desirable for its own sake. By surrendering himself to this purpose (not by 'using' it), religion becomes an 'intrinsic' value for the individual, and as such is comprehensive and integrative and motivational" (*Patterns and Growth in Personality* [New York: Holt, Rinehart and Winston, 1961], pp. 300–301).

28. MacIver, *op. cit.,* p. 20.
29. See Erikson, *Insight and Responsibility,* "Human Strength and the Cycle of the Generations."
30. This exercise is adapted from an approach used by Viktor Frankl in his practice of logotherapy.
31. From a discussion with William Genné, summer, 1958.
32. Erikson, *Insight and Responsibility,* p. 133.
33. Ross Snyder, *Inscape* (Nashville: Abingdon Press, 1968), p. 42.
34. *Ibid.,* p. 21.
35. *Ibid.,* p. 19.
36. Howe, *Herein Is Love* (Valley Forge, Pa.: Judson Press, 1961), p. 88.
37. Snyder, *Inscape,* pp. 16, 15.
38. MacIver, *op. cit.,* p. 132.

10 *The Outreach of Intimacy: Marriage and Society*

> What creates you as aliveness?
> The primary answer is—"to be caring." Sensitively engaged in what's happening. Not cautious about life, but interested in nurturing life.
>
> Ross Snyder, *On Becoming Human*[1]

"The restriction of intimacy to the family creates serious problems in marriages."[2] To be truly alive and growing, an individual must move beyond self-fulfillment as his impelling motive to what Gordon Allport called "self-extension"—the investment of oneself in another person, cause, or object.[3] The attempt to achieve individual fulfillment without consideration of the cost to others is self-defeating. It results in a head-on collision with a fundamental principle of the psychic life—he who saves or hoards his life ends by losing it. He loses the very things he sought—happiness, the esteem of others, the good taste of life fully lived. These values come as by-products of self-investment in relationships and the willingness to give freely as well as to take.

An apt book title describes marriage as "self-other fulfillment."[4] Growth takes place as one invests himself in relationships. Only as one contributes to the fulfillment of others will one's own potentialities be discovered and fulfilled. Only as one enters into relationships of mutual giving in which one is aware of and strives to satisfy the needs of the other, are one's own needs met. It is more than *quid pro quo* (you scratch my back and I'll scratch yours). Truly enlightened self-interest must transcend egocentric interest; it must involve genuine caring for another. Genuine caring means caring about the satisfaction of the other person's needs and about his growth.

In a period of family centeredness the principle of individual self-extension needs to be applied more broadly. Good family life is a valuable achievement. It is appropriate to focus on the family as the initial setting for personality growth. But exclusive marriage-centeredness or family-centeredness becomes ingrown and stagnant. Self-fulfillment is accepted as the gospel by millions in our society; family-fulfillment is probably an even more widespread guiding image. Both concepts highlight significant goals, but goals which can be realized only in a broader context. The family which operates on the principle, "We'll make our home an island of sanity and the world be damned," will itself be damned to psychological isolation. Isolated couple or family fulfillment is not full, healthy intimacy. Outreach to the needs of the extended family, to the community, to the world stimulates the family to transcend the confines of the nuclear boundaries. This transcendence is essential to the wholeness of a family.

The healthy closeness of a marriage and a family as social organisms is directly related to the vitality of the relationships and concerns beyond the family. Some persons who suffer from painfully low self-acceptance and high anxiety in relationships can relate closely to one person—usually a spouse, parent, or child. But there is a sticky, leaning dependency in such relationships which betrays a lack of interpersonal health. The attempt to overcome all loneliness in one relationship leads to an overloading of the circuits along which need-satisfying communication should flow freely. Overinvestment in a marriage increases the mutual demand load of that relationship in a way that results in less mutual satisfaction, not more. Gibson Winter's insight makes clear that "the restriction of intimacy to the family creates serious problems in marriages." When a marital partner feels the other is saying by his actions, "If you leave me (emotionally or physically) I'll die," there is a trapped feeling which suffocates spontaneity, autonomy, and the inner freedom to choose to stay in the relationship. Marital and family narcissism, like personal narcissism, leads to increased isolation from the perspective-giving, need-satisfying relations with those outside the family. Diminishing returns inevitably result.

To be vital and growing, a marital pair needs mutual investment in children (their own or those children who are deprived of adequate parenting by the tragedies of their lives). To be vital and growing, a family unit needs to be invested in persons and causes outside itself. The size of the life space of a family is enhanced by increasing the variety, breadth, and depth of extra-familial relationships. Families who treat themselves as their own objects of ultimate concern—family idolatry—are impoverished families; those who care about persons outside their circle become enriched by the family's investment in society. The web of meaningful relationships becomes a supportive structure, undergirding family crises and deepening family joys.

A research project which focused on the characteristics of healthy families discovered that most of them were invested in wide circles of outside concern. The researchers conclude:

It may be that he [man] cannot fully develop his personal identity and social potential solely within the family. He needs the large society as well as the more intimate family group in order to satisfy the multiplicity of his nature. Pleasure is derived through a process of involvement with kinfolks, neighbors, community, and the nation, and with other national groups.[5]

It behooves a couple or a family to become socially aware and involved, both because our troubled society needs the spiritual penicillin of enlightened caring and because a family can fulfill its potential only by transcending itself. One couple discovered that some of their most precious moments occurred when they were investing themselves together in a cause bigger than their own mutual-satisfaction and happiness. They agreed that "we have never felt closer than in the sharing of the defeats and successes of the struggle in our community for open housing." To be related to the real neels of a wretchedly lonely, broken world gives marital partners a sense of the ongoing significance of their partnership. Commitment intimacy, in this sense, is an ultimate dimension of marital intimacy. Shared dedication to meeting the crying needs of society's rejects, young and old, gives marriage closeness an ongoing significance that deepens and enriches it.

Every marriage needs something outside itself that enthuses both partners. The exciting awareness, "We *can* make some difference, small but significant, in the world of today and tomorrow!" is the spiritual ambrosia of family life. The heavy dailiness of life, the awareness of the brevity of one's existence with those whom he loves, the sad sense of the continuing lack of completeness in all relationships—these facts of finitude need to be offset by the transcendence of mutual commitment to values which will continue after our families and we ourselves have ceased to exist. Self-investment is an essential ingredient in the positive answer to finitude. To find something that excites a family is therefore a crucial need of every family. To reach out to others is a natural response for a healthy family. To have many friends, interests, and concerns outside its own circle is a spontaneous expression of the energy and vitality that mutually affirming family relations produce. *Thus, outreach is both an evidence of family health and a way of increasing it.*

Some families respond to unhappiness among themselves with compulsive involvement in outside causes. The frustrated wife who loses herself in church or P.T.A. work, the husband who attends a meeting every night, however worthy the cause, the family whose members are flying frantically in different directions seem to be coping with their impoverished relationships by keeping busy. Such involvement has a driven quality stemming from its underlying motivation—escape. There is little of the glad givingness which flows from the awareness that relationships with significant others are rich and good. Thus, the helping and caring work which such persons try to do is often manipulative and sometimes destructive. The inner celebration which comes from feeling that "my cup runneth over" in a marriage and family produces a very different quality of outreach. What is needed is a "balance between the *in-turning* and *out-turning*"[6] in marriage and family life.

Deepening family relationships provide a well-spring of energy and motivation for involvement in the urgent problems of one's community and world. The safe and dependable quality of the intra-family connections frees the individuals to move out from the family into wholehearted involvement in the extra-family world. A young husband said to his counselor, "The unhappiness in our marriage hangs like a dark cloud over my mind. It takes the meaning out of everything else that happens." In contrast, the wife of a couple who had grown closer through a marital growth group declared, "It's as though we are with each other even when we're apart." Her husband nodded, "Yes, I feel the warm glow of our new relationship even when I'm in an aggravating sales conference." Thus, for better or for worse, the quality of a marriage colors the total existence of the partners. A loving, esteem-raising family climate liberates the children to use their fullest potentialities in school and in relationships with peers and with nonfamily adults. Creative intimacy in the home is the launching pad and the propellant which allows one to orbit effectively outside the home. Satisfying experiences outside enrich family relationships, through the enjoyment of sharing them and through the enhancement of individual self-esteem which results from them. A middle-aged husband said, "I didn't like my feeling of competition with my wife's job when she first went back to work; but I've discovered that she's more of a person since she's had a life of her own. That's made things better between us."

NEW NEEDS IN A NEW SOCIETY

Realism demands that another aspect of family-society inter-relationships be taken into account. Outreach occurs continually in the natural course of the husband's (and often the wife's) employment, the school experiences of children and youth, and the contacts of family members with the institutions of society. These ongoing outreach relationships create opportunities for utilizing the creative energies which grow in intimate relationships. But this outreach into the world creates new needs which must be satisfied in family interaction. The overscheduled, high-pressure, bureaucratic, depersonalizing impact of our society's institutions takes a huge toll of creativity. Thus, the refueling, rehabilitative function of marriage-family relationships is essential if family members are to continue contributing constructively to the world outside the family.

In a searching discussion of "The Outlook of the American Family," sociologist Otto Pollak says, "Marriage is not only a counterpoint to organizational life in a bureaucratic world, but it is also a rehabilitative institution which generates new coping power in the encounter of modern man with social change and thus enables him to use what our world has to offer."[7] Bureaucracy demands conformity and restraint of spontaneity. The family is one of the few places where nonconformity, expressiveness (of feelings), and individuality can flower. These adults and children should be free to be *themselves*—joyfully and fiercely, and with respect for each other's right to be different. This is a vital contribution of the family to mental health. Conformist families which mirror our assembly-line society neglect an indispensable function.

Many functions, formerly performed largely by families and clans, have been taken over by society's institutions, including government. Generally, this represents progress; but new problems are always created by solving old ones. As never before in history, the family today must cope with the pressures of outside institutions impinging on more and more areas formerly the prerogative of family life. Social advances and the bureaucratic way of life which accompanies them create new needs which only families can meet. Pollak summarizes the new functions of marital partners created by these new needs: "1. Orchestration of such institutions as school systems, social security, and health care services; 2. determining priorities for use of time; 3. sexual synchronization over an extended life span; 4. economic co-ordination of the earning power of two adult earners; 5. out-let and rescue for hostilities created and suppressed in bureaucratic existence; 6. therapeutic cooperation with the health care services."[8] By performing these functions in our new society, families release their members to be change-agents and creative catalysts in that society.

THE EXTENDED FAMILY

Sociologists describe the concentric circles of kin and close friends just outside the nuclear family as the "extended family." These are the trusted ones to whom the family turns spontaneously when it needs support or help in a crisis. It is essential that the outreach of a family start with the building of an undergirding network of meaningful relationships. Since many families are isolated from relatives by geography, the family clan is not available to provide an instant extended family; it is necessary for them to work at building their supportive network of interlocking concern. A need-satisfying church provides many opportunities for cultivating an extended family, as transplanted people find new roots in small groups and make new friends relatively quickly. This is one of the most important human functions of a church in a highly mobile society. It behooves a family to make the continuing investment in time and concern which is required to keep their extended family relationships in robust condition. The dividends of such an investment include the joy of sharing family fun with friends in the wider circle. The availability of adults, *in addition* to parents, in whom children can feel trust is a tremendously security-giving experience for them. It reduces the impact of the haunting fear—"What will become of me if something happens to my parent or parents?" It does this by broadening the base of dependable, need-satisfying relationships in the children's lives. The crucial role of the extended family is most obvious when a family experiences one of the many losses which are woven into the fabric of all human existence. When the entire family is staggering emotionally and spiritually under a cruel blow of bereavement, the presence of those who really care but are not so deeply hurt by the loss can make all the difference in the world. The tightly closed or isolated family can depend only on its own internal resources; it is always easily hurt. In contrast, the open family whose boundaries are permeable and which is surrounded by a group with whom it exchanges mutual caring has a coping resource of immense utility and value.

The extended family constitutes an opportunity as much as a necessity. The opportunity is to satisfy the inescapable human need to *give* love and to make one's life count. The circle should include other families and also persons who currently lack family ties. Helping to meet the needs of such persons is an important, satisfying way of making one's family count in the world. Sharing the valleys and heights and plateaus of family life with at least one other family brings help and perspective to varied experiences. The opportunity to have ongoing relatedness with the lonely ones in the community—unmarried older relatives; "parents without partners"; single young adults separated from their families by military service, college, or job circumstances; older couples who have no children nearby; adolescents who are alienated from their parents but who need relationships with stable adults; children who have lost one or both parents; etc. The opportunity to sustain such friendship enlarges the horizons and sharpens the sensitivity of family members as well as meeting the needs of lonely people. Providing additional sources of relationship satisfactions removes the pressure felt by those who try to make their families all-sufficient.

Effective family involvement in social problems is made more likely when there is a significant extended family. Emily Mudd and her associates report: "The diverse evidence . . . suggests that concern about the healthy status of the community flows more naturally from a healthy kinship network than from a nuclear, socially isolated family unit."⁹ The mutual strengthening that comes from interaction with the extended family is particularly important when a couple or family attempts to pit the ounces of its influence against the forces of social injustice, economic exploitation, and discrimination. Being able to turn to friends or relatives who share one's convictions and may even be involved in the struggle for a better community is reassuring and supportive when the going is rough and discouraging. An idealistic couple in their twenties was deeply committed to action designed to open more job opportunities to minority groups. In reflecting on their discouragement in what proved to be an uphill job, they said, "The fact that two couples to whom we feel close are involved in similar projects in their communities, is one thing that keeps us going when the gains are nil or disappointingly small."

It is well to emphasize that vigorous, functional extended family relationships ordinarily do not just happen. One reason many of us do fail in this area is that we are too preoccupied with personal or family goals to invest continually the time and caring that are required. But clan or substitute-clan relationships flourish only when there are interaction, communication, and mutual need-satisfaction—the same basic requirements as for flourishing marriages. The hectic whirl of family life tends to insulate it from depth relationships beyond the inner circle as well as within it. Consequently, most families have to work hard at keeping their extended relationships in good repair. A conscious, planned effort to provide opportunities to relate is essential. "Friendships have usually filled the middle ground between family life and the less personal dealings of the larger community." It takes time to develop friendships. We are too hurried to take this time. "We are so uprooted we have few if any friends."¹⁰

Fortunate is the young family which has or creates opportunities for trans-generational relationships. A suburb in which almost all the adults are within a ten-year age span is an area in which mutual enhancement by relating across generation lines is constricted to two generations. It is particularly strengthening to the sense of well-being of children to relate to loving relatives, including older relatives. Such older persons are often more accepting and less demanding than parents, who feel most acutely the responsibility of guiding the child. Some who read this page may recall with a warm inner glow visits or vacations with doting grandparents.

Erik Erikson says it well when he writes:

> The individual ego can be strong only through a mutual guarantee of strength given to and received by all whose life-cycles intertwine. Whatever chance man may have to transcend the limitations of his ego seems to depend on his prior ability in his one and only life-cycle, to be fully engaged in the sequence of generations.[11]

In spite of the generation gap, a gap that is Grand Canyon-like in this period of lightning-swift social change, productive communication can and does occur between those in interlocking generations. It takes place when the interpersonal climate of a family allows for openness and respect for the right of each individual to be himself. Communication can bridge the generation chasm, allowing the younger and the older generations to learn from each other. Those who have lived longer and lived with self-awareness do have time-tested wisdom regarding values and relationships that is relevant to the young, even though they live in a different world. A popular newspaper advice-giver spoke a true word when she wrote: "There's hardly a man alive who couldn't retire comfortably in his old age if he could sell his experience for what it cost him."[12] Relatedness to the young can help older persons avoid hardening of the arteries of social concern, idealism, and zest for living. Furthermore, there is some evidence to suggest that people can relate better to others two generations removed than to those of an adjacent generation.

The optimum extended family should include both relatives and nonrelatives. There are deep and special bonds that human beings feel with those to whom they are genetically linked. The experience of personal closeness with those joined by blood ties has a security-giving effect on children. The ancient custom of pledging loyalty between friends by actually mingling blood points to this depth sense of closeness. All this makes it particularly tragic when alienation occurs within families. The loneliness of being cut off from real communication on things that matter with parents, siblings, and other relatives is a painful ache in the soul. On the other hand, a mark of emotional maturing is the ability, in Jesus' words, to "leave father and mother"—to cut the exclusive dependence on kin and clan (which is emotional incest), to take the risk of growing depth relationships with a variety of non-relatives, and to be surprised by the joyful discovery that the most important family is the family of man, which makes every person a relative.

OUTREACH TO THE COMMUNITY AND THE WORLD

In his searching discussion of the worldwide phenomenon of uprootedness, Erik Erikson says, "Roots are torn out or are brought along, dry up in transit or are kept moist and alive, find an appropriate soil, or fail to take hold and wither."[13] He describes those who have lost childhood soil and home, and who have not been able to put down roots in a new environment: "Their common symptoms betray a common state in their ego which has lost active mastery and the nourishing exchange of community life."[14] Creative family intimacy is made difficult for many by the anxiety of insulation from the nourishing exchange of community life. Urban families often protect themselves from the lonely impact of faceless society by withdrawing into the citadel delimited by their family boundaries. This self-protective reflex intensifies the loneliness which produced it.

As interaction with the extended family provides the supportive foundation for the nuclear family, interaction with the community nurtures and supports both the inner and outer families. One illustration of the function of the community and its institutions is the role of peer relationships in school, club, and church in the maturation of adolescents. These friendships provide an invaluable platform on which the young person can place his foot as he engages in the crucial struggle to relinquish his childhood dependency on family and clan. Relationships with nonfamily adults in these institutions, and with the ideology of the institutions (which always differs to some extent from the parents' ideology), provide experiences and values which supplement those that were deficient in the family, thus furthering emancipation and maturation. Ingrown families without permeability of the boundaries which encourages continuing two-way transactions with community institutions seriously restrict the use of the community's institutional resources for personal growth.

Erik Erikson's profound insights about the development of basic trust include the recognition that this trustfulness at the core of one's being (which is the fundamental resource in all intimate relationships), requires an "integration of the individual life cycle with some meaningful wider belongingness."[15] He points out that basic trust develops "within the trusted framework of their culture's life style."[16] But, in our time of kaleidoscopic social change, culture styles are ambiguous, conflicted, and in flux. Thus, it is difficult to know and to trust the life-style of one's culture and subculture. Families separated from their indigenous culture by emigration are only slightly more exposed to cultural shock than many families whose culture has changed so rapidly around them as to constitute almost a foreign land. Stable values confirmed by general community consensus are increasingly hard to find in our society; thus the family is thrown on its own resources in the difficult task of finding dependable values upon which they can agree and by which they can guide their life-styles. This makes more crucial the role of churches and temples as centers for the discovery of life-steering values from our heritage which are viable for the present and future.

Families and couples need to be needed by their communities. They need to have a vivid awareness that no family is an island,

and that meaningful family life requires a sense of effective involvement in the problems, celebrations, tragedies, and struggles of the community. "If institutions are to move effectively to serve man, educative efforts need to begin early in families of all classes of American society, as to their role and responsibility in shaping the character of such public and private institutions."[17] Dynamic family relations require a two-way flow to and from the inner circle, the extended family, and the community. The potential values derived from this flow stretch far beyond the mere satisfactions of being helpful to the needy and a part of community-improvement efforts. The integrating, unifying effect on families of a common dedication to a family-transcending purpose, cause, or ideal is clearly evident in times of national crisis when a country is mobilizing to resist some force which is perceived as a threat to the total well-being. How much better when families can experience this cohesion as a result of common commitment to a cause such as world peace; the United Nations; the eradication of poverty and hunger, injustice and disease; the control of an exploding population which threatens mankind with mass starvation. When parents are involved in a cause and demonstrate by words and actions that they regard it as worthy of the investment of their precious hours, days, and years, children will be deeply influenced, and unless they are rebelling adolescents, will usually make the cause their enthusiasm too.

The ultimate importance of community involvement is that it provides the couple and the family with a way of enhancing the health of the society, which plays a substantial role in determining the health of the family. In *The Sane Society,* Erich Fromm explores the ways in which societies influence the mental and emotional health of persons: "Whether or not the individual is healthy, is primarily not an individual matter, but depends on the structure of his society."[18] Working for a more just, loving, person-valuing society, beginning with one's own corner of the local community, is thus seen as an expression of enlightened self-interest on the part of a family.

To be involved in church and community groups engaged in action and study aimed at needed social change broadens a family's horizons by letting them see "how the other half lives," and by providing a deeper awareness that we are all affected by and are responsible for the problems of our community.[19]

The sense of involvement in humanity and in the sordid problems which perplex our world is particularly needed by children and adults who have lived and matured in suburban islands of privilege and plenty. To break out of the self-congratulatory, comfortable state of mind which characterizes the suburban ghetto is a salutary emancipation for such persons. It is a discovery of the burdened world of which we are all a part and which is a part of all of us. To recognize that man's evolution is unfinished—in terms of both interpersonal relationships and the injustice-breeding structures of society—makes a major contribution to a family's sense of corporate purpose. It does so because it opens the possibility of becoming participants in the process of working to complete creation, to move man's cultural evolution toward the goal of a just, loving society.

It is well to remember that much of the suffering of individuals is caused by the structures of injustice built into our social institutions—e.g., substandard schools in slum areas, corrupt political machines, court procedures which discriminate subtly against the poor, a welfare system that crushes the already tattered self-respect of recipients, bureaucracies (big labor, big corporations, big military), which depersonalize their employees, etc. Therefore, changing individuals is never adequate in itself as a strategy for producing a just, relating society. It is necessary to get at the roots of the problem by direct efforts to change person-damaging institutional practices. This usually requires political and economic power rather than simply personal persuasion, education, and therapy.

Many of the problems which are encountered in one's community are widespread, even universal maladies. Although outreach should never ignore the local community, it should recognize that world problems demand broad-scale approaches to solution. Those who have achieved depth relationships in their families have a large stake in reducing the massive problems which make it next to impossible for millions of people even to take an interest in deepening their relationships. War, poverty, and the population explosion are striking examples. The latter two problems are deeply interwoven. The economic gains of most underdeveloped nations have been offset to a large extent by their runaway population increases. Whereas it took some 800,000 years to reach a world population of three billion, it is estimated that the growth from three to six billion will occur in as few as forty years. The consequences of forced physical intimacy on an overcrowded planet will make it more and more difficult for the majority of the world's people to achieve anything resembling emotional intimacy. Those who value the opportunity for depth relationships and desire the same opportunity for others, now and in the future that is constantly being born, should be investing time, influence, and money in the struggle to find better ways of reconciling economic resources and population gains so that all children will have a birthright.

The haunting specter of nuclear war hanging like an ominous cloud on the horizon of man's consciousness threatens all things of value, including the fulfillment of marital and family relationships. In the junglelike struggle among those few peoples of the world who would survive an all-out holocaust, there would be no time or energy for focusing on relationships. Those who lull themselves with the "it's too terrible to happen" illusion should remember that mankind killed 100 million of its fellow human beings (combatants and civilians) in two world wars using weapons which, for the most part, were mere toys in comparison with the nightmarish bombs and chemicals now available. What is the subtle impact on our consciousness, our consciences, and our close relationships of this nuclear sword of Damocles under which we all exist? What is the impact of the well-known fact that the United States has destructive nuclear force equal to 35,000 tons of TNT for every human being alive? What is the effect on the spirits of children and youth of these grim facts? What does it mean that the present generation of youth is the first which has grown from childhood with the knowledge that a considerable percentage of mankind could be wiped out within minutes? No one really knows the full answers to these questions, but it seems certain that world problems such as those mentioned must detract from the capacity of mankind to have loving, secure, intimate relationships. Intimacy requires awareness, low anxiety, and time to relate. Gigantic problems such as poverty, war, environmental pollution, and overpopulation wear these qualities away by steady attrition. Tournier quotes Tina Keller: "The same warfare that unfolds on a world-wide scale has its effects in the family, and in the individual soul."[20]

It behooves persons with the ability to relate to be involved in social action for many reasons. Not the least of these is the live probability that some of the skills and insights which they have learned in individual, family, and small-group relationships may be applicable in restoring communication and resolving conflicts on a larger scale. In an article on adolescents, Sylvia Sacks concludes:

> Perhaps, as we continue to try to understand man's touch with his personal needs and his love, with his family and his past heritage, we may help to illuminate the heritage youth carries to his future family. For in his family must reside still the dignity and hopes for each man enabling him to reach towards and become part of the Family of Man.[21]

The concern of a couple for a world in which all persons have an opportunity to fulfill their God-given potentialities through creative relationships is a part of their responsibility to the future. In his lectures on the ethical implications of psychoanalytic insight, Erikson suggests that the motif around which humanity may find a new unity may be "the responsibilities which each generation of men has for all succeeding ones."[22] The future-focus of the outreach of intimate relationships is well-expressed by Ross Snyder in a paper for married couples: "You have chosen to journey together down the earth valley in the brief moment of Time that is yours. From this day forward, you become a unit of life that will bring forth futures."[23] Responsible intimacy must include this sense of one's potential influence on unborn futures. When couples achieve a strong degree of creative closeness and then together use the power and the insight that flows from it in reaching out to widening circles of caring, the zest is sustained in their marriage through the quickly passing years. Their investment in their relationship, in other people, and in the needy world is an investment in raising the stream of humanity which will continue long after they are gone. This sense of the eternity in the now of marriage gives a relationship special richness and meaning.

The growing marital closeness which a couple can achieve is a priceless gem within the reach of a relationship. It is of inherent and abiding value in itself; it is also the foundation for the ability to meet the needs of persons in a widening circle of caring. The family's closeness warms the cold loneliness of human existence, and this warmth can kindle the fires of caring for those far beyond its inner circle. This outreaching concern enriches and deepens creative relationships within the family.

These lines by Howard Thurman carry the central message and meaning of caring:

> I know I cannot enter all you feel
> Nor bear with you the burden of your pain.
> I can but offer what my love does give:
> The strength of caring. . . .
> This I do in quiet ways
> That on your lonely path
> You may not walk alone.[24]

To offer what the love of man and wife, parents and children can bring—the strength of caring for those who lack the daily bread of loving relatedness—this is the ultimate test and fulfillment of creative closeness. "Marriage then becomes a great adventure, a continuous discovery both of oneself and one's mate. It becomes a daily broadening of one's horizon, an opportunity of learning something new about life, about human existence, about God."[25]

TAKING ACTION

How a family implements its outreach into the community depends upon the particular unmet needs they find there. In deciding where you want to "invest the ounces of your influence" as a couple or a family, become aware of the things that need changing in the institutions of your community—the injustice, ineffectiveness, racism, person-damaging practices—as well as the symptoms of these social problems in the suffering of individuals. Use an action-research approach, beginning with some of the pressing needs of your neighborhood, community, state, nation. Decide which needs:

1. Are most urgent
2. Arouse your interest
3. Offer reasonable possibilities for you to make an impact.

Consider concentrating some of your action on the level of *causes* as well as *effects*. It may be more important in the long run to work to elect a school board that will improve sub-standard ghetto schools than to provide tutoring for ghetto children and youth. Both are important; it is crucial to work at both sides of the problem simultaneously when possible. It may be helpful to talk with community leaders and make several on-the-scene visits in order to decide where to begin. Investigate organized groups which are already involved in social change to see whether they offer the most effective opportunities for channeling your outreach.

After choosing the problem area which fits the three criteria listed above, a strategy conference in which the whole family participates can be held. Here are some of the relevant questions to raise in making decisions about how to get involved:

At what points might we have or acquire leverage to make our efforts as change agents count?
What social action organizations are most effectively changing the causes of human suffering? Which are mainly ameliorating

the painful symptoms? How can we ally ourselves with the organizations which will enhance our own power to move toward the goal we have chosen?

In what groups or agencies will we have the maximum opportunity to develop relationships with persons unlike those with whom we usually associate?

Is the best strategy political power (e.g. a letter-writing campaign), economic pressure (e.g. a boycott of a discriminatory food chain), personal negotiation, persuasion, education or therapy?

How can we use our particular interests, aptitudes, relationships and connections as a couple or family?

At this stage of our family cycle, what type of community action involvement is realistic?

Having chosen goals and developed strategies, move into action. Regular feedback sessions to evaluate what is happening and re-strategize plans, are essential.* Above all, remember—the hour is late! The needs are urgent! The issues facing our world no longer allow us the option to choose between apathy and involvement. They are literally matters of life and death.

NOTES

1. Snyder, *On Becoming Human* (Nashville: Abingdon Press, 1967), p. 23.
2. Gibson Winter, *Love and Conflict* (Garden City, N.Y.: Doubleday and Co., 1958), p. 71.
3. Allport, *Patterns and Growth in Personality* (New York: Holt, Rinehart and Winston, 1961), pp. 283–285.
4. Donald L. Porterfield, *Marriage and Family Living as Self-Other Fulfillment* (Philadelphia: F. A. Dan Co., 1962).
5. Emily Mudd, Howard E. Mitchell, Sara B. Taubin, *Success in Family Living* (New York: Association Press, 1965), p. 212.
6. George B. Leonard, "The Man and Woman Thing," *Look,* December 24, 1968, p. 72.
7. Pollak, "The Outlook of the American Family," *Journal of Marriage and the Family,* Vol. 29, No. 1 (February, 1967), p. 203.

* For a fuller discussion of the roles and strategies of laymen and clergymen as change-agents, see Harvey Seifert and H. J. Clinebell, Jr., *Personal Growth and Social Change* (Philadelphia: Westminster Press, 1969).

8. *Ibid.,* p. 193.
9. Emily Mudd, *et al., op. cit.,* p. 222.
10. Winter, *Love and Conflict,* pp. 180, 181.
11. Erikson, *Insight and Responsibility* (New York: W. W. Norton, 1964), p. 157.
12. Abigail Van Buren, writing to "Too Smart Too Late," November 11, 1966.
13. Erikson, *Insight and Responsibility,* p. 88.
14. *Ibid.,* p. 89.
15. Erikson, *Childhood and Society* (New York: W. W. Norton, 1963), p. 249.
16. *Ibid.,* p. 249.
17. Mudd, *et al., op. cit.,* p. 222.
18. Fromm, *The Sane Society* (New York: Rinehart, 1955). He continues: "A healthy society furthers man's capacity to love his fellow men, to work creatively, to develop his reason and objectivity, to have a sense of self which is based on the experience of his own productive powers. An unhealthy society is one which creates mutual hostility, distrust, which transforms man into an instrument of use and exploitation for others, which deprives him of a sense of self, except inasmuch as he submits to others or becomes an automaton" (pp. 72–73).
19. "The awareness of one's affinity with all of humanity makes one vulnerable to sharing the pain of humanity through empathy. But the lack of this awareness produces an impoverished life." Nathaniel Hawthorne gives this description of such a life in *Ethan Brand:* "[His heart] had ceased to partake of the universal throb. He had lost his hold of the magnetic chain of humanity. He was no longer a brother-man, opening the chambers or the dungeons of our common nature by the key of holy sympathy, which gave him a right to share in all its secrets; he was now a cold observer, looking on mankind as the subject of his experiment, and, at length, converting man and woman to be his puppets . . ." (Elizabeth L. Salomon, "Humanistic Values and Social Casework," *Social Casework,* Vol. XLVIII, No. 1 [January, 1967], p. 26.)
20. Paul Tournier, *To Understand Each Other,* p. 27.
21. Sylvia Sacks, "Widening the Perspectives on Adolescent Sex Problems," *Adolescence,* Vol. 1, No. 1 (Spring, 1966), p. 89. For a fuller discussion of the relationship between counseling and social action see Seifert and Clinebell, *Personal Growth and Social Change* (Philadelphia: Westminster Press, 1969).
22. Erikson, *Insight and Responsibility,* p. 24.
23. Ross Snyder, unpublished paper, p. 32.
24. Adapted from a poem by Howard Thurman; used by permission.
25. Paul Tournier, *To Understand Each Other* (Richmond, Va.: John Knox Press, 1962), p. 30.

A Final Word

Thus concludes the account of one couple's thoughts and experiences with the many-faceted diamond of intimacy—an account unfinished as our journey to intimacy is unfinished. Wherever you are as a couple on the marital journey—at the beginning, along the way, or near the end; on the main road, at a dead-end, or on a detour—we hope we have tempted you to new efforts in the struggle and discovery, the pain and joy which together create a marriage. From our own struggles, we counsel courage and patience when floundering against the barriers which are never fully eliminated. We wish you the joy of ever more frequent moments when soul touches soul. Reaching toward each other, reaching up and reaching out together—always reaching, often touching, sometimes joining as "the new person—us," this is the intimacy of marriage.

Bibliography: For Reading and Reflection

(Books with "P" in front of the author's name are of interest primarily to professionals in the field of marriage and family counseling.)

(P) Ackerman, Nathan W., M.D., *The Psychodynamics of Family Life, Diagnosis and Treatment of Family Relationships.* New York: Basic Books, Inc., 1958.

A discussion of family dynamics and therapy.

Bach, George R., and Wyden, Peter, *The Intimate Enemy: How to Fight Fair in Love and Marriage.* New York: William Morrow and Co., 1969.

A guide to constructive fighting in close relationships.

Baruch, Dorothy W., *How to Live with Your Teen-Ager.* New York: McGraw-Hill Book Co., 1953.

A practical guidebook for parents of adolescents.

Baruch, Dorothy W., *New Ways in Discipline.* New York: McGraw-Hill Book Company, 1949.

An insightful book on the emotional needs of children.

Baruch, Dorothy W., *New Ways in Sex Education, A Guide for Parents and Teachers.* New York: McGraw-Hill, 1959.

A readable and clearly illustrated guide to sex education which deals with each of the ages and stages of growth of children and adolescents.

Baruch, Dorothy W., and Miller, Hyman, *Sex in Marriage, New Understandings.* New York: Harper and Row, 1962.

A manual for understanding the physical and emotional dimensions of sex in marriage; included is a discussion of the initial sexual adjustment, keeping love alive, pregnancy, childbirth, and sex in the later years.

(P) Becker, Russell J., *Family Pastoral Care.* Englewood Cliffs, N.J.: Prentice-Hall, 1965.

A discussion of the role of minister and congregation in helping families to cope with crises and to live constructively.

(P) Bell, Norman W., and Vogel, Ezra, *A Modern Introduction to the Family*. New York: The Free Press, 1960.

> A symposium by sociologists dealing with the family and external systems, internal family processes, and the family and personality.

Berne, Eric, *Games People Play, The Psychology of Human Relationships*. New York: Grove Press, 1964.

> Includes a description of marital games.

(P) Berne, Eric, *Transactional Analysis in Psychotherapy*. New York: Grove Press, 1961.

> Includes a discussion of the application of structural and transactional analysis to marriage problems.

(P) Berther, Ruth and Edward (eds.), *An Analysis of Human Sexual Response, The Masters and Johnson Study*. New York: Signet Books, 1966.

> Includes a section on the practical implications of the findings of the Masters and Johnson study for counseling in sexual problems.

Calderone, Mary S., *Release from Sexual Tensions*. New York: Random House, 1960.

> A book on making sex a constructive force in marriage.

(P) Carrington, William L., *The Healing of Marriage*. Great Neck, N.Y.: Channel Press, 1961.

> A handbook on marriage counseling for ministers, doctors, and other professionals.

Chess, Stella, et al., *Your Child Is a Person*. New York: Viking Press, 1965.

> Application of findings of research on the effects of child-rearing practices on children from birth to age nine.

(P) Clinebell, Howard J., Jr., *Basic Types of Pastoral Counseling*. Nashville: Abingdon Press, 1966.

> Various chapters discuss marriage counseling, family group therapy, and crisis counseling.

Clinebell, Howard J., Jr., *Mental Health Through Christian Community*. Nashville: Abingdon Press, 1965.

> Chapter 9 discusses "Fostering Mental Health by Strengthening Family Life" through the church program.

Duvall, Evelyn M., *Family Development*. New York: J. B. Lippincott, 1957.

> An exploration of the developmental needs and goals of the various stages of family life.

Duvall, Evelyn M., *Why Wait Till Marriage*. New York: Association Press, 1965.

> A frank discussion of the case for premarital chastity; written for youth.

Duvall, Evelyn M., and Hill, Reuben, *When You Marry* (Rev. ed.), New York: Association Press, 1953.

> For those anticipating marriage—what it means to be married, the making of a family, changes in family life in contemporary society.

Eckert, Ralph, *Sex Attitudes in the Home.* New York: Association Press, 1956.

> A book for parents who want to help children to develop healthy sexual attitudes.

Egleson, Jim, and Egleson, Janet Frank, *Parents without Partners, A Guide for Divorced, Widowed or Separated Parents.* New York: E. P. Dutton and Co., 1961.

> Based on the personal experiences of single parents in the organization, Parents without Partners.

(P) Eisenstein, Victor (ed.), *Neurotic Interaction in Marriage.* New York: Basic Books, 1956.

> A symposium including articles on subjects such as psychoanalysis and marriage, neurotic factors in the choice of mates, the spouse of the alcoholic, and family diagnosis and treatment.

Eichenlaub, John H., *The Marriage Art.* New York: Dell Publishing Co., 1961.

> A most helpful discussion on the art of sex in marriage.

Ellzey, W. Clark, *How to Keep Romance in Your Marriage.* New York: Association Press, 1954.

> Discusses the various stages of romance in marriage as these relate to sex, money, emotional maturity, parenthood.

Ginott, Haim G., *Between Parent and Child.* New York: Avon Books, 1965.

> How to relate to your child and understand his feelings; practical guidance for everyday parent-child problems.

Ginott, Haim G., *Between Parent and Teenager.* New York: The Macmillan Co., 1969.

> A guide for parents who desire to "stand, withstand and understand" their teenagers; suggests methods of dealing with many problems in these relationships.

Gittelsohn, Ronald B., *Consecrated Unto Me, a Jewish View of Love and Marriage.* New York: Harper and Row, 1965.

> The marriage relationship from the Jewish perspective.

(P) Glasser, William, *Reality Therapy.* New York: Harper and Row, 1965.

> New approaches to counseling and psychotherapy; useful to teachers, ministers and others; emphasizes responsibility and facing reality.

(P) Green, Bernard L. (ed.), *The Psychotherapies of Marital Disharmony.* New York: The Free Press, 1965.

> Articles on sociological and psychoanalytic concepts of family diagnosis, couple counseling, conjoint family therapy.

Fairchild, Roy W., and Wynn, John C., *Families in the Church: A Protestant Survey*. New York: Association Press, 1961.
> Findings of a study concerning how families think, live and interact with their churches.

Greenblat, Bernard R., *A Doctor's Marital Guide for Patients*. Chicago: The Budlong Press, 1959.
> A discussion of sexual adjustment which is useful in pre-marital and marital counseling.

Howe, Reuel L., *The Creative Years*. New York: Seabury Press, 1959.
> On making the most of the years between completing one's preparation for one's work and retirement.

Howe, Reuel L., *Herein Is Love*. Valley Forge, Pa.: Judson Press, 1961.
> A study of the biblical doctrine of love in its bearing on relationships.

Howe, Reuel L., *The Miracle of Dialogue*. New York: Seabury Press, 1963.
> An exploration of the nature, purpose, barriers, and fruits of genuine communication.

(P) Hudson, Lofton, *Marital Counseling*. Englewood Cliffs, N.J.: Prentice-Hall, 1963.
> Techniques and methods of marriage counseling.

(P) Johnson, Dean, *Marriage Counseling: Theory and Practice*. Englewood Cliffs, N.J.: Prentice-Hall, 1961.
> Techniques and methods of marriage counseling.

(P) Kirkpatrick, Clifford, *The Family as Process and Institution*. New York: The Ronald Press, 1963, second edition.
> A sociological study of the nature, origins, social changes, life cycle, crises and reorganization of the family.

Jourard, Sidney M. *The Transparent Self*. Princeton, N.J.: D. Van Nostrand, 1961, Insight edition.
> Includes a discussion of the importance of openness in the marriage relationship.

(P) Kirkendall, Lester A., *Premarital Intercourse and Interpersonal Relationships*. New York: Julian Press, 1961.
> A research study of interpersonal relationships based on case histories of 668 premarital intercourse experiences of 200 college males.

Klemer, Richard H. and Margaret G., "Sexual Adjustment in Marriage," Public Affairs Pamphlet No. 397, Public Affairs Committee, New York, 1966.
> A brief discussion of the problems and possibilities of sex in marriage.

(P) Klemer, Richard H. (ed.), *Counseling in Marital and Sexual Problems, A Physicians Handbook*. Baltimore: The Williams and Wilkins Co., 1965.

> A symposium covering a wide range of marital and sexual problems, by leading authorities in the field; includes sections on premarital counseling; counseling on parent-child problems; counseling with the widowed, divorced and unmarried; counseling with alcoholics and their families; counseling with infertility problems; counseling with cases of sexual incompatibility; extra-marital pregnancies and marital infidelity.

Knight, James, *For the Love of Money*.

> Useful for understanding the dynamics of the financial dimension of marriage.

Levy, John, and Monroe, Ruth, *The Happy Family*. New York: Alfred A. Knopf, 1956.

> A study of the factors which contribute to happiness in family relationships.

Lewin, S. A., and Gillmore, Josh, *Sex without Fear*. New York: Medical Research Press, 1950.

> A discussion of the physiology of the reproductive system, the art of intercourse, pregnancy, menopause, etc.

Mace, David, *Success in Marriage*. Nashville: Abingdon Press, 1958.

> An introductory book for couples on the principles, adjustments and problems of a successful marriage.

May, Rollo, *Love and Will*. New York: W. W. Norton, 1969.

> A study of the myths and symbols of sex and love, as these relate to the overcoming of alienation and the achievement of relationships that are more alive and dynamic.

McGinnis, Tom, *Your First Year of Marriage*. New York: Doubleday and Company, 1967.

> A guide for newlyweds and premarital couples.

(P) McHugh, Geiolo, *Marriage Counselor's Manual and Teacher's Handbook for Use with the Sex Knowledge Inventory* (Form X Revised). Durham, N.C.: Family Life Publications, 1968.

> A manual for use with the SKI, an instrument for premarital and marital counseling on sexual problems.

Missildine, Hugh, *Your Inner Child of the Past*. New York: Simon and Schuster, 1963.

> A discussion of the child side that is in everyone and how to take care of it.

(P) Moore, Allen J., *The Young Adult Generation, A Perspective on the Future*. Nashville: Abingdon Press, 1961.

> A book for helping young adults understand themselves and for helping the older generation understand them.

(P) Mudd, Emily H., *et al.* (eds.), *Marriage Counseling, a Casebook.* New York: Association Press, 1958.

> Forty-one cases by members of the American Association of Marriage Counselors.

Mudd, Emily H., Mitchell, Howard E., Taubin, Sara B., *Success in Family Living.* New York: Association Press, 1965.

> An analysis of factors which contribute to successful functioning of one hundred "normal" families.

Mudd, Emily H., and Kirch, Aaron, *Man and Wife.* New York: W. W. Norton, 1957.

> Seventeen authorities explore problems in marriage.

(P) Nash, W. M., *et al., Marriage Counseling in Medical Practice.* Chapel Hill: University of North Carolina Press, 1957.

> Aimed at physicians but useful for persons in the other helping professions as a discussion of the physical, and interpersonal-emotional factors in marriage counseling.

Elof, Nelson G., *Your Life Together.* Richmond, Va.: John Knox Press, 1957.

> A book for engaged couples.

(P) Oates, Wayne E., *Premarital Pastoral Care and Counseling.* Nashville: Broadman Press, 1958.

> Useful for clergymen in their premarital guidance work.

Otto, Herbert, *More Joy in Your Marriage.* New York: Hawthorne Books, 1961.

> Techniques for "waking up" a marriage.

Peterson, James A., *Married Love in the Middle Years.* New York: Association Press, 1968.

> A book on the crisis of the mid-years and how to make the most of marriage in maturity.

Peterson, James A., *Toward a Successful Marriage.* New York: Charles Scribner's Sons, 1960.

> Discusses choosing a mate, courtship, the engagement, setting the pattern of a marriage, money, sexual relations, children, and marriage during the last half of life.

Porterfield, Austin L., *Marriage and Family Living as Self-Other Fulfillment.* Philadelphia: F. A. Davis Co., 1962.

> A sociological approach to the family life-cycle; love; work; children, social values and family interaction; psychological processes in family interaction.

Rainer, Jerome and Julia, *Sexual Adventure in Marriage.* New York: Julian Mesner, 1965.

> Keeping the sexual side of marriage adventurous and lively.

(P) Rutledge, Aaron L., *Premarital Counseling.* Cambridge, Mass.: Schenkman Publishing Co., 1966.

> A discussion of the objectives and methods of premarital counseling.

(P) Sanctuary, Gerald, *Marriage under Stress.* London: George Allen and Unwin, 1968.
> A comparative study of marriage counseling in various countries.

Schutz, William C., *Joy, Expanding Human Awareness.* New York: Grove Press, 1967.
> Describes new awareness techniques which can be used in encounter groups and by couples.

Shostrom, Everett L., *Man, the Manipulator.* Nashville: Abingdon Press, 1967.
> Describes the movement from a manipulative life style to actualization.

(P) Skidmore, Rex, *et al., Marriage Consulting: An Introduction to Marriage Counseling.* New York: Harper and Bros., 1956.
> The background, aims, importance and methods of marriage counseling.

Snyder, Ross, *Inscape, Discovering Personhood in the Marriage Relationship.* Nashville: Abingdon Press, 1968.
> A poetic book with searching insights about marriage.

(P) Stewart, Charles W., *The Minister as Marriage Counselor.* Nashville: Abingdon Press, 1961.
> Discusses premarital counseling, marriage counseling, divorce and post-divorce counseling, family counseling, and family-life education in the context of the church.

(P) Taylor, Donald L., *Marriage Counseling, New Dimensions in the Art of Helping People.* Springfield, Illinois: Charles C. Thomas; 1965.
> Discusses the nature, goals, philosophy and methods of marriage counseling; and such topics as communication, feelings, and the nature of a loving relationship.

Tournier, Paul, *To Understand Each Other.* Richmond, Va.: John Knox Press, 1967.
> A beautiful book filled with understanding of the marital relationship.

Winter, Gibson, *Love and Conflict: New Patterns of Family Life.* Garden City, N.Y.: Doubleday and Co., Dolphin Book, 1958.
> Discusses the relationship of love and conflict in marriage and the changes in family life due to the shifts in male-female roles.

(P) Wynn, J. C., *Pastoral Ministry to Families.* Philadelphia: Westminster Press, 1957.
> An overview of the many opportunities of the clergyman to enrich family life.

Wyse, Lois, *Love Poems for the Very Married.* Cleveland: World Publishing Co., 1967.
> Tender, sensitive poems about married life.